ROMANCING THE OLD

TRUE AFRICAN STORY

AMA NKRUMAH

UNA LLC

Copyright © 2025 AMA NKRUMAH

All rights reserved

This work presents a true story, though the names of characters and locations have been crafted by the author, serving as a means to protect the identities of the real individuals involved. Any similarities to actual persons, whether living or deceased, as well as events or places, are coincidental and unintentional. The narrative seeks to convey genuine experiences while ensuring the privacy and anonymity of those mentioned. Readers are invited to immerse themselves in the tale, recognizing that while the essence of the story is rooted in truth, in other not to compromise the integrity of this real-life story and the people behind it, specific details reflect the author's imaginative interpretation.

No part of this book may be reproduced, or stored in a retrieval system, or transmitted in any form or by any means, electronic, mechanical, photocopying, recording, or otherwise, without express written permission of the author and the publisher.

ISBN: 979-8-9921951-3-2

In dedicating this book to the cherished memory of my late parents, Mr. J.B. Morrison and Mrs. Rebecca Morrison, I reflect on the profound impact they had on my life. Their unwavering love, support, and guidance shaped me into the person I am today. Each word I write is infused with gratitude, as I remember the countless sacrifices they made for my happiness and growth. I carry their legacy with me always, holding them in my heart and thoughts. Thank you, Papa and Maa-me, for your endless devotion and the foundation you built for my life. Your influence will forever resonate within me, guiding my journey as I navigate the world without you by my side. This book is a tribute to your love and an acknowledgment of the invaluable lessons you imparted.

"WHILE THE WORLD STILL STANDS, TANTALIZING THRILL OF MYSTERY WILL FILL IT"

AMA NKRUMAH

CONTENTS

Title Page
Copyright
Dedication
Epigraph
Introduction
Preface

ROMANCING THE OLD	1
CHAPTER ONE	2
CHAPTER TWO	11
CHAPTER THREE	48
CHAPTER FOUR	67
CHAPTER FIVE	89
CHAPTER SIX	113
CHAPTER SEVEN	157
CHAPTER EIGHT	173
CHAPTER NINE	208
CHAPTER TEN	232
CHAPTER ELEVEN	276
CHAPTER TWELVE	312

CHAPTER THIRTEEN	357
CHAPTER FOURTEEN	382
CHAPTER FIFTEEN	431
CHAPTER SIXTEEN	456
Acknowledgement	509
About The Author	511
Books By This Author	513

INTRODUCTION

In this heartwarming real-life story, three families from diverse backgrounds embarked on a journey of friendship and resilience. At the center was Abeba, a spirited girl with dreams larger than life, found solace in her bonds with Njeri a wise and empathetic friend, and later with Ayanda, whose vibrant energy uplifted those around her. After navigating the turbulent waters of college, they found real life facing them. Abeba vanished without a trace after a night's party, leaving her friends in a state of confusion and worry. With Abeba gone, the atmosphere shifted from joy to despair. Njeri had always believed herself to be resilient, navigating the challenges of life with grace and determination. But when the most powerful woman in her world unexpectedly undermined her efforts, pulling the rug from under her feet, Njeri found herself in uncharted territory. Confused and betrayed as she grappled with the sudden shift in her reality. With her foundation shaken, Njeri knew she had a choice: either succumb to despair or rise to the occasion. Drawing on her inner strength, she sought allies and crafted a plan to reclaim her power.

Ayanda, drawn by her unquenchable quest for wealth, became entangled with the ambitious and manipulative third most powerful man in the land. As she delved deeper into this dangerous alliance, the stakes rose, and her humanity put to the test. Faced with a choice that could either elevate her to newfound affluence or compromise her integrity, Ayanda grappled with her identity and values. Will she succumb to the allure of wealth and influence, or will she muster the courage to stand up for her dignity, reclaiming her strength in a world that threatened to consume her? In this distressing journey, she must confront the true meaning of power and the essence of self-respect.

Ayanda's predicament will leave readers captivated and contemplative. As she navigates through the challenges of her unique situation. The questions linger: could anyone ever encounter a circumstance as perplexing and transformative as Ayanda's? Readers will likely reflect on the implications of her circumstance, questioning the boundaries of wealth and power.

PREFACE

In the dance of nature, the sun will rise, casting its warm glow, while the moon follows, illuminating the night with its silvery light. The stars will twinkle in the vast expanse above, and the clouds will drift lazily, painting the sky with their soft shapes. The winds will carry whispers of change, and the rain will nurture the earth, reminding us of life's cycles. Yet amid these certainties, the love we seek from others can often feel elusive and uncertain, a dizzying whirlwind of emotions. It is crucial to remember, however, that the most steadfast love is the one we cultivate for ourselves. Embracing and nurturing self-love lays the foundation for all other connections, allowing us to appreciate and share love with the world. We must not overlook this essential truth; self-love is the light that guides us through both clarity and confusion.

In this Book, "Romancing The Old" the aim is to inspire and uplift all of humanity by reminding us that there is a time and season for everything in life. There are moments when it may seem like the clouds of despair and challenges are never going to fade away. However, since the dawn of creation, we have seen that clouds - whether dense or papery, always move on. Just as they gather in the sky, they eventually drift away, leaving behind clear horizons. This recurring nature of existence serves as a powerful reminder that no matter how daunting the trials we face, they too shall pass, and brighter days are always on the horizon. This book offers a powerful exploration of life's journey, recounting the authentic experiences of real people growing up in a small town in Africa. It delves into the countless challenges and triumphs faced from childhood to adulthood, highlighting the universal struggles for survival and resilience. Through vivid storytelling, the author captures the essence of determination, emphasizing that despite the differences in personal narratives, a common thread unites: "the struggle continues, unabated." Just as with the changing seasons, hardships may emerge and dissipate, but it is our response to these challenges that ultimately shape our lives. Readers will find themselves reflecting on their own journeys, understanding that whether our experiences are alike or vastly different, the power to navigate our struggles lies firmly within us.

One profound truth that should be a guide: no trouble or problem faced is unique to one person; others have navigated similar struggles throughout history. The Earth, ancient and vast, has witnessed countless challenges long before our time: hardship is a shared human experience. With each new obstacle, one should find solace in the collective wisdom of those who have come before, and remember, that resilience is a timeless trait. The echoes of past troubles resonate in the present, encouraging us to face our own with courage and the understanding that, through perseverance, we can emerge stronger, having learned from those who endured before us. Through the journey of these three families, let us embrace hope and resilience, understanding that we are not alone in our experiences.

ROMANCING
THE OLD

TRUE AFRICAN STORY

BY
AMA NKRUMAH
MD. USA

CHAPTER ONE

"The Calabash Is Broken; Why Cry?"
(No Sense in Crying over Spilled Milk)

Abeba stood in the vast cornfield, the heat devils shimmering above her like ghostly mirages in the relentless early morning sun. At just six years old, she was brimming with excitement and curiosity, having recently passed the hand-over-ear test with flying colors. This achievement marked a significant milestone in her young life, signaling that she was ready to embark on the adventure of school. With bright eyes and a contagious smile, she looked forward to meeting new friends, learning new things, and exploring the world around her. Her parents cheered her on, proud of her accomplishments and eager to support her as she took this first big step.

School days filled with laughter, creativity, and discovery awaited her, and she couldn't wait to dive into this exciting new chapter of her life.

It was late August and the heat was intense, as she shielded her eyes from the blinding morning sunlight reflected by the leaves, which glinted like fierce green mirrors. Desperate to navigate her way through the field, she extended her hands, hoping to find the familiar boundary by touch, but the uneven ground betrayed her - a rough patch snagged her feet, and she stumbled, falling hard. The impact sent a jolt through her body, and she grazed her knees against the unforgiving soil. With a grimace, Abeba took a moment to gather herself, the sunlight bearing down relentlessly, reminding her of the steamy sun's grip. Despite enduring worse tumbles in the past, this particular fall left her feeling utterly humiliated, tears welling up in her eyes.

"Don't be such a baby," a voice chastised

her. She tried to regain composure. She shut her eyes tightly, hoping to block out the words; the soft rustle of leaves, the murmur of the wind, and especially the chastising voice, yet, the persistent crackling voice grew louder, a sound of determining arms pushing aside the foliage with an urgency. It was a reminder that she was not alone, that someone was following her, and eventually, whether she wanted to or not, she would have to face whoever, and the reality that awaited beyond her hidden refuge. With her eyes shut, she sensed an imposing shadow as someone approached her. She could hear the rustling of leaves and the distant call of birds, but her mind was elsewhere, lost in thoughts that felt too heavy to bear. "I know you can see and hear me," the voice said. Abeba finally opened her eyes, caught between the mayhem of the moment and the impending revelation of whose voice she was hearing.

The world around her felt both familiar and strange, as if she were on the brink of an adventure yet to unfold. "What are you doing down there? Did you faint? Are you okay?" the voice laced with worry asked. It was a strange moment, one that felt out of place. Abeba blinked slowly, trying to gather her thoughts and disorientation. She was a girl just like her, her hands hovered near her as if unsure whether to assist or just reassure her that everything would be alright. The surreal ambiance wrapped around them, blending concern with the ordinary act of grooming. As she sat on the ground, tears streaming down her face, she looked up at her and sobbed, "I just fell, but I'm okay, I only wrecked my dress." Her voice quivered as the weight of her ruined attire sank in. The elegant fabric, once a beautiful reminder of a special occasion, was now stained, and she felt utterly embarrassed.

The strange girl knelt beside her, gently stroking her hair to comfort her. "It's just a dress," she assured her with a warm smile. Slowly, she helped her to her feet, encouraging her to shake off the fall. Despite the mishap, she reminded her that what truly mattered was; she was safe and sound. With her support, she began to wipe away her tears, realizing that even a ruined dress couldn't steal her joy. "It's no surprise you tripped while wearing this ridiculous long dress in the field. Its essential to prioritize safety, especially when walking in areas that might not be foot-friendly. Next time, please hold onto your dress firmly, especially if it has a long train to prevent any accidents." The first day of first grade was more than just a new beginning; it was a special occasion that allowed children to express themselves without the constraints of a uniform. This day was a canvas where creativity thrived, and every child had the chance to shine in their own unique way, setting the tone for a year filled with discovery, learning, and self-expression. The classroom transformed into a vibrant tapestry, reflecting the rich diversity of the little ones eager to embark on this exciting new chapter together.

As Abeba sat up to assess the situation, she noticed the long streak of dirt marring the pink lawn of her dress, a beautiful dress made especially for her first day at school. The bruise on her knees stung, but the sight of her masterpiece - the gifted dress featuring a delicate pocket edged in rose fold - was what truly hurt. Now, feeling defeated, she wondered if she could ever reclaim the pride she felt when parading herself in it just a day before. As she rose, a sharp sting shot through her knees. With each hesitant step, she limped toward the gigantic corn, which loomed like a green leafy fortress around her. The stranger stood there, her eyes shifting with empathy, absorbing the weight of the moment unfolding before her. Her heart ached for her and with every tear that glistened in Abeba's eyes, she was reminded of the fragility of her own falls and the harsh realities that often accompanied it as she spoke. "My name is Njeri, and I'm sorry about your dress," she said, her voice a mix of regret and uncertainty.

Abeba in the stunning dress with elegance that seemed innate, offered a gentle smile in response. "It's okay, my name is Abeba," she replied, her tone warm and forgiving. But Njeri, unable to hold back her thoughts, interjected, "I know, you are the rich doctor's child." The admission, perplexing and filled with unspoken feelings.

Abeba's smile faltered for a moment, revealing the weight of expectations and perceptions, a complex web of social dynamics was laid bare, hinting at the contrasts between their worlds and the silent judgments that often accompany privilege. "Thank you for helping me up." They both walked deeper into the field, where sunlight flickered through the leaves, casting playful shadows on the ground. They took a few dozen steps, and soon the familiar outlines of their house and outbuildings faded from their view. They could see the transporter; the canoe that was to carry them across the calm river, where the buzz of school life never stopped among the school children in the nearby town.

Abeba starred up at the collection of sky filtered through the leaves and tassels. The corn stood tall, as if guarding some secret, yet it offered little refuge from the relentless sun overhead. The leaves were too sparse to form a comfortable shelter, but the two young girls maneuvered closer to the sturdy stalks, letting the delicate foliage shield their faces from the scorching rays. As the sun peered through the corn, they found themselves packed together with a group of children into a canoe, their laughter echoing across the calm waters. With paddles in hands and hearts full of excitement, they embarked on a journey to school that surpassed the challenges they faced. Whether they traveled by smooth strokes of the paddle or through the occasional bumpy strainers, the thrill of learning awaited them on the other side.

Each ripple in the water mirrored their enthusiasm; the chance to gain knowledge was a treasure far more valuable than any inconveniences they might encounter. In that moment, the canoe became their vessel of dreams, carrying them toward a brighter future filled with endless possibilities. The joy of education, regardless of the means, was a priceless gift they cherished deeply.

CHAPTER TWO

"No Man Can Paddle Two Canoes at the Same Time"
(A Thing at a Time)

Dr Fray was a man of noble character, embodying integrity in all aspects of his life. Growing up in a humble environment, he faced the harsh realities of poverty, which shaped his values and determination. Despite the challenges of his early years, he persevered and worked tirelessly to improve his circumstances. As he transitioned into adulthood, the struggles of his childhood became distant memories, replaced by a life marked by success and respect. Throughout his journey, Dr Fray remained grounded and committed to helping others, ensuring that his integrity and noble spirit shone brightly in the community he lived. His story was a testament to the power of resilience and the importance of staying true to one's principles, no matter the circumstances.

Despite being impoverished and overlooked by society in his early years, he demonstrated remarkable resilience and determination in his adult life utilizing his limited earnings to provide for his family. His unwavering dedication and remarkable skills as a doctor not only enabled him to provide a comfortable life for his family but also instilled a deep sense of pride and accomplishment within them. Through his craftsmanship, Dr Fray meticulously sharpened his medical expertise, transforming his passion for healing into a lifeline for those in need. Each patient he treated became a testament to his ingenuity, reflecting the countless hours of study and practice he committed to his craft. Each day he wove a fabric of hope and healing in the community he served through his unwavering dedication and love. He as well ensured that his children would have a foundation built on strength, creativity, and the belief that they could overcome any obstacles life presented.

Regardless of his numerous achievements and contributions to the medical field, Dr Fray found himself grappling with a salary that fell short of his expectations. Having dedicated years to rigorous education, countless hours in surgery, and a deep commitment to patient care, he anticipated that his financial rewards would reflect his efforts and expertise. However, the reality was disheartening; his earnings were modest and did not adequately compensate for the sacrifices he made along the way. This stark contrast between his professional accomplishments and financial compensation left him pondering. While the salary was sufficient enough to cover his personal expenses, it was hardly enough to support his family; himself included. Each month, he found himself juggling bills and expenses, often feeling the weight of financial strain, leaving him to wonder if advancing further up the corporate ladder would truly remedy the situation.

Sitting at his desk, Dr Fray stared blankly at the scattered papers and opened notebooks that surrounded him. The afternoon sunlight streamed through the window, and his mind was clouded with uncertainty. He knew he needed to make a decision, but the weight of the choices before him felt overwhelming. Would he take the risk and pursue a new opportunity, or stay in the safety of his current situation?

As he tapped his fingers rhythmically on the desk, he began to visualize the possibilities ahead. Each option held promise but also the potential for disappointment. Time seemed to stretch on, and with every passing moment, the urge to act grew stronger. He realized that the pursuit of a higher salary was not just about ambition, but about providing a better life for his loved ones. Every day felt like a struggle, and the realization struck him that he could no longer rely on others to define his financial future. With a fierce determination to change his circumstances, he decided it was time to take control of his life. Becoming his own boss was not just a dream; it was a necessity. He envisioned a future where he could set his own terms, create something meaningful, and, most importantly, earn enough to sustain himself and family comfortably.

The thought of independence stirred a mix of apprehension within him. However, he recognized that the sooner he embraced this crucial decision, the better equipped he would be to forge his own path. Each passing day served as a reminder that freelance required courage and resilience, and he was determined to find strength in his newfound pursuit, knowing that this journey, though daunting, would ultimately lead to personal growth and a deeper understanding of himself. With a clear roadmap guiding his efforts, he embarked on this exciting journey, fully aware of the challenges but unwavering in his determination to make a significant impact in the lives of those he longed to serve. The path would be tough, but the promise of freedom and self-sufficiency fueled his commitment to make it work.

Drawing from his extensive experience and deep understanding of medical practices, he created an environment that fostered trust and open communication between practitioners and patients through innovative approaches and continuous improvement. As he navigated the complexities of establishing his practice, he encountered obstacles in administrative policies and patient acquisition, which hindered continuous professional development. Despite the initial excitement about attracting new patients, the practice grew at a disappointingly slow pace. Nonetheless, undeterred by the sluggish start, he remained committed to his goal of delivering outstanding care.

Subsequently, his dream turned into a

significant burden for his family; challenges mounted, and financial instability began to take its toll. The pressure of erratic income and the uncertainty of the future led to heightened stress and anxiety within the household. Instead of providing the anticipated freedom and prosperity, his dream started to feel like a heavy weight, straining family relationships and creating a rift that seemed overwhelming, leaving him to wonder if the sacrifices were truly worth the cost. Despite his optimism and the promises of future opportunities, success remained elusive, and he felt increasingly frustrated. Each day was a reminder of the passion he once had for his work, overshadowed by the pressures of financial uncertainty and professional stagnation.

While Dr Fray yearned for a breakthrough that would finally allow him to focus on building a thriving practice, he continued to navigate the complexities of his career, hoping for brighter days ahead. Upon the daily hurdles, he clung to the belief that brighter days were on the horizon, determined to rise above the uncertainties and build the thriving practice he had always envisioned. His passion for helping others remained a guiding light, urging him to persevere in the face of adversity. While he appreciated the sporadic income, the lack of a solid foundation left him yearning for a more secure and fulfilling professional practice. With each challenge he faced, he refused to be disheartened; instead, he embraced the idea that behind every closed door could lie new opportunities. Each setback only strengthened his resolve, and through his dedication, he remained optimistic that his efforts would one day bear fruit, allowing him to truly make a difference in the lives of those he sought to help.

Some opportunities came his way through friends and regular customers who appreciated his reliability and skill. Each job, regardless of size, provided him with not only financial support but also a sense of community and belonging. His versatile approach to care allowed him to build lasting relationships, creating a network of trust and mutual support among clients and friends alike. As he continued to navigate this patchwork of opportunities, he discovered the joys of helping others while carving out his own humble path in the bustling world around him.

After months of unwavering perseverance and countless late nights, he slowly but surely made progress in his endeavors. Each step he took was fueled by the dreams that danced in his heart, lighting his path even in the darkest of times. At long last, after countless trials and moments of doubt, the breakthrough he had long anticipated arrived, sparkling like a beacon of light at his doorstep. This was the moment he had envisioned in his mind. As he stood before the opportunity, a sense of gratitude and determination surged within him, propelling him forward into a new chapter filled with endless possibilities and hope. The milestone was not just a piece of paper; it represented the pinnacle of his hard work, steadfast dedication, and unshakeable belief in his vision.

Signing the contract overwhelmed him with relief, overshadowing the tension that had weighed him down for months. The ink barely dried on the page before he felt an incredible sense of freedom, as if a burden had been lifted from his shoulders. The months of negotiation, the sleepless nights filled with uncertainty, and the endless doubts evaporated in an instant. He had faced obstacles that tested his resolve, but now, with his signature sealing the deal, a new chapter awaited him. The future stretched out before him, vibrant and full of possibilities, and for the first time in a long while, he could breathe deeply, embracing the promise of what was to come. The once daunting prospect of change transformed into an exciting adventure, igniting a fire of ambition within him that he hadn't felt in years.

Dr Fray was a man of dreams and ambitions, his aspirations, once distant stars in the night sky, had gradually transformed into tangible realities. Every challenge he faced became a stepping stone, propelling him closer to his goals. Through hard work and determination, he claimed victories both big and small, weaving them into the fabric of his existence. As each dream materialized, he found himself not just dreaming of a better future but actively crafting it. His journey became a testament to the power of perseverance, leaving a legacy that inspired those around him to chase their own ambitions. In the end, Dr Fray not only came through but thrived. He finally realized his dream of providing a stable and comfortable home for his family.

After much anticipation, he finally purchased a stunning home nestled in a prestigious community renowned for its beauty and serenity. The charm of tree-lined streets, where each whispering leaf seemed to tell a story, captivated him from the moment he arrived. The neighborhood exuded sophistication alongside a warm sense of community, where friendly faces greeted each other and vibrant interactions flourished. To celebrate this new phase in his life, he decided to indulge his family with a luxurious car, serving as a testament to his newfound success. This transformation represented a pivotal moment for them, as they embarked on a lifestyle brimming with opportunities, adventures, and experiences that promised to enhance their journey together.

Dr Fray quickly became the envy of his peers, captivating everyone with his remarkable talents and undeniable charisma. With a wealth of opportunity at his fingertips, he seemed to effortlessly turn dreams into reality. People began to associate his hands with the touch of King Midas, believing that whatever he touched flourished and prospered. His once humble beginnings were overshadowed by his newfound success, leaving those around him to marvel at his uncanny ability to achieve greatness. As admiration turned into jealousy, a silent competition brewed among his old colleagues, each one longing for just a taste of the fortune and favor that seemed to follow him wherever he went. His extraordinary ability to provide medical care and a healing touch truly distinguished him from others. Patients who sought his assistance often left not only with improved physical well-being but also with a sense of emotional comfort that was hard to find elsewhere. Whether through a gentle touch or a calming presence, his approach went beyond traditional methods.

Many badged him a beacon of hope in challenging times, as he navigated the complexities of health with remarkable skill and empathy. Dr Fray's unique gift stood as a testament to the power of caring and the importance of holistic healing in patient care. His remarkable talent not only made him wealthy beyond imagination but also opened doors to exclusive circles that were once inaccessible to him. He eagerly joined clubs where only the elite mingled, and engaged in conversations with the most influential people of his time. In those luxurious venues, he could share his insights and experiences, rejoicing in the admiration of others who envied his fortune. However, beneath the surface of his gilded existence, he often pondered whether his newfound status was a blessing or a curse, questioning if true friendship could ever be forged in a world where wealth dictated worth. Each interaction left him wondering if people valued the man he was or merely the esteem he brought into their lives.

Dr Fray indulged in the glow of his club membership, a gateway to a world of lucks and favors that transformed his life into a dream come true. Every evening, he strolled through the club's lavish halls, where laughter echoed and friendships blossomed effortlessly. Exclusive events, delightful surprises, and unexpected opportunities seemed to follow him at every turn. The sense of belonging fueled his spirit, making him feel invincible and elated. With each passing day, he celebrated the thrilling highs of his newfound status and the privileges it brought him. Life could not be any better; he had the perfect blend of excitement and fulfillment, living his dream on grand scales. The sky was his limit, and he was determined to cherish every moment of this remarkable chapter in his life.

Mrs Elizabeth Fray, affectionately known as Betsy by her husband and closest family and friends, was a respected Matron at one of the city's colleges. Her warm demeanor and nurturing spirit made her a beloved figure among students and staff alike. With a dedication to fostering a supportive environment, Betsy played a crucial role in the lives of countless young people, always ready with a comforting word or a helping hand. Her commitment to education and her genuine care for others left a lasting impression on the school community, making her not just a Matron, but a cherished mentor and friend. Through her efforts, Betsy helped create an atmosphere where students felt valued and encouraged to thrive.

Long before Dr Fray secured his breakthrough, and success began to flow in his direction, it was Betsy who served as the lifeline of the family. With unwavering determination and an endless supply of love, she held everything together during their toughest times. While her husband struggled to find his footing, she single-handedly managed the household. Her resilience and spirit shone brightly, instilling hope in her family when it felt like the world was against them. Her sacrifices laid the groundwork for the eventual prosperity that followed, highlighting her crucial role in their journey.

Notwithstanding the fact that Dr Fray's achievements grew, Betsy's strength and support continued to carry the day in the hearts of the family. She understood the struggles of living on her husband's limited wages, which often fell short of meeting the needs of their family. Despite the challenges, she was determined to ensure that her loved ones always had enough to eat. With her resourcefulness and creativity, she stretched their budget by planning meals carefully, opting for seasonal produce, and making the most of what they had on hand. She took pride in her ability to provide nutritious meals, often cooking in bulk and recycling leftovers to minimize waste. Her dedication not only filled their plates but also brought a sense of warmth and togetherness to their home. Through her efforts, she instilled in them a sense of pride and understanding.

Despite Dr Fray's strong opposition to the idea, Betsy found herself in moments of need, turning to her parents for support. While her husband's disapproval lingered in the background, her connection with her parents provided her with a sense of comfort as she was the only child in the family. They listened patiently to her concerns, offering guidance that sometimes conflicted with her husband's beliefs. Betsy and Dr Fray shared a connection that was unbreakable, rooted in mutual loyalty and trust. They faced life's challenges hand in hand, always prioritizing each other's happiness and well-being. Their commitment to one another remained steadfast. Dr Fray admired Betsy's unwavering support during tough times, while Betsy cherished his ability to bring joy and light into her life. Together, they created a sanctuary of love, where honesty and understanding flourished.

As they navigated life's ups and downs, their dedication to each other served as a testament to the beauty of true love. Finding solace in the knowledge that they would always be there for one another, they chose to defy the norm by openly sharing their affection and love for each other. Whether in the quiet moments of the morning or amidst the hustle and bustle of daily life, their warmth radiated. In the secluded neighborhood where everyone seemed wrapped up in their own lives, the Fray family appeared to fit the perfect picture of happiness. Neighbors often admired their seemingly perfect life, unaware of the struggles that unfolded behind closed doors. They worked tirelessly to provide for their children, juggling multiple jobs while trying to maintain a sense of normalcy. Despite their hardships, the family wore smiles that masked their fatigue, making it nearly impossible for others to see the weight of their challenges.

Betsy and Dr Fray shared a special bond, a love story that blossomed amidst lockers, homework, and teenage dreams. Their laughter echoed through the hallways, and they shared countless memories, from attending school dances to studying together under the flickering fluorescent lights. Their shared experiences in the same classrooms and hallways paved the way for a deeper connection, filled with mutual memories and dreams for the future. Each moment spent together deepened their bond during their teenage years. They graduated together from the same school in the same year. This milestone not only marked the end of their academic journey but also the beginning of their life together. They supported each other through the challenges of schoolwork and the excitement of new opportunities. As they celebrated their graduation, their love story blossomed amidst the backdrop of their academic achievements, creating a unique chapter in their lives that continued to influence their journey together. Graduating side by side symbolized the enduring partnership they had cultivated, as they look forward to the many adventures that lay ahead.

While their paths diverged a bit after graduation, the memories of their youthful romance stayed put, reminding them both of the innocent dreams and aspirations they had together. Time may have changed many things, but the essence of their first love remained etched in their hearts, a testament to a beautiful chapter of their lives that shaped who they became.

Betsy graduated as a culinary student, marking a significant milestone in her journey toward becoming a professional chef. Enthusiastic about her new skills and knowledge, she quickly entered the job market and secured employment with one of the colleges in the city right after her graduation. This opportunity not only allowed her to apply her culinary expertise but also enabled her to inspire and teach aspiring chefs in a dynamic educational environment. Her passion for cooking and commitment to excellence were evident as she embarked on this exciting chapter of her career, where she refined her craft and contributed to the culinary community. With each dish prepared, she did not just fill plates but also shaped the next generation of culinary talent.

Growing up as the only child, she

wallowed in the comfort of her parents' love and attention. With every wish and whim granted, her life unfolded like a fairy tale, and everything she desired was presented to her on a silver platter. Betsy became a culinary wizard in the making. Her aptitude for combining two simple ingredients into a remarkable dish was nothing short of magical. She had an innate ability to envision flavors and textures that would surprise anyone. A dash of this, a sprinkle of that, and suddenly a simple meal transformed into a gourmet experience. She delighted her friends and family with her creativity in the kitchen. Her passion for experimenting with flavors made her a star in her culinary class, inspiring others to see the beauty and the joy of cooking.

The first meal she prepared for Dr Fray whilst dating was an experience that remained inscribed in his memory forever. The aroma filling the room with warmth and comfort as he took his first bite while the rich flavors danced in his stomach. A harmonious blend of spices and ingredients that spoke to her culinary prowess. Every mouthful was like a warm embrace, reminding him of the love and care that went into its preparation. Betsy's cooking had a way of making Dr Fray feel at home, no matter where he was. It was not just the food she prepared; it was the laughter shared around the table, and the memories that made that first meal unforgettable. Betsy's dish was more than just a meal; it was a cherished moment in time.

After years of friendship filled with laughter and late-night study sessions, their relationship blossomed into something deeper. Just two years after they graduated, they decided to take a monumental step together and tied the knot. Their marriage celebration was a heartfelt affair, radiating love and warmth surrounded by friends and family who had witnessed their journey from classmates to life partners. As they exchanged vows, the joy in their hearts reflected the dreams they had nurtured together during their time in school. This new chapter marked not just the union of two individuals, but also the merging of hopes and aspirations for their future. With every promise made, Betsy and Dr Fray embraced the adventure of married life, ready to support each other through all of life's challenges and triumphs.

Betsy became a truly hands-on bride who made her wedding day special in every possible way. She infused her personality into the celebration, taking on the ambitious task of preparing most of her own wedding dishes. This wasn't just about food for her; it was about creating a heartfelt experience for her guests. She spent countless hours in the kitchen, experimenting with recipes that reflected her favorite flavors and family traditions. From savory appetizers to desserts, she poured her love into each dish, ensuring that everything was perfect for the occasion. The result was not just a meal but a tapestry of memories woven through taste, making her wedding a unique and unforgettable event and more meaningful for everyone involved.

On their second anniversary, Jabari, the oldest child of the family was born, marking a joyous milestone in their lives. The Frays were thrilled as they prepared for the arrival of their first child. Over the years, they diligently saved every penny, knowing that significant occasion would not only change their lives but also bring immense joy and responsibility. Their home was filled with love and anticipation, each corner adorned with baby clothes, toys, and a cozy nursery waiting for its new occupant. Friends and family showered them with advice and support. Dr Fray often imagined the day he would hold his son for the first time, while Betsy feasted in the thought of the countless memories they would create as a family.

As the due date drew near, their hearts brimmed with love and dreams for the future, eager to embark on this beautiful journey of parenthood together. Jabari's arrival filled their home with laughter and love, as they celebrated not just their love for each other but also the beginning of their journey as parents. Jabari quickly became the center of their world, bringing new challenges and experiences that deepened their bond. Each day was a discovery:from his first smiles to his first steps, and they cherished every moment. Dr Fray and Betsey reflected on how their lives had changed since that special day, two years ago, and were grateful for the joy their son brought into their hearts. As they looked ahead, they eagerly anticipated creating countless more memories as a family, knowing that Jabari would always be a reminder of their love and commitment to one another.

Before the Fray's breakthrough, life for Jabari and his family was filled with challenges, yet they managed to create a stable environment with their himd. Although they did not live in luxury, they found contentment in their simplicity. Jabari was fortunate enough to attend one of the city's best private schools, where he received an excellent education and formed lasting friendships. They prioritized his upbringing, ensuring that he was exposed to opportunities that would help him flourish. They understood the value of a good education and instilled in him the importance of hard work and perseverance. Dr Fray always believed that good education was a choice he would not trade for anything. Growing up, he understood the invaluable lessons that knowledge could provide, shaping not only his mind but also his character. Throughout his life, he tirelessly pursued learning opportunities, whether through formal schooling or self-study. He often reflected on how this choice opened doors to new experiences and broadened his perspective of the world. For him, education was not simply about acquiring facts; it was a lifelong journey that empowered him to think critically and made informed decisions.

Dr Fray frequently shared his belief with

his peers that education extends far beyond the confines of the classroom. He passionately encouraged everyone in his circle to delve into any reading material they could find, emphasizing that the pursuit of knowledge could unlock vast opportunities. To him, information was akin to wealth, a treasure that could enrich one's understanding of the world. Whether it was a book, an article, or even the news, he advocated for continuous learning as a means to empower oneself. His motto, "knowledge is power, and ignorance a massive casualty." He firmly believed that the pursuit of knowledge could liberate individuals from the shackles of ignorance, empowering them to make informed decisions and contribute meaningfully to society. In a world rife with misinformation and complacency, he viewed ignorance as a significant threat, leading to societal regression and individual disenfranchisement.

Jabari lived in a world where dreams

came true after his parents' breakthrough. He had the toys that sparked his imagination, from shiny cars to fantastical action figures that came to life in his mind. His room was a treasure trove of wonders, filled with books that took him on magical journeys and games that challenged his skills. He enjoyed countless adventures in the great outdoors, climbing trees, riding his bike, and exploring every corner of his neighborhood. With a loving family supporting him, echoes of laughter filled his life. Surrounded by friends who shared his joy and curiosity, he never felt alone. In every moment, Jabari realized he lacked nothing; he was truly living the childhood dream, a life brimming with happiness, love, and endless possibilities. Each day was another page in his story, filled with excitement and wonder and the attention that came with being the sole focus of his parents' affection.

Suddenly, the spotlight that once shone brightly on him dimmed as his parents' attention became divided. Everything shifted dramatically with the arrival of his baby sister. The joy he once felt began to wane as he grappled with feelings of jealousy and confusion. While he loved his sister dearly, he struggled to adjust to this new reality where his every whim was no longer the top priority. In time, Jabari would learn to embrace his role as an older brother, but the transition from the pampered life he knew to sharing everything with his sibling was an adjustment he didn't anticipate.

Jabari became the protective older brother, boasting six years of wisdom over his younger sister, Abeba. This age difference meant that he often took on the role of a mentor, guiding her through childhood adventures and life lessons. He was a constant source of support and encouragement. Abeba looked up to him, admiring his confidence and sense of humor. With enough resources to meet their basic needs, their parents were able to focus on creating a supportive atmosphere for them.

They took pride in providing a comfortable home filled with love and care, ensuring that they both had a solid foundation to grow up on. With Jabari's basic needs sufficiently met, he thrived in an environment designed to nurture his growth and well-being. Dr Fray, liberated from financial worries, channeled his energy into creating a nurturing environment that promoted Jabari's exploration and self-expression. Feeling a profound sense of love and security, he engaged with the world freely, fostering his curiosity and personal growth.

Soon, a significant change was about to unfold; signaling a bigger shift on the horizon for Jabari and his family. Dr Fray, who had quietly held a limited share in the private practice he founded, faced mounting pressure from the other shareholders. They were adamant that he relocate to a newly established facility situated in a remote part of the country. This impending move not only jeopardized the family's stability but also posed risks to the relationships and community ties they had built over the years. As the shareholders pushed for the move, the Dr Fray found himself at a crossroads, uncertain about the impact this relocation would have on his family and the future of the practice that had been their lifeblood. Tensions mounted as he weighed the benefits of the move against the heartache of leaving behind their familiar surroundings.

Dr Fray stood at a crossroad, contemplating a significant transition that could redefine his family's future. As he weighed the pros and cons of raising their children in the serene embrace of rural areas, he grappled with the allure of simplicity against the potential challenges of limited access to resources. The quiet charm of nature and a close-knit community beckoned to him, promising a different pace of life. However, he worried about educational opportunities and social interactions that urban environments typically offer. Each option carried its own set of possibilities and sacrifices, leading him to question what kind of upbringing would best shape his children's values, experiences, and dreams. While he held reservations about the limited opportunities and lifestyle that the countryside offered, he was equally hesitant to lose his shares in the private medical practice which he had put immense effort and dedication into establishing, facing countless challenges and setbacks along the way. The thought of relinquishing his shares felt like a betrayal to his hard work and vision, not to talk of the bustling life he had built around his private medical practice.

While he appreciated the serene landscapes and slower pace of rural living, he couldn't shake off the nagging reservations regarding the limited opportunities it presented. This internal conflict left him at a crossroads, weighing the allure of a simpler life against the fear of losing the professional identity that had consumed his life for sometime. Balancing these competing desires,

Dr Fray grappled with the question of what truly defined success and fulfillment for his family. He understood that the charm of rural living came with challenges, but he was determined to find a balance between his aspirations and the nurturing environment he wanted for his children. As he navigated his options, he pondered how to create a fulfilling life that enabled his children to thrive while also safeguarding his financial future. He tried to convince Betsy what living in rural areas offered. Numerous advantages, one of the most significant being access to fresh and healthy food. Residents often enjoy locally made produce that is not only fresher but also packed with nutrients. Many rural communities have farmers' markets where they could purchase organic fruits and vegetables directly from local growers, ensuring that their meals are wholesome and free from harmful chemicals."

Betsy equally reminded him of the challenges, particularly with access to quality education and essential resources like clean drinking water. Despite the serene landscapes and close-knit communities that often characterize rural life, residents frequently find themselves facing significant limitations. "The absence of good schools can hinder the educational opportunities available to children, leaving them at a disadvantage compared to their urban counterparts. Child education is a fundamental pillar that cannot be jeopardized." Betsy pressed on.

Dr Fray found himself in a dilemma as the prospect of relocating to a rural area weighed heavily on his mind. He understood the importance of a solid educational foundation for their children and was equally apprehensive about how a move might impact this critical aspect of their family's future. While he was attracted to the potential investment opportunities in the rural setting, his concerns about access to quality education overshadowed any financial incentives. The thought of uprooting his children from the city they had come to love weighed heavily on his heart. He knew that staying in the city was paramount, yet abandoning his investment felt like a daunting path. The challenges of navigating this change loomed before him, creating a mix of anxiety and hope.

As the days passed, the urgency of the situation mounted, and he found himself at a crossroads, contemplating how to strike a balance. The need for a decision grew stronger, urging him to seek a solution. With just a month remaining, he felt the pressure mounting; the clock ticking, and every moment counted as he weighed the pros and cons of relocating. He envisioned the consequences of failure - a complete loss of everything he had put in. With stakes this high, he knew he had to act swiftly and strategically, gathering all the necessary information while exploring possible avenues to safeguard his interests. Time was not on his side, and he understood that his next steps would determine not only the fate of his investment but also his financial future.

CHAPTER THREE

"Men Who Make Sport of a Monkey in a Cage
Will Not Spare the Carrier."
(Associate with Fools and You'll
Be Treated like a Fool.)

◆ ◆ ◆

The following day was Wednesday, a day typically reserved for the men's group club meetings in the neighborhood. Just when Dr Fray arrived, he spotted his childhood friend, Professor Simpson, chatting with a few other members. Memories of their shared past flooded back, and he felt an overwhelming urge to confide in him about the struggles he had been facing recently. Although he hesitated for a moment, pondering the potential weight of his troubles on their friendship, he sensed that sharing his ordeal could bring both relief and support. With a deep breath, he approached Prof, as affectionately called, ready to open up about the challenges that had been weighing heavily on his mind. The warmth of their brotherliness reassured him that maybe sharing his burden could lighten the load.

Growing up in the same neighborhood, Professor Simpson and Dr Fray shared a tie that went beyond friendship; they were like brothers. From their early childhood adventures, where they built wooden playhouse in the backyard, to teenage escapades that ignited a lifelong friendship making their connection deeply rooted in shared experiences and mutual respect. Their lives unfolded around school days, family gatherings, and the inevitable challenges of growing up, but through it all, they remained inseparable. Their laughter echoed through the years, each moment reinforcing the notion that they had found in each other a kindred that would last a lifetime.

Even as adults, the lessons learned and the memories made together kept their bond strong, showcasing a friendship that was a true testament to brotherhood. The interrelated lives of the Simpsons and the Frays painted an authentic picture of longstanding family connections. Prof's older brother shared a classroom with Dr Fray's older sister, solidifying their bond during their formative years that evolved into a close-knit friendship circle that crossed generations. Family gatherings became lively reunions filled with shared memories and laughter, drawing on the experiences that had woven their families together. The legacy of this friendship not only enriched their lives but also laid the foundation for future generations.

In their world shrouded in secrecy and unspoken truths, they found solace in their friendship. Each bore the weight of hidden secrets, burdens that felt too heavy to share with the outside world. Yet, within the sanctuary of their shared confidences, Prof and Dr Fray discovered a bond that went beyond mere acquaintance. Late-night conversations and whispered confessions became their refuge, a sacred space where vulnerability was met with understanding. They knew the contours of each other's hidden lives; the fears that haunted them and the dreams they dared not voice. Trust blossomed as their friendship built on shared secrets, became a lifeline.

As Dr Fray reminisced about the many years spent alongside his trusted friend, he decided it was time to confide in him. He explained the plight that had been weighing him down, revealing the truth about his private medical practice that had long been hidden. "With barely a month to make a decision, I feel the weight of responsibility pressing down on me. Jabari is currently navigating the early stages of his primary education, laying the groundwork for his future learning and development. This initial phase is crucial as it will equip him with essential skills and knowledge that will serve him throughout his academic career, especially with focus on foundational subjects such as literacy and numeracy. Unfortunately, I find myself in a difficult position, as the prospect of sending him to a rural school feels out of reach. Every day counts, and I am acutely aware that his early learning experiences will shape his future. I want the best for him, but the options are limited. I am desperate to find a solution that ensures he gets the education he needs while balancing the constraints of our situation. Time is ticking, and I must act quickly to secure a brighter path for him.

Abeba, my little sunshine who fills my days with joy and laughter is currently in a stage of early childhood where she is not yet of school-going age. Her days are filled with play, exploration, and learning at home, as she engages in activities that stimulate her curiosity and creativity. She enjoys the freedom of these formative years, where the focus is on discovering the world around her. I find comfort in knowing that her bright future awaits and often imagine how it will be when she finally puts on her school uniform, ready to embark on new adventures. I can't help but think about the time when I will return to the city, ready to navigate the bustling life again. By then, I hope to have found my footing, ensuring that Abeba's journey is filled with as much love and support as possible. Until then, I cherish every moment with her, understanding that these early years are as precious as the education and experiences that lie ahead." After Dr Fray narrated his plight, a sense of relief overwhelmed him, knowing that he had someone who understood his struggles.

Prof listened intently as his friend recounted the troubling news about his family's situation. The information weighed heavily on him, but Prof refused to let despair take hold. With a reassuring tone, he said, "don't worry, we will figure something out." He had always been the steadfast pillar in their friendship, ready to lend support in times of need. Ideas began to swirl in his mind, each one more hopeful than the last. He knew they had faced challenges before, and together, they could overcome this too. Prof's words weren't just empty promises; they were a vow to stand by his friend, no matter the hurdles ahead.

Dr Fray, however, was less optimistic, he frowned in concern as he retorted, "what can we possibly figure out?" the atmosphere was full with despair. While Prof, with unwavering determination worked hard to lift the spirits of his friend, offering words of encouragement and glimmers of hope, Dr Fray was lost amidst the overwhelming darkness that surrounded him. He remained trapped in a web of desolation, unable to escape the gnawing sense of helplessness that clung to him. Every effort to ignite optimism in him seemed futile. The contrast between Prof's anticipative demeanor and Dr Fray's internal struggle highlighted the profound complexity of his situation. While Prof sought to break free from the chains of despair, Dr Fray found himself entangled within its suffocating grip. With a shared determination, they began to brainstorm solutions, believing that with friendship and resourcefulness, brighter days lay just around the corner. Prof sat across from his friend, concern imprinted on his face. "I promise you, something will definitely be done about this situation," he reassured him, his voice steady and calm. He could see the worry in his friend's eyes, and it only fueled his determination to act. He knew the challenges ahead were daunting, but he was ready to face them head-on.

"Let's not lose hope," he continued, his tone filled with conviction. "Together, we can find a way to resolve this. I won't let you down." With that, he reached out, placing a reassuring hand on his friend's shoulder. Prof understood how important it was to uphold that promise, and he was prepared to put in the work required to bring about the help his friend desperately needed. In a moment thick with tension, Prof turned to Dr Fray, his voice carrying both concern and disbelief. "Have you forgotten my own circumstances?" he pressed, recalling the weight of a past decision that still weighs heavily on him. "Do you remember the challenging crossroads I encountered when I accepted my political appointment? It meant leaving my only son behind in the States, a sacrifice that was both professional and profoundly personal. The choice was not made lightly, as it severed the everyday bonds that parents cherish with their children.

Your situation echoes within me, a reminder of the complexities of duty and family that we all navigate in our lives. My only son, who is now eight years old, is currently staying with my brother in the States. The prospect of moving to another country filled me with dread, as I wanted stability for him. I felt the weight of that choice heavily on my shoulders, knowing how crucial it was for Malik's upbringing. My brother and I grappled with the decision of what was best for his early development. Understanding the critical importance of early childhood education, we deliberated on various options. Ultimately, my brother stepped in, and proposed Malik stayed back with him while I fulfill my national obligation. He took Malik as part of his own family. This arrangement brought some solace to me, allowing me to fulfill my national obligations while ensuring that my son remained in a loving environment.

The challenges of balancing career and family life would always be present, but family and friends' support would make a significant difference. I believed it was essential for him to have a strong bond with family, and I trusted my brother to provide guidance and support during that period. Although I miss him dearly, I am comforted by the thought that he is in good hands, gaining new experiences and memories that will last a lifetime. I look forward to hearing all about his adventures and the lessons he learns while we are apart.

Currently, Jada and I find ourselves without a child in our care. I plan to have a conversation with her about your situation to explore possible solutions. Perhaps we can arrange for Jabari to stay back with us in the city, allowing for some stability while we figure things out. We want to ensure that his needs are met and that he feels comfortable. By discussing this together, we can come up with a plan that works for everyone involved. It's important for us to remain flexible and supportive during this time, and I'm hopeful that we can find a suitable arrangement soon." Prof proposed a creative approach to help his friend.

Dr Fray found himself torn between loyalty and concern. Despite being Prof's closest confidant, the thought of leaving his child in the bustling city filled him with dread. He could hardly fathom the dangers and distractions that city life offered, and it pained him to imagine his little one navigating such a chaotic environment without his protection. The bond he shared with Prof was strong, forged through years of friendship and shared experiences, yet the welfare of his child outweighed those sentiments. he felt a deep sense of unease, although he understood that circumstances had forced his hand, the thought of entrusting his precious son to Prof filled him with apprehension. He pondered whether his choice would permanently alter the course of his child's life and if he had any alternatives that could allow him to remain present. Dr Fray was torn between his career responsibilities and the desire to be an active part of his child's formative years, leaving him grappling with guilt and worry. "Thank you for your understanding and willingness to help" Dr Fray said. After exchanging thoughts for a while, they parted ways, each lost in thoughts, reflecting on the likelihood that lay ahead and the importance of collaboration in making informed choices.

As the evening began to wind down, Dr Fray realized he needed to have a conversation with Betsy about the possibility he and Prof had considered earlier. The night air felt crisp and cool, and he knew that the next conversation with Betsy would be crucial in shaping their path forward. Her perspective was important, and he wanted to ensure he had all the information before making a final decision. That night, Dr Fray gently stirred Betsy awake, knowing that the conversation ahead was crucial. As the darkness of the room surrounded them, he touched on the delicate subject of leaving Jabari behind, considering the impact it would have on their family. The possibility of entrusting him to his bosom friend, Prof weighed heavily on their minds. He voiced his own concerns about Jabari's well-being and the importance of having a stable environment during such uncertain times. Betsy listened intently, her heart racing as she contemplated the implications of their choice.

Together, they navigated the emotional landscape of their decision, weighing the risks and rewards of leaving Jabari in the care of someone they trusted. Although the night air was full with tension, their dedication to doing what was best for their son guided them through their challenging moment. Betsy was initially taken aback by the notion of leaving their young son in the care of the Simpsons in the city. The mere idea caused her to feel a rush of anxiety, conjuring up fears about safety and trust. She envisioned all sorts of scenarios that made her heart race, imagining what could go wrong in a thronging environment. However, Dr Fray managed to calm her nerves, patiently discussing Jabari's benefits of the arrangement. With reassuring words, he laid out how the Simpsons were capable and trustworthy, emphasizing the importance of their shared goals. Gradually, Betsy began to see the situation from a new perspective. Eventually Dr Fray's support and understanding helped her come around to the idea, transforming her initial hesitation into a sense of cautious optimism about their son's future.

The two families gathered the Sunday to engage in a thoughtful discussion about the best way to ensure Jabari could remain in the city with the Simpsons. As they sat around the table, filled with optimism and concern, each member contributed their ideas and preferences. The Frays shared their perspective, emphasizing the benefits of having Jabari close, while the Simpson family contemplated the implications for his schooling and social life. They contemplated various options, considering everything from logistical arrangements to emotional well-being. As the conversation unfolded, it became clear that everyone was committed to finding a solution that would work for Jabari. By the end of the meeting, they felt more united and hopeful about crafting an arrangement that would allow Jabari to stay and thrive with the Simpsons in the city.

Three weeks after the necessary arrangements were made, Dr Fray and his family embarked on a new chapter in their lives, moving to a serene rural area with their young daughter, Abeba. This decision marked a tearful transition for the family, as they left behind their oldest child. The countryside promised tranquility and a fresh start, yet the absence of Jabari weighed heavily on their hearts. Dr Fray and Betsy hoped that their new surroundings would provide a nurturing environment for Abeba, filled with nature's wonders and a slower pace of life. However, the emotional struggle of leaving Jabari behind lingered, as they grappled with the complexities of family dynamics and the bittersweet nature of their choice. While the rural life beckoned with its promises, the separation from their oldest child cast a shadow over their new beginnings.

Formal adoption was neither common nor widely recognized, nonetheless, Jabari found solace in the home of the Simpson family.

The warmth and affection that filled their household made it clear that Jabari was as good as their own child. The Simpsons embraced him wholeheartedly, providing the love and support that every child needs to thrive. In their eyes, Jabari was not just a boy taken in out of circumstance; he was a cherished member of the family, weaving a new narrative of connection and love that would last a lifetime. Jada, the devoted wife of Simpson, exhibited the essence of the western lifestyle alongside her husband. Together, they found joy in the good fellowship of their tight-knit community, where neighbors lent a helping hand and friendships thrived. Jada's spirit mirrored the wild beauty of the West, as she and Prof built a life rich with adventure, love, and the enduring charm of their chosen lifestyle. In their community, their western lifestyle and unique experiences set them apart as symbols of class and sophistication. With an appreciation for modern amenities intertwined with traditional values, they embraced a way of life that reflected both elegance and authenticity. Their gatherings were marked by refined tastes, from gourmet cuisine to well-chosen decor, showcasing a blend of cultural influences that impressed neighbors and friends alike. This distinction elevated their status, as many sought to emulate their style and grace.

As they steered through the complexities of contemporary living, they remained grounded in the values of kindness and respect, ensuring their classy reputation was not merely about appearances but also about genuine connections. In the fullness of time they became role models, embodying the essence of what it meant to thrive in a fast-paced world while honoring their roots.

Transitioning to a new school can be daunting, and Jabari's was a significant turning point in his life. The modern school he joined was a world away from his previous environment, filled with diplomats and affluent families who brought their own set of expectations and social dynamics to the school. But for Jabari, the journey became one of discovery and growth, thanks in large part to the Simpsons. Amid the swirling chaos of unfamiliar faces and challenging coursework, he found a beacon of support and care in their unwavering commitment while navigating the complexities of his new surroundings. They helped him adjust to his peers and fostered his confidence, ensuring he felt valued and accepted. Together, they cultivated a sense of belonging that allowed him to thrive academically and socially, making this chapter of his life, one filled with both challenges and personal growth. With the Simpsons by his side, Jabari learned the importance of family, friendship, and resilience in the face of change.

CHAPTER FOUR

"A Wanderer Who Is Determined to
Reach His Destination Does Not Fear the Rain"

The Frays now living in a remote rural area where the communication system was painfully inadequate. This hindered their ability to maintain connections with the Simpsons. They could only connect with them sporadically by traveling miles away and each conversation, albeit infrequent, became precious moments woven with significance. With each discussion, Prof shared updates on Jabari's progress, aspirations, and challenges, hoping that those snippets of his life would resonate with his friend and keep their connection alive despite the vast distance that separated them. Though the gaps between ther communication often left Dr

Fray and Betsy anxious and longing for a deeper connection, they cherished every brief moments, understanding how vital they were for maintaining their family bond and sharing the joys and challenges of childhood. Despite the obstacles, the Frays remained hopeful that one day, improvements in the communication network would allow them to keep in closer touch with his friend, ensuring that news about Jabari and other life events would flow more easily between them.

In the tenth year of their journey, the Frays had became an integral part of the rural landscape, weaving their lives into the fabric of small communities. Their presence brought a profound transformation, as they engaged with local traditions and contributed to the vibrant lifestyle of rural life. The once quiet villages began to pulse with new energy, fueled by the Frays' initiatives and collaborative spirit. Farmers shared their knowledge, artisans showcased their crafts, and children laughed in the fields as the Frays fostered an environment rich in connection and creativity. Through community events, workshops, and shared experiences, those years marked a discerning evolution, highlighting the power of collaboration and the beauty of rural resilience.

The Frays, in their steadfast dedication, not only celebrated the land and its people but also cultivated lasting bonds that would echo through generations to come. Life for them was comfortable and simpler; finding contentment in their simpler lifestyle. Yet, despite the appeal of a quiet in the rural existence, they craved the vibrancy and excitement that city living offered. The pulse of the city promised adventure and connection; a stirring curiosity about what lay beyond their small town often left them daydreaming.

Dr Fray stood as a beacon of hope for the residents, embodying the lifeline that many depended upon. As the sole medical doctor serving around fifteen to twenty neighboring villages, his presence was invaluable. The villagers relied on his expertise not just for medical treatment, but for comfort in times of distress. He dedicated himself to his craft, often going beyond his duties to ensure the well- being of each patient. His warm smile and gentle demeanor made him not only a healer but also a confidant for many. As news of illness spread from one home to another, the community's collective anxiety transformed into relief with the mere thought of his arrival. In an area where healthcare was scarce, Dr Fray's unwavering commitment and compassion lit the path to better health for all who sought his care.

For Abeba, being the only child of a prominent doctor certainly came with its own set of privileges. She was often at the center of attention wherever she went. Even on her first day of meeting Njeri, her very first day of school, where she stumbled and fell on the field, only to be met with a kind smile and helping hand from Njeri, her soon-to-be best friend. Their friendship blossomed from that moment, rooted in a shared understanding and mutual support.

Njeri always knew how to lift her spirits, reminding her that she was cherished and important, whether through shared experiences or heartfelt conversations, each moment strengthened the connection between them, transforming an awkward first day into the beginning of a beautiful friendship that would last a lifetime. Abeba thrived in this nurturing environment, her confidence blossoming as a result. With every act of kindness and consideration, the people in her life reinforced her importance, creating a union that made her feel not just special, but loved.

Her father's esteemed profession and status opened doors to exclusive events and gatherings, where she had the opportunity to meet influential people from various fields in the community. This privileged upbringing, no matter how little or simple, nurtured

Abeba's aspirations and provided her with inspiration, as she witnessed firsthand the impact of her father's work on countless lives. Balancing the advantages and the responsibilities of being a doctor's only child was a unique journey that shaped Abeba's identity and ambitions. From an early age, she was accustomed to being treated with special attention that few, if any of her peers could imagine. The villagers treated her with a blend of reverence and admiration; they would often bow down as she passed by, acknowledging not just her father's esteemed position, but also as a symbol of prestige and admiration that her family represented and the social status that came with it. In the eyes of the community, she was more than just a girl - she was a symbol of prestige, someone whose presence was associated with respect and gratitude for the medical services her father provided. This adulation, however, sometimes felt suffocating, as it created an invisible barrier between her and the few friends she longed to connect with more intimately.

Amidst the bows and accolades, she often wondered what life would have been like had she been just another child in the village, free from the weight of expectation. While her friends often envied her lifestyle, she carried the weight of expectations that accompanied her family's reputation. She often felt the pressure to succeed, balancing the privileges of her upbringing with her desire for genuine friendships and personal achievements. Yet, out of the advantages, she sought to carve her own identity, striving to be more than just " the doctor's daughter."

Abeba was a bright young girl, her discerning intellect shone through from an early age. Her curiosity knew no bounds. She was endlessly fascinated by the wonders of local science experiments, observing the intricate patterns of plant growth. She immersed herself in hands-on learning. Subjects such as Mathematics captured her imagination; she saw numbers not just as symbols but as keys that unlocked the secrets of understanding to oneself. Each problem she solved felt like a small victory, fueling her desire to explore and understand the world around her. Her inquisitiveness drove her to seek knowledge in every form, making her a true seeker of understanding, often tackling small challenges that seemed daunting to her peers. With each passing year, she not only excelled in her studies but also developed a strong sense of self and a desire to make a difference in the world. Those around her recognized her potential, and as she continued to grow, it became clear that she was destined for greatness.

Abeba was a remarkable beauty, captivating all who crossed her path with her enchanting presence. As she blossomed into a young woman, her allure only grew stronger, drawing admiration from those around her. Her striking features were complemented by a sharp intellect, making her not only a vision of beauty but also of substance.

Conversations with her revealed her depth of thought and insight, earning her the respect and admiration of peers and elders alike. Her ability to balance grace and intelligence set her apart in a world where both qualities are often undervalued. As a young woman, she became a symbol of empowerment, inspiring others to recognize the strength that lies within beauty and intellect combined.

Despite her many gifts, she found herself in the stark and undesirable hinterland with her parents, a place that seemed to stifle her potential. Surrounded by the rugged landscape, she often daydreamed about the opportunities and adventures that lay beyond the skyline. Her brilliance and charm shone brightly, yet they appeared to be overshadowed by the isolation of her surroundings. She yearned for a life filled with new experiences. She believed deep down that she was meant for more than the quiet, unassuming life her parents had embraced.

Every day, she held onto the hope that one

day she would break free from the confines of the hinterland and step into a world where her brilliance could truly flourish. Betsy, her mother always found herself lost in thought, her mind racing with worries about Abeba's future. Each day in the village felt like Abeba's precious moment slipping away, and the uncertainty of when they would leave weighed heavily on her heart. The old-fashioned village, with its tranquil charm, felt both like a sanctuary and a cage. Betsy longed for her daughter to experience the vibrant city life, filled with opportunities, diversity, and the pulse of modernity. Yet, each day spent in the village was a mix of remembrance and anxiety. Betsy worried about the timing of their departure and whether they would find the right moment to embark on a new chapter. The streets of the city beckoned with promises of adventure, and the thought of her daughter missing out weighed heavily on her heart. With each passing day, she envisioned her daughter stepping into a vibrant world filled with diverse experiences, where affluence and elitism offered pathways to success. She knew that the transition would be challenging, but she remained hopeful that one day they would embark on this transformative journey together, setting her daughter on a course for a brighter future.

Meanwhile, Jabari's social life took a remarkable turn when Prof introduced him to Malik, who resided in the United States. This connection opened up a whole new world for Jabari, allowing him to explore diverse cultures and ideas that he had only previously read about. Malik, with his vibrant personality, quickly became an inspiration for his growth, encouraging him to step out of his comfort zone and engage with a wider circle of friends. In their time together, they engaged in profound conversations, sharing remarkable experiences that shaped their connection. Each discussion was a journey into their thoughts, dreams, and memories, revealing layers of understanding and intimacy that deepened their bond. They explored diverse topics, from their personal histories to their visions for the future, each exchange rich with insight and emotion. Through their dialogue, they uncovered not only each other's perspectives but also gained a clearer understanding of themselves.

Their conversations became a sanctuary, a space where both felt heard and valued, leading to a bond that would withstand the test of time. Jabari's horizons expanded as he embraced new opportunities and tales often shared by Malik about his school experiences and the simple joys of life in the State. He painted a vivid picture of the freedom he enjoyed - long afternoons spent playing outdoors, exploring nature, and forming unbreakable bonds with friends. Each story highlighted the carefree spirit that characterized his youth, filled with laughter and adventure as he navigated the joys and challenges of growing up. For Malik, this was a cherished period, a representation of every young child's dream, where possibilities seemed endless and the weight of the world felt distant.

Jabari wondered at Malik with curiosity and asked, "So, what do you do when it gets cold?" I heard it can really get chilly during some seasons; is that right?" Malik leaned back, recalling the biting winds and frosty mornings. He nodded, a smile creeping onto his face as he began to share stories of winter activities, cozy nights by the fire, and the joy of hot cocoa. He explained how he loved to bundle up in layers, enjoying the snow when it fell, and the magic that the cold season brought along.

Jabari listened intently, eager to learn about the charm of winter that he had only heard about and never experienced himself. He couldn't help but bombard Malik with a series of ludicrous questions, all stemming from his genuine curiosity. "How do you walk in the snow?" he inquired, his forehead wrinkling in deep contemplation. "Do you need to wear special boots or something to help you navigate the icy terrain?" It was as if Jabari believed that there was a secret art to traversing snowy landscapes that he had yet to learn. Malik chuckled at the absurdity, realizing that Jabari's innocent questions were just a reflection of his whimsical nature. Instead of dismissing them, he decided to indulge his curiosity, explaining the simple mechanics of walking in snow and the importance of proper footwear.

While Malik continued to chuckle softly, Jabari, curious and slightly perplexed, asked, "what's so funny?" With a playful grin, Malik replied, "Oh, it's nothing really, I just enjoy hearing your voice and how inquisitive you are about everything." His words lingered between their banter that filled their conversations. Jabari smiled, "I look forward to the day we meet face to face, where I can show you just how breathtaking it is when nature wraps the world in its frosty embrace. Until then, these images will have to suffice, capturing the beauty of a winter wonderland that we can one day explore together."

Malik captured numerous pictures and videos that showcased the enchanting transformation of his surroundings. Each snapshot told a story of delicate snowflakes dancing through the air, while the ground was adorned with spotless white coat. He shared those beautiful moments with Jabari through postage, offering a glimpse into the magic of snowfall. Each day, during their conversations, Malik couldn't help but ask Jabari the same question: "why won't Daddy bring you here to spend the vacation with us? It's so much fun! you'll really enjoy the States." His enthusiasm was very distinctive as he painted vivid pictures of all the adventures they could traverse together - exploring parks, visiting amusement attractions, and indulging in new foods.

Malik couldn't help but imagine the laughter and memories they would create during the vacation. He believed that having Jabari by his side would make the experience even more special. Each day, he eagerly awaited the chance to share his excitement, hoping that he would soon join them for the unforgettable break ahead. "How old are you now?" Malik asked Jabari. Jabari chortled softly, amused by Malik's inquisitiveness "Well, it seems like I've always been a bit older than you, right?" Malik teased. Jabari scratching his head and his brow slightly furrowed, replied playfully, "but age is just a number." Malik rolled his eyes, knowing that Jabari loved to dodge a straightforward answer. "Come on, just tell me," Malik urged, half- laughing. Jabari's grin widened, and he leaned back. "Alright then, let's just say I'm old enough to know better but young enough to still have fun." Their light-hearted banter continued.

Malik leaned back in his chair, a mischievous smile playing on his lips as he refused to drop the subject "I clearly have more candles on my birthday cake than you do, I only can't help but wonder just how many?" Jabari's curiosity evoked, "if you're bold enough, maybe you should ask Dad, he might spill the beans about our age gap," he continued, a twinkle in his eye. Malik enjoyed the playful banter and with a voice laced with impatience he shot back, "You think I haven't already?" "And what did Daddy say?" Jabari pressed further, mirroring the same urgent curiosity. Tension mounted as Malik sighed, knowing the conversation was headed in circles.

"What's the big deal about your age anyway? Is it some kind of forbidden question, or what?" he asked, a hint of playfulness in his tone. He leaned back, clearly intrigued by the mysterious mood surrounding Jabari's reluctance to share such a simple detail. To Malik, age was just a number, a mere fact of life that shouldn't dictate how one was perceived. Yet, Jabari's reaction suggested it held significance. "Just like you are doing now," he continued, irritation seeping through his words, "Daddy has been dodging around the question, not giving a straight answer. It's like he's scared of what will be found." They both understood there was more to the story, but unraveling it felt like chasing shadows, elusive and frustrating. As the evening grew darker, the clock signaled the late hour, prompting them to wrap up their phone conversation. "It's getting late over here," Jabari remarked, his voice influenced by the weariness of the day. They agreed to catch up again the next weekend, eager to continue their discussions then. With a familiar warmth in their interaction, they exchanged good nights. "Good night, Jabari," Malik replied, feeling a sense of comfort in their connection, while Jabari echoed the sentiment back. As they hung up, the tranquil silence of the night engulfed them, both looking forward to their next chat.

A few months later, Jabari began receiving unexpected mails at school. Each envelope held a collection of vibrant pictures showcasing Malik enjoying the winter wonderland, walking gracefully through the snow-covered landscape. The images captured the essence of winter, with Malik's laughter echoing through the serene frosty air. Alongside the personal snapshots were postcards, featuring prominent places throughout the State, each one depicting the beauty and charm of the local scenery. The postcards, with their stunning views and messages, evoked a sense of longing in Jabari, who couldn't help but wish he were there, sharing in Malik's adventures.

The mails became a delightful surprise that brightened Jabari's days, linking him to his friends and sparking his curiosity about the winter escapades that filled those chilly days. He beamed with pride as he showcased the pictures to his friends and the rest of the class. Each image captured a moment filled with laughter and joy, telling a story that resonated with everyone present. His classmates leaned in closer, their inquisitiveness aroused, while their eyes sparkled with admiration for his beautiful images. With every snapshot, Malik recounted the memories behind them, allowing Jabari and his friends to share in his excitement. The atmosphere buzzed with enthusiasm as they discussed the details and shared their own experiences. For Jabari, these moments were not only about the pictures but also about the connections he forged with those around him, strengthening the bonds of friendship and love within the classroom.

Malik was the epitome of charm and good looks, a striking figure whose presence turned heads wherever he went. With his captivating smile and magnetic personality, he seemed to be the guy every girl dreamed of. Among those enchanted by him was Mimi, who found herself utterly mesmerized by his charisma. From the moment she spotted his pictures, she felt a spark igniting within her - a feeling she had never experienced before. Malik's pictures resonated in her mind, making her forget everything else in the world. Captivated by his charm, she pleaded with Jabari to lend her one of his pictures, wanting to gaze at him whenever possible.

As Jabari watched Mimi's eyes light up at the sight of Malik's pictures, a knot tightened in his stomach. Despite knowing that Mimi was just a good friend, he couldn't shake off the unsettling feeling that maybe showing the pictures was a mistake. Doubts crept into his mind about their relationship, leaving him to wonder if Mimi's newfound admiration for Malik would alter the dynamics between them. The joy he initially felt began to fade, replaced by an unforeseen insecurity.

Jabari had always known that he was not the biological son of Prof and Jada Simpson, although they never once hinted at the truth of his origin. He relished the privileges that came with being a child of affluent parents. His life was enriched by educational opportunities and extracurricular activities. His upbringing, surrounded by comfort and abundance, shaped his outlook on life, giving him a unique perspective on both privilege and responsibility.

CHAPTER FIVE

"If We All Know What Tomorrow Brings
There Wouldn't Be Any Mysteries Behind The Wall"

In an old village situated near the village of the Frays, resided an elderly woman who everyone referred to as Madam Feli. She was often misunderstood by the townsfolk who couldn't fathom the joy she found in her conversations with the birds and the whispering leaves of her beloved garden. With flowers of every hue stretching toward the sun, her spirited sanctuary seemed to sparkle with life, a stark contrast to the scornful whispers that labeled her a witch. Yet, in her world, magic thrived not in spells but in the simple connections to nature - each bloom, a testament to her nurturing spirit. As she tended to her plants, she listened to the gentle chirps and rustles, finding wisdom and companionship in the natural world. While others turned away, she held fast to her unique gift, knowing that true enchantment lay in the beauty of her garden and the melodies of the wild around her.

Madam Feli had a distinctive charm when it came to calling her beloved chickens. In the open air, her chickens made their home among the sturdy branches of the trees, creating a serene and natural habitat. Every morning, as the dawn was ablaze with sunlight, she would wander into the yard and click her tongue against her cheeks in a rhythmic pattern. This unique sound echoed through the branches, drawing her feathery friends closer with every click. Responding to the melodic call that only she could produce, they would flap down in excitement to see her. Her bond with her chickens was special, rooted in her playful method of communication that turned an ordinary chore into a delightful experience shared with the lively birds that brought joy to her days. Although she lived alone, Madam Feli's home was filled with the scent of freshly baked bread, a treat she frequently prepared for those who stopped by. The children adored her stories of yesteryear, filled with magic and adventure.

In defiance of being labeled a witch, she carried an unyielding spirit that shone brightly through the whispers of her neighbors. Her hut, small and unassuming, stood on the hill at the outskirt of the village. Inside it was adorned solely with the essentials: herbs hanging from the rafters, jars filled with potions, and a small abode that crackled with warmth. To many, she was perceived poor, yet her wealth lay in the wisdom of her years and the love she gave to those in need. Madam Feli was rich in wisdom and kindness. With no children to share her days and no relatives to visit, her world was often filled with silence. She found companionship in the creatures of the forest - the chirping birds outside her window and the curious squirrels that ventured close in search of nuts. Often, she would spend her afternoons tending to her flower garden, whispering stories to the blossoms as if they were her dear friends.

Despite her loneliness, she carried a light within her, radiating warmth and kindness to anyone who happened to cross her path. She may not have had a family, but in her heart, she embraced the beauty of life and the simple joys that surrounded her, finding solace in the quiet moments and the gentle rustle of the leaves.

Madam Feli woke up one morning feeling unusually weak. At first, she brushed it off as a simple cold, but as the day went on, her condition worsened. She struggled to eat her favorite meals and the usual commune with nature and the laughter that filled her heart was replaced by an unsettling silence. Her distant relatives were far away, caught up in their own lives, leaving her vulnerable and alone. Despite her usual resilience, she found it difficult to muster the strength to face the days ahead. As the sun set each evening, she longed for the simple comforts of companionship - a hand to hold, a voice to reassure her. It was during those moments of solitude that she realized the importance of family and the need for care in times of distress. If only someone would come to check on her, perhaps the burden of illness would be a little lighter, and the way back to health a little clearer, she thought. Despite her vibrant spirit and the warmth of the memories she cherished, the outright isolation became a heavy burden during her illness.

Once a vibrant woman who captivated others with her intuition now grappled with the heavy burden of neglect from her community. The laughter and cheers that once filled her days had faded into distant memories, leaving behind a stark reality where isolation prevailed. Each passing hour seemed to deepen the pit between her and the world she once thrived in. With every missed hello and every unattended gathering, the weight of indifference pressed down on her spirit, dimming the light of her once-bright personality. She yearned to reclaim the connection she had lost, to share her tales once more, but found herself adrift in a sea of apathy that threatened to extinguish her spark forever. Hope flickered faintly, as her heart still held the desire for warmth and companionship amidst the cold silence.

Two weeks had passed since Madam Feli had fallen ill. During the time that Dr Fray was about to conclude his day and retire to the comfort of his own home, he noticed a small hut perched on the hill at the outskirt of the village. It had been a long day filled with patient visits for him, yet something about that house drew his attention. Curiosity stirred, he found himself reconsidering his plans, feeling an inexplicable urge to investigate further. Perhaps there was someone inside who needed his help, or maybe it was just a fleeting thought. Nonetheless, the hill seemed to call him, urging him to take one last detour before he returned to the solace of his village.

Madam Feli's hut had a charm on its own, huddled away from the main roads and surrounded by a clump of trees that made it somewhat difficult for unacquainted to find. The narrow path leading to her front door was often obscured by overgrown shrubs and wild-flowers, creating a sense of adventure for anyone brave enough to seek it out. The small and old structure seemed to blend seamlessly with the nature that surrounded it, telling stories of years gone by. Dr Fray set out on his trip up the hill, the winding path was lined with tall trees, their leaves whispering secrets in the cool evening breeze. Curiosity sparked within him; he wondered if anyone resided at the hut. Longing for a connection in the solitude of the landscape, each step brought him closer to the hut. Arriving at the top, he paused, taking in the breathtaking view while his heart raced with the anticipation of discovery. The thought of finding someone inside filled him with hope as he ventured further, wondering what secrets this serene hill might unveil. He stood at the foot of the hill, the anticipation of discovery whistling in his veins. With each step, the cool breeze whispered secrets of the unknown, urging him onward.

Arriving at the weather-beaten door, he hesitated only for a moment before raising his hand and knocking firmly. "Knock, knock, anybody in here?" he called out, his voice echoing through the still air. The eerie silence that followed sent a shiver down his spine, but curiosity overcame his apprehension. This secluded place held mysteries he was eager to uncover, and he couldn't shake the feeling that someone - or something - was waiting just beyond that door. With determination, he prepared to venture inside, ready to face whatever might lie ahead. After several knocks, each echoing in the stillness of the hallway, Dr Fray's face wrinkled in concern as there was no response from within, only the heavy silence that lingered. As if holding his breath, he glanced at his watch, noting the passage of time, a sense of urgency began to bubble within his calm nature. Realizing that something might be amiss, he took a deep breath and carefully turned the knob. With a slight push, the door creaked open, revealing the dimly lit room beyond. Dr Fray stepped inside, his heart racing as he prepared to confront whatever awaited him in that silence. As he ventured closer, he was met with a revealing clear-cut scene that sent chills down his spine.

There, on the bare floor, lay Madam Feli, her expression vacant, unable to voice her thoughts or fears. The room felt heavy with unspoken words, and the air thickened with an unsettling presence. Dr Fray rushed to her side, his instincts kicking in as he knelt beside her, searching for any sign of life. The tension of the moment was obvious, and in that instant, he knew he had to act quickly to understand what had transpired and to ensure her safety.

Madam Feli lay on the bare floor, her frail body still and silent. Dr Fray knelt beside her, concern etched on his face as he examined her with urgency. The room was filled with an air of silence, the only sounds being the steady thumping of his heart. Despite his efforts, she could not respond, her eyes closed, and breath shallow. Knowing time was of the essence, he made a decisive choice: he carefully prepared to administer resuscitation, focusing on each movement with precision and care. The hope was real as he worked, determined to awaken her from this unnerving stillness. Pouring all his focus and energy into each push, seconds felt like hours, but his determination never wavered. After several intense cycles of compressions, a flicker of hope emerged; she finally responded, her body beginning to show signs of life. Slowly, her eyes waggled, revealing a faint glimmer of awareness. The once still room erupted in a mixture of relief and cautious hope for him. With every beat of her heart, Dr Fray's assiduity grew stronger, his commitment unswerving. As she began to breathe more steadily, the possibility of recovery transformed his tension into a sense of optimism. This critical response was not just a victory for her, but also for Dr Fray who fought against the odds to bring her back.

Dr. Fray couldn't bear the thought of leaving Madam Feli alone in such a desolate place. The loneliness surrounding her weighed heavily on his heart. With tenderness he lifted her into his arms and carefully carried her to his truck. The journey was filled with compassion, as he ensured her comfort in the vehicle, knowing that he had to take responsibility for her well-being. He drove her to his doctor's quarters, a place where she could find solace and care through her recovery. Madam Feli, despite the uncertainty of her situation, felt a glint of hope knowing she would no longer face her solitude alone.

Betsy was a remarkably kind-hearted person who dedicated herself to taking care of Madam Feli during her time of need. With her gentle demeanor and nurturing spirit, she provided not only physical care but also emotional support, ensuring that Madam Feli felt loved and comfortable. Day after day, she attended to her needs, preparing meals, reading stories, and sharing comforting words that helped lift up her spirits. Thanks to Betsy's unfaltering dedication and compassion, Madam Feli gradually regained her strength and wholeness. When the time came for her to return to her own home, she left with a heart full of gratitude. Betsy's kindness had made a lasting impact, and she cherished the memories of their time together, knowing she had made a dear friend in Betsy. Dr Fray made it a point to visit Madam Feli every time he found himself in the village. His visits were not just routine; they were inspired with a special significance, as he recognized that she had no nearby relatives to care for her.

The villagers often spoke of the warmth that Dr Fray's presence brought to her modest home, where laughter and stories filled the air during those precious moments. Dr Fray would listen intently as Madam Feli recounted tales from her younger days, her laughter intertwining with the rustling leaves outside. He believed it was important to ensure she felt valued and cherished, particularly in her solitude. Each visit was a testament to his kindness and dedication, reminding Madam Feli that even in her twilight years, she was never truly alone. Their bond blossomed into a beautiful friendship, providing her with companionship and joy that she so deeply cherished.

On a warm day, Dr Fray set out on his usual house-to-house calls, his heart filled with the familiar rhythm of his routine. As he approached Madam Feli's hut, the air was thick with the vibrant sounds of birds chirping, and a gentle breeze rustling the leaves. Madam

Feli's old little home, adorned with blooming and welcoming flowers, stood as a testament to her nurturing spirit. Dr Fray had found solace in her stories and laughter during his visits, knowing that each encounter not only brought him joy but also allowed him to offer care and attention to her. As he knocked on the door, he prepared himself for another delightful afternoon filled with warmth, tales of yesteryears, and perhaps a taste of her famous homemade cookies waiting inside. Madam Feli, with her warm smile and wise eyes, called him into her living room. She wasn't unwell; in fact, she felt better than ever, but there was a particular task that had burdened her mind for quite some time.

As they settled into her chairs, Madam Feli explained with gentle urgency that she wanted him to help her with something. She looked at him with a gentle smile, her eyes sparkling with warmth and wisdom. "My dear son," she began softly, her voice carrying the weight of countless memories, "I have seen much goodness in you over the years. Your kind heart and unwavering spirit have always filled me with pride." She paused for a moment, her gaze turning forlorn as she gathered her thoughts. "As I approach the end of my journey, there is one last wish I hold close to my heart I wish for you to carry for me." She turned to Dr Fray, and spoke with a blend of serenity and acceptance, "I know that very soon the good Lord will call me home." Her eyes sparkled with the wisdom of her many years, and there was a certain peace in her words. For her, the end of life was not something to fear but rather a gentle transition into a new existence. Madam Feli had lived a full life and in that moment, she embraced the inevitable with grace, confident that her spirit would endure beyond this world.

Dr Fray listened attentively, touched by her acceptance and the profound truth in her statement, understanding that often, the strongest souls face the end with open hearts.

The room was filled with an atmosphere of understanding and love as she expressed her wishes for when the inevitable day comes. "All said and done," she continued, her voice steady despite the weight of the topic, "this is what I would like for you to do when I pass away." Her request was both simple and heartfelt. Dr Fray nodded, though a hint of uncertainty flickered in his eyes, the weight of the moment pressed down on him, making his hands feel slightly shaky.

Madam Feli, sensing his hesitation, offered a reassuring smile, her voice gentle yet firm. "Don't be afraid," she said, her words wrapping around him like a warm blanket, "I would not ask you to do anything unwarranted." Her confidence was infectious, and slowly but surely, Dr Fray felt some of his apprehension fade away. Trusting her wisdom, he leaned in closer eager to hear what she would say next. "Always remember, my dear, that goodness is a gift that multiplies when shared." With that, Madam Feli reached out, holding Dr Fray's hand tightly, sealing their bond with a promise of enduring love.

The room felt warmer, filled with the quiet comfort of acquaintanceship. "Wait here, I will be right back," she said with a gentle smile, her voice reassuring. Dr Fray watched as she moved with purpose, her presence a calming balm in his swirling thoughts. The uncertainty that had clouded his mind began to dissipate, replaced by a growing sense of hope. He took a deep breath. As he waited for her return, he felt a renewed sense of resolve ready to confront whatever challenges lay ahead. He could almost feel her presence guiding him through his thoughts, reminding him of the strength they shared. Anticipation built as minutes passed; he was ready to face whatever challenges awaited him. Finally, the door creaked open, and Madam Feli stepped back into the room, her eyes twinkling with mischief. In her hands, she held a box tied tightly with a rope, its contents unknown. A sense of excitement mixed with curiosity surged within him as he wondered what lay hidden inside. He instinctively knew that with her by his side, they could tackle anything together.

In her weathered hands, Madam Feli held a box, strained by the tightness of the rope that bound it. The mystery of its contents lingered in the air, a curious promise wrapped in secrecy. "Here, my son," she said, her voice a blend of warmth and authority, as she gently extended the box toward him. Her eyes sparkled with a hint of mischief as she handed over the box. "This is my gift to you and your family," she said, her voice filled with warmth and sincerity, a gentle smile graced her lips. The moment felt heavy with emotion, an unspoken bond between them strengthened by her intentions. "I would like you to open it when I pass away," she added, her eyes glowing with a mix of hope and pensiveness. It was more than just a present; it was a piece of her heart, a lasting reminder of love and connection that would transcend time. As the weight of her words settled in, she knew that this gift would carry her spirit, offering comfort and solace in the days to come. It was a promise of enduring love, a legacy meant to be cherished, and a reminder of the moments they shared.

As she spoke, her eyes glimmered with a depth of emotion; her words thick with suspense, a beautiful promise of connection and love. She paused, taking a deep breath. With every pause, she drew him in deeper, creating an electric tension that kept his hearts racing. It was as though she held a secret just out of reach, and continued, "I would like you to bury me like you would with your mother." Her request; both saddening and profound. The room felt heavy; Madam Feli's voice was soft yet filled with a weight of sincerity as she shared her wish. "And whatever is left in this is yours after I am buried," she continued, her eyes searching his for understanding. "Do not open it now, and do not tell anyone except your family about this." Dr Fray nodded solemnly, recognizing the weight of her request. He felt a combination of nervousness and responsibility as he promised to honor her wishes.

Returning home later that evening, he carried the secret not just of the item, but also of the trust placed in him. His heart weighed heavily with the burden of unspoken thoughts but he knew he must protect the legacy she had entrusted to him, keeping it close to his heart until the time was right to reveal it to his family. The following day, Dr Fray resolved to visit Madam Feli once again, driven by a mix of excitement and concern for her well-being. Approaching her charming little hut, memories of their previous conversations flooded his mind, filling him with anticipation. He cherished the way she wove her wisdom into heartwarming stories, each one a precious glimpse into her life. As he knocked gently on the door, his heart raced; he hoped today would bring a smile to her face and a few enchanting tales from her past. Yet, alongside his eagerness, a sense of fear began to creep in, leaving him anxious about what he might find behind the door. He took a deep breath, reminding himself of the joy their meetings usually brought, while he continued to wait for her familiar voice to greet him.

The silence that followed his knocks left him on edge. As the stillness grew heavier, doubt began to cloud his mind, but he held on to the hope of hearing her usual voice. Finally, after several unanswered knocks, he steeled himself and slowly turned the doorknob, ready to confront whatever lay beyond - a mix of anticipation and dread rushed through him as he prepared to enter. Dr Fray hurriedly called out Madam Feli's name as he moved through the dimly lit room of her hut.

The air was thick with worry, and his heart raced as he made his way to her bedroom. Concern gripped him, wondering if she might be feeling unwell or if something had happened that required immediate attention. He pushed the door open, half-expecting to find her resting quietly or just in need of assistance. He couldn't shake the feeling that every moment mattered, and he hoped that his fears were unfounded, wishing instead to find her safe and sound. The echoes of his last call faded into the background, swallowed by the weight of impending loss.

As he entered the room, the sharp reality hit him like a wave - she was no longer there. Madam Feli had peacefully moved on to join her ancestors, leaving behind a lingering warmth and countless cherished memories. Time seemed to stand still; Dr Fray was engulfed by a tide of emotions: sorrow for her absence, gratitude for the love they shared, and a profound respect for the journey she had taken. It was both a heartbreaking farewell and a reminder of the enduring bond that ties generations together, transcending even the boundaries of life and death.

Dr Fray took it upon himself to make the necessary arrangements for her burial, ensuring that everything was handled with the utmost care and respect. In a gesture of respect and compassion, he honored his promise to ensure that Madam Feli received a burial that truly befitted her memory. The funeral was a heartfelt affair, filled with the wonders of nature. Family and the community gathered to celebrate her life. Each detail was meticulously planned, from the beautiful flowers that adorned her casket to the soft music that echoed through the cemetery. Dr Fray stood by, radiating a sense of calm as he took in the scene, knowing he had fulfilled his vow; Madam Feli's legacy would live on in the hearts of those she touched, ensuring that she would never be forgotten.

The villagers took immense pride in Dr Fray's presence. In their hearts, a remarkable man lived among them, embodying virtues that inspired admiration and reverence. They often spoke of his kindness and wisdom in hushed, worshipful tones. To some, he was a saint, a beacon of hope and compassion who brought light to their darkest hours. Others proclaimed him God-sent, believing his arrival was a divine gift meant to uplift their community. His gentle demeanor and selfless acts of service left an indelible mark on the hearts of those who knew him. Conversations buzzed with tales of his generosity, and a sense of unity blossomed among the villagers as they embraced the extraordinary legacy he was creating.

CHAPTER SIX

"A Guest Who Breaks the Dishes of His
Host Is Not Soon Forgotten"
(We Live on and Are Remembered by Our Deeds)

A few months after Madam Feli's burial, whispers swept through the fifteen to twenty villages which Dr Fray served. The news of Dr Fray's impending return to the city became the talk of the community, stirring a mix of emotions among the villagers. Some felt a deep sense of loss, as he had offered not just medical care, but also comfort and hope in their times of need. Others pondered the implications of his departure, realizing that they would be left without a trusted healer. As they gathered around the communal fire in the evenings, tales of Dr Fray's contributions began to circulate, highlighting the bond he had formed with the villagers. His absence would create a void, prompting many to reflect on the future of their healthcare and the enduring legacy of Madam Feli in their lives. As the communities grappled with the implications of his departure, they reflected on the legacy of compassion and commitment he instilled in the realm of medicine. His contributions were not merely professional; they represented a genuine investment in the well-being of others, fostering hope and healing.

As good as the news of Dr Fray's return to the city was, he found himself grappling with an inner sense of loss. The village, with its close-knit community and tranquil environment, had become a second home to him. The laughter of children playing outside his window and the familiar greetings from neighbors filled his days with warmth and purpose. Moving back to the city, despite the professional opportunities it promised, felt like leaving behind a cherished chapter of his life. He couldn't help but reminisce about the simple pleasures and strong connections he had forged in the village. Dr Fray faced a bittersweet dilemma: advancing his career meant sacrificing the comforts of a life that had deeply enriched him. He found himself yet at another crossroads, his career aspirations clashing with the cherished relationships he had built over the years. The prospect of advancement shimmered enticingly before him, promising new opportunities and recognition, yet it came with an emotional toll. Each step toward his professional goals felt like a step away from the comfort and warmth of the life he had cultivated.

As he weighed the importance of success against the heartbreaking thought of leaving behind those he had come to know and love, his heart overflowed with guilt pulling at his emotions. He was torn between ambition and affection. He began to understand that the path to his progress often demanded sacrifices that weighed heavily on his conscience. He had brought them not just knowledge, but a healthier way of living, and in doing so, had forged strong bonds that entwined his identity with theirs. This connection made him reflect on the true cost of his aspirations; was achieving his goals worth potentially losing the very relationships that had enriched his life? As he grappled with this internal conflict, he realized that the heart of his journey lay not just in success, but in the love and trust he had cultivated within the community.

As he observed the vibrant lives around him, the weight of his evolving priorities became clear; a deep yearning for his own family's well-being, particularly for his daughter, Abeba. She was a bright spark in his life, and he wanted her to have the finest education, one that could open doors and shape her future. She deserves the best opportunities that life can offer, particularly in the realm of education. A quality education from a reputable school would provide her with the foundation she needs to unlock her full potential. With the right educational environment, Abeba could develop the skills and knowledge necessary to pursue her aspirations and positively impact her community. The weight of his decision pressed heavily on his shoulders, a burden he could hardly bear. He felt the stakes rising, not only for Abeba, whose future seemed intertwined with his choice, but also for his son, Jabari whom he had entrusted to his best friend, Simpson.

With each passing day, the urgency to reunite with him grew stronger, fueling his determination to secure a brighter tomorrow for his children. Dr Fray's ambition and responsibilities as a father left him questioning the path forward. Ultimately, he understood that true success would be measured not just by accolades, but by the lasting impact he would have on both his family and the community that embraced him. It was a delicate balance, one that required careful consideration and perhaps a change in direction.

With determination driving him, he resolved to seek out his friend Simpson, hoping to gain insight into how to provide Abeba with the quality schooling she deserved and, his son, Jabari, whose potential could align with Abeba's aspirations. With each passing day, the urgency to reconnect with Simpson and his son intensified, igniting an unwavering determination within him. He envisioned a future where both Abeba and Jabari thrived, fueling his resolve to bridge the gap that had grown too wide, striving to secure a brighter tomorrow for his beloved children. Memories of Jabari haunted him, a fleeting image of laughter and innocence now overshadowed by the years that had stolen away those moments. Time seemed both a friend and foe, reminding him of the distance that had molded their lives apart. As he navigated the complexities of his current life, the echoes of his past whispered the same plea: to reconnect with Jabari, to learn whether the boy he once knew had grown into a contented man. With hope in his heart, he set out on a journey fueled by love and the relentless pursuit of reunion.

Meanwhile, Abeba blossomed into a remarkable young woman, her beauty shining brighter each day. He felt a deep sense of responsibility to prepare her for the challenges ahead, believing that the zest and challenges of the city could offer her invaluable experiences. In the midst of his quest for closure and a brighter future for Abeba, he found that reconciling his past with the present played a crucial role in shaping his decisions. The journey was not just about moving forward; it involved reflecting on his experiences, understanding the lessons learned, and acknowledging the mistakes made along the way. Fortunately, Abeba was in her final year of high school, making the transition to college in the city a natural progression for her. With her determination and resilience, she was ready to embrace the opportunities that lay ahead, steering through the complexities of urban life while forging her own path in the world.

The prospect of college, with its endless possibilities, ignited a flame of determination within Abeba. With each moment she envisioned herself navigating the lively streets, forging new friendships, and absorbing knowledge that would empower her future. The city's energy mirrored her aspirations, a place where she could transform her ambitions into reality. For her, this was not just an opportunity; it was the beginning of a remarkable adventure, one that would test her limits and inspire her to soar. With unwavering resolve, she embraced the excitement ahead, ready to carve out her unique path in the heart of the metropolis. Additionally, Betsy believed that this transition would not only mark a significant milestone in Abeba's life but also provide her with the chance to embrace the lively city life fully. The thought of exploring new opportunities and meeting diverse individuals filled her with optimism. She was confident that Abeba would navigate the challenges with grace, making the most of her experience. There was no better time than now for her to take the leap, and she felt proud to support her daughter as she prepared for this exciting chapter ahead.

At last, the Fray family had made their decision, feeling a mix of excitement and anxiety about their journey ahead. With the moving day approaching, they found themselves surrounded by boxes, tapes, and memories, knowing they had a lot of packing to do. With every box filled and each memory carefully wrapped, laughter transformed what could have been a daunting task into a shared celebration of their time spent in the neighborhood. The community turned the farewell into a meaningful ritual. Though the move signified an end, the friendships forged and the love exchanged illuminated their hearts, reminding them that goodbyes often open the door to new beginnings. The Frays although were leaving behind a home, they were not alone in this transition. The support from neighbors and friends not only lightened their load but also added warmth to the bittersweet experience of saying goodbye. Together, they created a beautiful farewell filled with shared moments and promises to stay connected in the future.

As they prepared to take their next steps, they felt deeply grateful for the connections that made their departure sweeter amidst the sadness. The connections they had forged during their time together provided warmth and comfort. Each shared laugh, encouraging word, and heartfelt conversation echoed in their minds. With each goodbye, there was a promise to cherish the memories and a hope for future reunions. They knew that although they were parting ways, the friendships they had nurtured would remain.

As Abeba prepared to say goodbye to her friends, a bittersweet feeling enveloped her heart. Each laugh shared and every moment spent together played in her mind. Among them, Njeri her best friend, a cherished companion whose laughter had often brightened her days. They both understood that their paths were diverging, yet the bond they shared felt unbreakable. Each moment they spent together had woven their friendship into a rich tapestry that would forever enrich their individual lives.

Abeba knew that while distance might stretch between them, the vibrant threads of their connection would continue to illuminate the journey ahead, offering warmth and resilience as they stepped into new adventures. Their friendship, a masterpiece, would thrive in their memories, reminding them that true companionship never truly fades, no matter the circumstances.

She recalled the day she first met Njeri,

when a clumsy fall had marred her beautiful dress intended for her first day at school. Their laughter had intertwined, creating a moment that felt both simple and profound, heralding the start of a friendship crafted like a masterpiece. Njeri was very kind and sweet. She was known throughout the community for her kindness and sweetness, traits that made her exceptional. Their friendship became the talk of the town, often sparking conversations about their strong bond and the delightful adventures they shared. Their relationship was a shining example of loyalty and unconditional support.

Njeri was a year older than Abeba. When both girls were admitted to the same class, Abeba's mother, Betsy, felt a wave of relief. She knew that Njeri's protective nature would help Abeba navigate the challenges of school life, providing her with a sense of security and support, especially in moments when she couldn't be there herself. It was a blessing to have such a loyal friend in Njeri, who would guide and support her through the ups and downs of school. Njeri was always there for her, offering guidance and encouragement. In return, Abeba took it upon herself to help Njeri with her class-work, recognizing that her friend faced difficulties that she herself did not.

Abeba's understanding and patience fostered an environment where both friends thrived - Abeba excelling in her studies while Njeri grew more confident with Abeba's assistance. As much as she longed for the thrill of city life, the longing for Njeri's laughter and support overshadowed it all. It was a bittersweet moment, torn between the promise of new experiences and the weight of leaving behind a piece of her heart. Ultimately, Abeba knew that no matter the distance or the paths their lives took, the memories of their laughter and adventures would echo in her heart forever. It wasn't just the fun they had together, but the unwavering loyalty and kindness that Njeri had shown her through thick and thin. Abeba couldn't help but wonder if she would ever encounter another friend who embodied such genuine warmth and support.

As Abeba reminisced quietly, her thoughts wandered back to that unforgettable day in the forest. It was a time when the world felt both mysterious and alive, and the air was thick with the scent of earth and leaves. The day was a declared day forbidden for farming. In their twelfth and thirteenth years, they felt both adventurous and invincible discovering hidden paths and secret clearings. Laughter echoed through the trees as they played. Though they were still young, they felt a strange curiosity about the world of prohibition that painted their surroundings in a veil of intrigue. Whispers of those who dared to defy the rules echoed through their small town, fueling their imagination. Yet, despite the vivid tales spun by older generations, they regarded those accounts with skepticism. To them, the stories felt more like fantastical myths than reality. They couldn't quite reconcile the thrilling adventures described by others, instead, their youth enfolded them in a bubble of innocence, where the rebellious spirit of prohibition seemed distant; a land of enigma they could only dream of but never fully grasp.

On a sunny day, Abeba and Njeri decided to venture into the forest, eager to explore its hidden wonders. The air was crisp, and the wind was calm, creating a serene atmosphere that welcomed them. As they walked along the winding trails, the sunlight filtered through the leaves, glistening on the forest floor. Each ray of light danced joyfully, brightening the earthy tones of the soil and the delicate flowers that peeked through, casting playful shadows on the ground. Each step brought new discoveries; from vibrant wild-flowers to the gentle rustle of animals in the underbrush. It was a perfect day to connect with each other and to the enchanting world around them, leaving behind the hustle and bustle of everyday life.

The forest felt like a magical escape, a place where memories were made and cherished forever leaving behind the bustling market, where sellers and buyers moved with purpose, engaging in lively conversations and exchanging goods that filled the air with the aroma of fresh produce and homemade delicacies. Children darted between stalls, their laughter mingling with the sounds of merchandising, while their parents navigated the crowd, equally occupied with their own daily routines. Amidst the hustle and bustle, the market served as a vital hub, connecting families and fostering a sense of community inspite of their busy lives. The rhythm of the day echoed in the laughter of children, the chatter of adults, and the symphony of vendors.

As Abeba and Njeri ventured deeper into the forest, a glimmer of gold caught Abeba's eye, gleaming softly amongst the greenery. She called out to Njeri, urging her to see the enchanting sight. The two friends hastened their pace, their hearts racing with anticipation and excitement. Branches brushed against them, and the earthy scent of damp leaves filled the air as they wove through towering trees. Each step brought them closer to the mysterious golden object, sparking their imaginations with possible treasures or hidden wonders.

The forest, with its symphony of rustling leaves and distant bird calls, seemed to hold its breath as they approached the glowing beacon that had captivated them, eager to uncover the secrets it might reveal. As they ventured closer towards the enchanting scene, a mother fowl whose entire body was covered in pure gold, shimmering brilliantly under the sun paraded proudly, her vibrant feathers glistening in pure gold, while her adorable chicks fluttered about, their downy feathers catching the rays against their tiny gleaming gems. The mystery was not in the sight of the fowl and her brood but rather in their gold nature that seemed almost magical against the backdrop of the earthy woods.

The mother fowl and her golden chicks strutted gracefully inside the forest like living pieces of art, captivating the attention of Abeba and Njeri. They began to follow them, entranced by their beauty, the mother fowl sensed their pursuit and decided to lead her little ones further into the wilderness. The closer Abeba and Njeri got, the more cleverly she moved with her golden chicks.

The chase turned into a game of hide and seek, a delightful spectacle where the mother fowl showcased her agility while her chicks fluttered closely behind. Despite their attempts to catch the enchanting sight before them, the allure of the golden family only deepened, motivating them to chase the elusive beauty just a little bit longer. The mother fowl, protective and attentive, ventured into the hollow of a sturdy tree. Peeking through the warm embrace of the wooden hollow, Njeri and Abeba were astonished to find a cluster of sparkling gold eggs. However, their excitement quickly turned to shock as they noticed a massive gold python coiled protectively around the precious eggs, its scales gleaming like treasure. Njeri and Abeba exchanged worried glances, realizing that retrieving the eggs would require a cunning plan to outsmart the formidable guardian of this golden bounty. With their hearts racing, they contemplated their next move, aware that this adventure was far from over.

An unsettling realization washed over them: they were lost. Panic bubbled within as they retraced their steps, each familiar landmark now seemingly distorted and alien. The once-comforting trees loomed menacingly, their branches twisting like fingers reaching out to snatch them away. Every rustle of leaves sent shivers down their spine, and the fading light dimmed their hopes further. Frantically, they scanned the treeline, searching for any sign of a path, a clue, anything to ease the rising dread in their chests. Time slipped away, each moment stretching into an eternity as the shadows deepened around them.

With hearts pounding and breaths quickening, they realized that the forest, once a place of adventure, had turned into an entanglement of fear where they no longer felt safe. The thrill of exploration had vanished, leaving only the stark reality of isolation and uncertainty: they were lost. Terror erupted trough them as they retraced their steps, only to discover that the familiar markings of their path had vanished, swallowed by the dense undergrowth. Each turn they took seemed to lead them deeper into the complex web of the forest, where rustling leaves and distant animal calls heightened their sense of disorientation. It was a surreal experience, as if the woods themselves conspired to keep them wandering with every landmark concealed by the dense foliage. With nightfall approaching, a chill gripped their hearts, and they could only hope that the rising moon would guide them towards a way out before darkness enveloped them completely.

With the appearance of night fall, an uneasy tension settled over the families of Njeri and her friend. Anxiety set in when Njeri's mother, familiar with the customs of their land, recognized the seriousness of the situation. In their culture, the disappearance of a loved one was a matter that demanded immediate attention and action. With heavy hearts, the two families gathered and made their way to the grand palace, where they sought an audience with the king. Their urgent footsteps echoed through the corridor, each step filled with fear and determination to uncover the truth behind their daughters' absence. The weight of their worry pressed down as they sought the king's assistance, hoping for a swift resolution to the mystery that night had cast over them. Desperation fueled their resolve, and they arrived at the palace, united in their plea for help.

As the tension in the palace grew, an elder stepped forward to share his account of the two families' distress over their daughters. He recounted how he had warned the girls against venturing into the forbidden forest, cautioning them about the dangers that lurked within its shadows. He had witnessed their initial thrust into the woods, and though they eventually retreated, he remained uncertain if they had truly turned back for good or succumbed to the forest's allure once more. His testimony added weight to the families' plight, prompting the king to consider the implications of the elder's words. The king sat in deep contemplation, his mind swirling with the weight of responsibility. The elder's report lay before him, a revelation that could hold the key to finding them. Time was slipping away, and with each passing moment, hope grew dimmer. In a tense moment, the king commanded a search group to find the missing girls from his realm.

The sunset and darkness fell, the resonant beating of a drum echoed through the kingdom, alerting every citizen to the urgent situation at hand. The air was thick with worry as families awaited news of the two girls. The search group gathered in the heart of the ancient forest, their voices mingling in a haunting chant as they performed the 'revelation ritual.' Despite their efforts, the forest loomed large and unyielding, its magic weaving a deceptive veil around the path where Njeri and Abeba had vanished. Shadows twisted and turned, dancing menacingly around them with every movement, as if the darkness itself sought to ensnare their very souls, cloaking their whereabouts in an impenetrable darkness that made the searchers feel increasingly disoriented and lost. Each step taken felt heavy with a sense of foreboding, the forest's enchantment disorienting them further. As the chant reached its climax, the air buzzed with anticipation, and a glimmer of hope ignited within the group, urging them on in their quest to uncover the truth hidden within the magical depths of the forest.

Right when despair threatened to settle in, the search groups' sense of hope emerged as midnight approached. They returned, their figures illuminated by the moonlight, bringing with them the joyous news: they had found Njeri and Abeba safe and sound. Relief washed over the kingdom, transforming dread into celebration.

Just as they dismissed the stories of the river goddess, who was said to emerge from the depths on certain days to bathe her children in the flashing waters, so did their tales of the golden fowl and her precious chicks, brought to light by Abeba and Njeri fall on disbelieving ears. As the two friends excitedly recounted their encounter, their families looked on with skepticism, refusing to embrace the magic woven into their narrative. Even as the river goddess remained a myth for most, so too did the story of the gold fowl and her protective gold python fade into the realm of fanciful imagination, overshadowed by practicality and doubt. Yet, in the hearts of Njeri and Abeba, the magic lived on, a treasured secret shared only between them.

Abeba recalled their adventures with tears in her eyes, she hugged Njeri tightly, not wanting to let go, fully aware that distance would soon separate them. But even in separation, they knew the memories they created together would remain a source of strength and comfort no matter the miles between them.

Njeri equally reflected on the incredible bond she shared with Abeba especially the unforgettable night she and Abeba spent together - a night that would forever live in their memories. The laughter, the shared secrets, and the warmth of their friendship: it was the evening they forged an unbreakable bond, whispered promises they made to keep their newfound secret hidden. Njeri felt an overwhelming sense of trust and loyalty, they both knew that the experience would shape their relationship in ways they could never have anticipated; it was a moment of pure connection, a testament to the depth of their friendship, and she cherished every detail, knowing that the essence of that night would remain with them always, a beautiful secret shared between two souls destined to be linked forever.

Njeri and Abeba, just seventeen and sixteen, found themselves at a crossroads in their lives. Once full of youthful exuberance and dreams, their paths took a dark turn as they succumbed to the pressures and temptations around them. The choices they made led them to a harrowing experience that left deep scars on their souls. It was a moment that would shape not only their present but also their futures, forcing them to confront the consequences of their actions. The vibrant laughter and carefree days seemed a distant memory as they navigated the aftermath of their decisions. Through their struggle, Njeri and Abeba learned about resilience and the importance of finding a way back to the light, even when the shadows felt overwhelming. One night, as the river's current gently lapped against the canoe, Abeba found herself on yet another adventurous outing with Njeri. Despite her lack of interest in the thrill of their usual off-shore escapades, Abeba felt an undeniable pull to keep pace with her friend. Njeri's excitement was infectious, and Abeba couldn't help but become her loyal tag along, even when a part of her yearned for a quieter evening. The moonlight shimmered across the water, casting a magical glow that made the night felt alive with possibilities. Though she didn't have the same zeal for the thrill-seeking life that Njeri embraced, Abeba cherished the bond they shared knowing that true friendship often meant joining someone on their journey, even if it wasn't their own preferred path.

That night, under the dim glow of

flickering streetlights, they stumbled upon a peculiar sight: a man they dubbed the 'Moswine,' (money swine). He was dressed in extravagant attire that spoke of wealth, there was an undeniable air of splendor around him, hinting at a life lived in luxury. The 'moswine' stood there, a crisp reminder of the fine line between wealth and destitution, captivating their imaginations.

As they settled into the cozy confines of his car, excitement danced in the air, and they felt a rush of curiosity as he drove them deep into a city that seemed like a hidden gem. The streets were adorned with twinkling lights, and the aroma of delicious food wafted through the open windows. An assortment of drinks and delectable treats awaited them, turning the evening into a feast for their senses. Njeri couldn't help but wonder how this charming stranger had evaded her notice for so long, realizing that fate had finally graced her with this unforgettable night. Laughter echoed around them as they shared stories and dreams, each seconds weaving a moment of joy. It was a night of pure magic, one that they would carry in their hearts forever, knowing they had experienced the best time of their lives together in this enchanting, undiscovered city. The next morning, Abeba and Njeri woke up to a scene that filled them with dread and confusion.

As they hung dangerously from the branches of ancient trees in the dark forest, their hearts raced with fear. How had they ended up in such a terrifying predicament? The memories of the previous night were vague and distorted, leaving them feeling lost and bewildered. The sunlight filtered through the leaves, casting eerie shadows that seemed to mock their situation. With their minds racing, they exchanged worried glances, silently communicating their shared anxiety. They had to figure out how to escape this bizarre nightmare, but first, they needed to gather their thoughts and assess their surroundings.

The forest, with its whispering winds and rustling leaves, felt both bewitching and foreboding, as if holding secrets that would either save them or trap them further. Fear gripped them as they clung to the branches, their hearts racing in the stillness of the forest. With every rustle of leaves, the reality of their predicament pressed down harder. They had to descend safely from the top of the tree, but the height seemed daunting. Glancing at each other, they knew they had to act quickly. Njeri suggested a cautious descent, inching down the rough bark while maintaining a steady grip. Together, they remained focused, determination overriding their fear, as they slowly made their way down to safety. Each movement was deliberate, every heartbeat echoing their resolve to escape the surrounding gloominess of the forest.

At last, they reached the ground, their bodies a patchwork of scrapes and bruises that told the story of their harrowing descent.

Each scratch and injury was a reminder of the challenges they had faced descending the treacherous tree. Breathing heavily, they exchanged glances fused with relief and exhaustion. Yet, amidst the pain and body aches, they were united by the thrill of their narrow escape. The air was filled with a mix of exhilaration and disbelief as they took in their surroundings, the adrenaline still coursing through their veins.

Underneath the slump tree, they spotted an old man with a knowing smile, as if he had been expecting them. He listened intently as they narrated their harrowing adventure, the words tumbling out in a rush. With every detail shared, the weight of their experience began to lift, and they found solace in the understanding gaze of the old man. Together, they stood beneath the sheltering branches, the bond of their escape weaving them closer. The man explained to them that they should consider themselves fortunate. The wealthy individual they had encountered was not just an ordinary person; he was a deity from their village, someone with the power to influence their lives. Their encounter with him had not been a mere coincidence but rather a significant warning meant to guide them. He urged them to reflect on their recent escapades and the reckless behavior they had embraced. The implication was clear: they needed to alter their ways, for the deity's presence was a reminder of the traditions and values they were at risk of forgetting.

Ignoring this warning could lead to dire consequences, making it crucial for them to heed the lesson and embrace a more respectful and humble approach to their lives. The old man continued his tale, his voice steady and filled with a weighty wisdom. He told them the mesmerizing city that had dazzled their eyes, the luxurious hotel where they had momentarily found refuge, and the delectable food and drinks that had seemed so real. Yet, beneath the surface of this enchanting facade lay a profound truth: everything they had experienced was merely an illusion, a cleverly crafted mirage conjured by the deity. This was no random act; it was a lesson intended to awaken their spirits and challenge their perceptions of reality. As the old stranger spoke, his words painted a vivid picture of a world where nothing was as it seemed, urging Abeba and Njeri to look beyond the superficial and to seek the deeper meanings hidden within their fleeting pleasures. It was a gentle reminder that life often holds more than what meets the eye. But as they opened their mouths to speak, eager to voice their appreciation to him for his sage advice, a strange chill surrounded the air, and they found themselves staring into the emptiness where the old man had stood moments before. He had vanished without a trace, leaving behind only the echo of his words and an air of mystery. Confusion mingled with gratitude as they tried to comprehend what had just occurred, feeling an odd sense of connection to the fleeting figure who had just advised them, though they would never see him again.

With their spirits lifted, they began the long walk home, their footsteps echoing in the quiet of the forest. The journey felt endless as they traversed unfamiliar paths, the shadows growing longer with each step. Finally, they arrived in their village under the blanket of night, the comforting sight of their homes glowing softly in the darkness. Their parents, aware of their whereabouts on the other side of the river studying for upcoming exams had prepared for their return, filling the air with the tantalizing aroma of dinner. Relief washed over them, knowing that the day's trials had come to an end, and they were safely back where they belonged.

As Njeri and Abeba hugged tightly, Njeri's mind raced with thoughts about the uncertain future ahead. Suddenly, amidst her worries, a spark of hope ignited within her. "Wait a minute," she murmured, pausing mid-thought, "we both applied for the same college in the city, right?" The realization lifted her spirits, yes, they were saying goodbye for now but not forever. The idea of attending the same school filled Njeri with excitement, painting vibrant images of shared experiences, late-night study sessions, and endless laughter in their college dorm. With a renewed sense of purpose, she felt the weight of her fears lighten, replaced by the promise of new adventures waiting just around the corner. Together, they would navigate this new chapter, transforming their dreams into reality. Even the fleeting chance of not getting admitted to the same school couldn't dampen her excitement. The journey ahead was uncertain, but the idea of navigating it together and forming new memories infused her with hope and a promise of new beginnings.

Whilst Abeba bubbled with excitement as she imagined the bright lights and new adventures that awaited, her heart was still heavy with the thought of leaving Njeri behind. The thought of saying goodbye felt unbearable; the weight of goodbye pressing on her hearts. Abeba promised herself she would carry Njeri's spirit with her, praying for a reunion that would bridge the distance. Every second apart would be a reminder of their bond, a connection that neither time nor space could sever. Njeri echoed her sentiments also, acknowledging the ache of parting but also the excitement of what lay ahead. Together, in the depths of their hearts, they understood that the moment was not the conclusion, but rather a brief interlude in their dynamic friendship.

"Daddy has vowed to get a phone for me as soon as possible." Abeba excitedly shared her father's promise with her friend. Njeri quickly interjected, "It's as if the world around us is in a constant race and we must adapt to its relentless pace. It is important we stay grounded amid the chaos. I believe that the bonds we have created should remain unwavering." Njeri couldn't shake off the feeling of unease as she thought about Abeba moving to the city. The bustling urban life, filled with sophisticated girls and social scenes, made her anxious that her friend would soon forget her. Memories of their laughter and shared dreams weighed heavy on her heart, but the realities of city life loomed large in her mind. Would Abeba still want to spend time with her, or would she be drawn to the elegance and allure of her new surroundings? Njeri found herself grappling with self-doubt and a fear of being left behind, wondering if their bonds could withstand the winds of change. The thought of losing Abeba to the city's glitter was daunting, and she hoped her friend would remember the roots that tie them together, no matter where life took them.

Abeba's reassuring smile cut through her concerns. "Don't worry, we shall definitely meet again. You are the best of friends I have ever experienced," Abeba declared, her voice filled with warmth and sincerity. Njeri chuckled, a playful glimmer in her eyes, and replied, "silly, I am your only friend;

I am all you know," trying to lighten the mood. Despite the teasing tone, there was an undeniable truth behind the words. Their friendship, though simple, was filled with countless cherished moments and inside jokes that only they understood, but a hint of worry crept into Njeri's voice. "Maybe when you get to the city and meet those sophisticated city girls, you will forget all about me."

Abeba felt a pang of sadness at the thought, realizing just how much Njeri meant to her. Their connection, built on shared memories and laughter, would never fade, even amid new experiences and faces. "You and I have faced so much together, we have shared countless experiences in this village, each moment weaving our lives together. We've faced challenges and celebrated triumphs, forging a bond that goes beyond mere friendship. Our journeys have intertwined in ways that reveal our true selves, allowing us to understand each other on a deeper level. From the tranquil mornings spent by the river to the long nights discussing our dreams, our connection has grown stronger with each passing season. We can sense each other's thoughts and feelings without needing to say a word." Abeba smiled, her eyes sparkling with sincerity. "Those city girls you talk about will never compare to you or me," she said, her voice filled with conviction. "What we have is something truly special - our friendship is unbreakable, and I promise nothing or no one can come between us."

With every shared secret and heartfelt conversation, their connection deepened, reinforcing the idea that their friendship was a sanctuary - a place where they could be authentically themselves, supported and cherished. Abeba knew that together, they could navigate the complexities of life, holding onto the belief that their friendship would always shine brightly amidst the chaos.

The evening air turned cooler, reminding Abeba that it was getting late. She could almost hear her parents' voices laced with concern as they wondered about her whereabouts. Njeri, always the devoted friend, offered to walk Abeba partway home to ensure she arrived safely. With each step they took, the bond of friendship was filled with laughter and shared secrets. As they reached a familiar intersection, Njeri turned to Abeba with a warm smile, "get some rest for your trip tomorrow," she urged gently. They exchanged heartfelt hugs, sealing their good nights with promises of adventures to come. With a final wave, Abeba felt a swell of gratitude for Njeri's kindness as she made her way home.

As Abeba stood at the parted junction, she felt a wave of sadness wash over her. She had just said her final goodbye to Njeri, her closest friend, and the pain of separation weighed heavily on her heart. Thoughts of worry lingered: she couldn't shake the worry that clung to her heart. The village, with its looming trees and quiet streets, felt so isolating, and she feared for Njeri's well-being in its depths. Would she find friends among the villagers, or would she be left to navigate the challenges of solitude? Abeba pictured Njeri's kind smile, the way her laughter could light up a room, yet she knew that not everyone could see the beauty within. With a heavy heart, she knew she had to reach out to Njeri soon to reconnect and ensure her friend wasn't facing her struggles in isolation. As she contemplated her next steps, the soft murmur of familiar voices reached her ears, snapping her from her thoughts. "We were just about to come and get you; it's late, and you need to get some rest."

"How did Njeri take your going away?" Dr Fray inquired, his tone filled with empathy. Abeba paused, thinking about Njeri's brave face and the promises they had made, realizing that the bonds they shared would remain, no matter the distance that lay ahead. As he asked about Njeri's reaction to the farewell, his voice was laced with genuine concern. Sensing Abeba's unease, he quickly reassured her, "Don't worry, we will talk all about it tomorrow. I'm sure that something will work out for the two of you." He bid her good night with warmth and sincerity, "good night Abeba", "good night father, good night mother."

The comforting exchange lingered in the air, wrapping them in a sense of togetherness. Amidst the uncertainty that lay ahead, Abeba felt a flicker of hope ignited by her father's reassuring words. His gentle tone reminded her that she was not alone in navigating the challenges to come. Her heart swelled with gratitude, knowing that even when the future seemed daunting, the support of her family would always guide her through the storm. With each passing moment, her worries began to dissipate, replaced by a belief that whatever obstacles they faced, they would tackle them together, stronger as a unit.

That night none of the Frays slept well. Whilst Abeba's thoughts drifted towards Njeri, Dr Fray sat quietly, contemplating the countless patients he had tended to over the years. His heart consumed by compassion for the fifteen to twenty villages he had dedicated himself to, each village holding stories of resilience and hope. The weight of his responsibility was both a burden and a privilege, reminding him of the lives he had touched and the trust bestowed upon him. Their lives seemed interconnected, bound by the threads of care and reflection. Meanwhile, Betsy was motivated by thoughts of the fresh start awaiting her daughter. She envisioned a brighter future for them both, dreams of reunions swimming in her mind, especially the moment she would see her son again after all this time apart.

Each one, in their own way, grappled with transitions - one leaving a cherished past and the other eagerly embracing the promise of new beginnings. Their journeys were intertwined by the threads of love, sacrifice, and the relentless hope of reuniting with family. In that moment, amidst the silence, they shared a common thread of longing and aspiration, each navigating their own quiet quest for connection and reassurance in a world filled with challenges.

CHAPTER SEVEN

"I Have No Hair On My Body," Said The Chameleon;
Therefore, I Need Not Fear The Razor."
(A Good Conscience Need Not Fear The Judge)

Professor Simpson was a man of considerable means, largely due to the fortunate circumstance of his inheritance. His commitment to academia was evident, as he dedicated countless hours to his work, striving for excellence in his field. He poured his energy into teaching and research, yet many whispered that his lifestyle was more reflective of his family legacy than of his own endeavors. Despite this, Professor Simpson embraced his affluent position, using his resources to support various educational initiatives and philanthropic causes. He believed in giving back to the community that shaped him.

Growing up amidst opulent surroundings and high societal expectations, he was well-acquainted with privilege. Their inherited lineage was steeped in wealth and elitism, tracing back generations, where each ancestor contributed to the illustrious legacy. Their lavish lifestyle and influential connections shaped not only their lives but also the communities they inhabited. Prof and his siblings attended prestigious schools and mingled with society's elite, all while inheriting the values tied to their family's reputation. Amidst Prof's background, it was his hard work and passion that ultimately defined his legacy. Balancing expectations with personal aspirations became a delicate journey for him, as he strived to carve out his unique path surrounded by the shadows of his ancestors.

He was a prominent figure in society, known not just for his considerable wealth, but also for his esteemed position as a

Professor and a Diplomat. His expertise in literature and the written word garnered him respect and admiration from his peers and students alike. People often sought his opinions on various literary works, and he was frequently invited to speak at conferences and seminars. His lectures were renowned for their depth and insight, allowing students to delve into the complexities of his work in a meaningful way. Beyond his academic achievements, he was often seen at social gatherings, effortlessly blending his intellectual pursuits with his affluent lifestyle, making him a well-rounded figure in both academic and social circles. His dual recognition as a wealthy individual and a learned scholar created a unique persona that left a lasting impression on all who encountered him. Though often engrossed in his work, he maintained a warm and approachable demeanor, making him both an esteemed mentor and a cherished friend. Through his endeavors, Prof demonstrated that intelligence combined with kindness could foster an environment of learning and growth.

Prof and Jada's relationship was a blend of intellectual companionship and deep emotional connection, making them an inspiring couple. Jada's beauty was not just skin deep; it radiated from her warm personality and insightful conversations that often sparked lively debates in academic circles. Together, they enjoyed exploring art galleries, attending lectures, and hosting lively dinner parties where ideas flowed freely. Their love story was a testament to the power of partnership, where mutual respect and admiration developed, allowing both to grow in their individual pursuits while supporting each other wholeheartedly. In every glance and every shared laughter, it was clear that Jada was not only the love of Prof's life but also his greatest muse, inspiring him in ways that was remarkable.

Jada's family, although not as wealthy as Prof's, prioritized education above all else. They understood the significance of knowledge and were determined to provide their only daughter with the opportunities they never had. Despite financial constraints, they made sacrifices, ensuring that Jada had access to quality schooling and resources. Her parents instilled in her the values of hard work and perseverance, encouraging her to pursue her dreams passionately. Through their unwavering support and dedication, Jada blossomed academically, proving that with determination and the right support, one can overcome obstacles. Their love and commitment to her education became the foundation for her future. Their belief in her potential empowered her to reach for the stars and chase her aspirations with confidence.

Jada was raised in a lively household, surrounded by the boisterous energy of her four brothers. As the youngest and only girl in a family of five, she often found herself in a unique position, balancing between the rough and tumble of boyish play and her own quiet moments of soul-searching. Her brothers adored her, sometimes teasing but mostly protecting her fiercely, creating an environment filled with both chaos and love. While she often looked up to them for strength and adventure, she also cultivated her own interests, becoming a strong individual in her own right. Despite being the youngest, Jada's voice mattered deeply in the family, ensuring that she left a mark that would be remembered by her siblings for years to come. Growing up in a modest home, she learned the value of perseverance and the importance of financial stability. Her upbringing instilled in her a strong work ethic and a sense of responsibility, motivating her to aim for higher education and better opportunities. Despite facing the typical challenges of a middle-income lifestyle, her family cultivated a supportive environment where dreams were encouraged. With each stepping stone, she built resilience, determined to rise above circumstances while cherishing the lessons learned from her upbringing. This foundation ultimately shaped her aspirations, inspiring her to strive for success in her personal and professional life.

Prof and Jada lived life in the lap of luxury, enjoying all the trappings of celebrity status when they relocated from the States. Their days were filled with the thrill of high-end living, cruising in luxury cars that turned heads wherever they went. Their beautiful mansion, a testament to their success, boasted exquisite architecture and lavish decor, making it the ultimate sanctuary for glamorous gatherings. Additionally, their wardrobes were a dazzling display of beautiful clothes, featuring designer pieces that showcased their impeccable taste and style. Every moment was an opportunity to indulge in the privileges that wealth afforded them, from lavish parties to exclusive events, where they were always the center of attention.

During Prof's studies in the United States, he encountered Jada, a dedicated student majoring in a different field. Their first meeting was significant. They were both participant in a rally at the State Capitol. Jada stood out as a distinctive student, enthusiastic and unyielding in her beliefs, while Prof was more focused on his academic responsibilities and the demands of his position. During the rally, tensions escalated rapidly, resulting in an alarming display of police brutality. As the situation intensified, both Jada and Prof found themselves caught up in the chaos, leading to their arrest alongside other protestors. The atmosphere was charged with fear and confusion as they faced a series of intense interrogations aimed at extracting information about their involvement. Despite the harrowing experience, they managed to maintain their composure, defending their right to peacefully protest. After hours of questioning, the authorities ultimately released them.

The harrowing experience of police brutality that both endured marked the unexpected beginning of their friendship. In the aftermath of the traumatic event, they found solace in each other's company, sharing their stories and emotions. This shared suffering forged a deep bond between them, as they navigated the complexities of trust and empathy in a world that had shown them its darker side. Through countless conversations and moments of vulnerability, they uplifted each other, discovering resilience in their shared narrative. Their friendship blossomed amidst adversity. Together, they became advocates for change, united by the belief that their voices could spark a movement towards a more just society. The brutal encounter, once a source of pain, transformed into a spur of hope and solidarity, forever altering the trajectory of their lives.

As graduation day dawned, Jada and Prof felt an undeniable spark that ignited a whirlwind romance. Their connection deepened amidst the joy and celebration of their accomplishments. With Jada's radiating beauty and determination, Prof realized the extraordinary woman before him, he could not bear the thought of losing her. With fervent passion, he sprang into action, orchestrating an unforgettable wedding that would become the talk of the town. Friends and family were invited to witness their love story come to life. The ceremony was filled with joyous laughter and heartfelt vows, marking the beginning of a lifelong journey together. That day, surrounded by loved ones, they promised to cherish each other, setting the stage for a love destined to shine brightly for years to come.

From that moment on, their love story was woven into the fabric of history. Jada thrived in her role as the lead accountant at a reputable accounting firm. Every day, she immersed herself in numbers and financial strategies, finding fulfillment in her meticulous work. She often reflected on her life's journey, grateful for the opportunities that had led her to this point. With each successful project and positive client interaction, her passion for accounting grew deeper. Jada couldn't have envisioned a more perfect blend of professionalism and personal happiness. As expected, she felt fortunate, cherishing the rewarding experiences that her career brought her, and the sense of purpose it instilled in her life.

Prof and Jada were overjoyed to welcome their wonderful son, Malik, into their lives. As Malik approached his eighth birthday, a significant opportunity arose for the young family - a political appointment in Prof's home country. Understanding the importance of maintaining a stable and supportive environment for their son during the transition, they made the difficult decision for Malik to stay behind. He would live with his uncle, who provided a nurturing home while Prof and Jada relocated to serve in their new roles. Although separated by distance, the family remained closely connected, united by love and communication as they navigated the challenges of this new chapter in their lives.

In their home country, Prof and Jada celebrated the excitement that accompanied their celebrity status. Despite their youth, their lives revolved around their only beloved child, Malik, who was living with his uncle in the States. While they enjoyed the perks of fame, they often found themselves yearning for a more complete family. Dr Fray's dilemma of his relocation, opened up a new chapter for them, this change turned out to be a blessing for Prof and Jada, as it brought little Jabari into their lives. This unexpected opportunity sparked hope allowing Malik to share in the joy and warmth of siblingship. The transition offered new experiences and challenges, yet it was the bond between Malik and Jabari that truly enriched their family dynamic.

As they navigated this new chapter together, Prof found joy in fostering rich memories and embracing the blessings of parenthood, ensuring that their home remained a place of love and support. After much persistent pressure from Malik, the Simpsons finally agreed to take Jabari along on their state's official visit, granted that Dr Fray approved. The decision came after considerable debate, with Malik championing Jabari's inclusion, emphasizing the importance of broadening his experiences and fostering connections. As the day approached, Jabari felt a mix of anticipation and anxiety, eager to step beyond his usual boundaries. With the Simpsons' support and Dr Fray's blessing, the journey abroad became a pivotal moment in Jabari's life and the prospect of venturing into the unknown ignited a spark of joy in him.

Both Jabari and Malik were thrilled at the prospect of their new adventure. They spent days discussing the sights they would see and the experiences they would share. Jabari, filled with anticipation, couldn't wait to explore new places and create unforgettable memories with Malik and his Uncle's family.

He looked forward to embracing the culture and adventures that awaited him on his journey. They bonded like brothers and Malik was always there to lend a helping hand with homework or play games that Jabari enjoyed. Their relationship showcased the love and responsibility that often defines sibling connections. With Malik as his guardian, Jabari blossomed, feeling secured and cherished in the nurturing environment created by Malik's uncle.

With endless time to explore their surroundings, they found joy in shared adventures, from discovering local parks to enjoying late-night talks under the stars. This chapter of their lives was not solely about learning in classrooms; it was a unique experience of brotherhood, forging memories that would last a lifetime and lessons that extended beyond textbooks.

With both children abroad, the Simpsons found themselves in a unique position to explore new social circles and interact with a diverse array of groups. This unexpected freedom allowed them to break away from the traditional expectations placed on married couples. Instead of settling into a predictable routine, they embraced a youthful spirit, often engaging in activities and relationships that mirrored the carefree nature of young couples. Their open-minded approach to life energized their relationship, fostering a sense of adventure and spontaneity that reinvigorated their bond. As they mingled with others, they discovered new interests and perspectives, enriching their lives and deepening their connection to one another.

Every moment became an opportunity for celebration, and their home transformed into a vibrant hub of joy and laughter. They hosted parties gathering friends and family to share in the spontaneous revelry that defined their new lifestyle. As they infused every gathering with creativity and vibrancy, the walls echoed with music, and the air was filled with the scent of delicious food and the sounds of laughter. Every weekend unfolded like a new chapter in their enchanting story, drawing friends and admirers into the warmth and magic of their gatherings. With laughter ringing in the air and bright smiles all around, it was impossible to find a reason not to enjoy themselves. Each gathering marked another milestone in their journey as a couple, filled with laughter, love, and the joyous chaos that comes with inviting friends and family to join in the festivities. This chapter was not just about their marriage; it was a celebration of life itself. As they shared their dreams and aspirations, their connection deepened, captivating those who witnessed their love story. Together, they built a vibrant tapestry of experiences.

CHAPTER EIGHT

"Men Who Make Sport of a Monkey
In a Cage Will Not Spare the Carrier"
(Associate with Fools and You'll Be
Treated like a Fool.)

Meanwhile the Frays were back in the city, a familiar and exciting place filled with opportunities. As Dr Fray settled back, he imagined reconnecting with his loved ones and friends engaging in the simple joys of family life. However, he quickly discovered that his transfer was not what he had expected. Instead of returning to the familiar urban landscape, he was reassigned to oversee a newly established private hospital in the countryside, where his partners relied on his expertise and compassion. One critical night, whilst deep in thought, he weighed the importance of his absolute independence against the temptation of enduring his investors, who envisioned turning him into a medical missionary, moving from village to village to stabilize a newly opened practice.

In the final analysis Dr Fray chose to prioritize his young family over his career. This decision, though difficult, brought him a profound sense of peace after years of unwavering dedication to his work. By focusing on his family's needs, he found a new purpose that reignited his passion for medicine. Determined to overcome any obstacles in his path to becoming the sole investor in his private practice, Dr Fray embarked on a journey of exploration and innovation. He meticulously researched potential funding sources, networked with financial advisors and fellow practitioners to gather insights and advice.

Each setback fueled his resolve, prompting him to consider alternative financing solutions, from private investors to small business loans. With a clear vision and unwavering determination, he mapped out a strategy that would ultimately turn his dream of self-sufficiency into a reality, allowing him to focus on providing exceptional care to his patients without the constraints of external partnerships. He sat in his small study, contemplating the conversation he had with his friend at the bank. The optimism in his friend's voice had sparked a flicker of hope within him; securing an investment loan could be the key to expanding his business dreams. However, that hope quickly dimmed as he remembered the catch – he lacked the necessary collateral to back the loan. Selling his old house before moving to the countryside had seemed like a wise decision at the time, yet it left him in a precarious financial position.

Time was of the essence, and he knew he needed to act quickly to find a way to bridge the gap between his ambitions and his current circumstances. As he was boiling up with the way he had been treated, a distant memory surfaced. He recalled the old box given to him by Madam Feli, a mysterious gift whose significance always eluded him. What secrets did it hold? could it be the key to unlocking his aspirations? Filled with uncertainty, he felt the weight of his choices pressing down on him, knowing that the answer he sought might just lie within that unassuming box. His heart raced with the thrill of anticipation as he thought about what Madam Feli might have known - some secret waiting just for him to uncover. With a blend of excitement and worry, he knelt before the old dusty box, its weathered surface spoke of countless untold stories, and he felt an irresistible urge to uncover its secrets. With a gentle tug, he began to untie the worn out rope that held it shut, each movement accompanied by delicate dust particles swirling into the air.

The air was thick with anticipation as he worked the knots free, wondering what treasures or mysteries lay hidden within. Finally, the last knot loosened, and he hesitated for just a moment, heart racing, before slowly peering into the depths of the box, ready to discover what had long been concealed. His fingers trembling as they brushed against the cool worn surface. As he peered inside, hope quickly turned into disappointment; the box was empty, yet he couldn't shake the feeling that there was more to Madam Feli's mystery than met the eye. Determined to uncover the truth, he resolved to dig deeper, to search for clues that might lead him to the hidden knowledge that seemed just out of reach.

The quest had only just begun, and he felt an unshakeable resolve to unearth whatever it was she had left behind. Dr Fray stared at the empty box, why would Madam Feli present him with something so seemingly useless? The box, had an air of mystery about it: was it a simple gesture, or did it hold deeper significance? He recalled the tales of her family she had told - a lineage of secrets and hidden treasures, perhaps Madam

Feli had intended the box to hold memories, stories yet to be written, or even dreams waiting to be realized. The emptiness felt profound, inviting him to ponder what it could become rather than what it was. As he continued to examined the box, a spark of inspiration ignited within him, the empty box transformed into a canvas for possibilities, a symbolic space created for new beginnings. With this newfound perspective, he began to understand the true gift hidden within Madam Feli's seemingly empty offering. As he lay in bed, he tossed and turned, his mind racing with curiosity about the empty box that had captured his imagination. Thoughts swirled around him, each scenario more intriguing than the last.

The first light of dawn found him restless, and he couldn't wait to share his discovery with Betsy. He called on her excitedly, unable to contain his enthusiasm, together, they examined the box. Glinting in the morning light, Betsy noticed something unusual there, a key bound to the very bottom of the box. "Maybe you will want to check it out" Betsy said. A very small piece of paper, carefully taped flat to the inside bottom of the box. It was almost invisible, blending seamlessly with the aged surface, but something about it felt significant. Betsy gently peeled it away, she discovered a delicate key nestled beside it, its purpose shrouded in mystery. A thrill of anticipation surged through them both, as the key hinted at secrets yet to be uncovered. What could it unlock? They were about to embark on an unexpected journey of discovery, igniting their imaginations further.

As Dr Fray and Betsy hastily unfolded the note, they were struck by the gravity of its content. Written by Madam Feli, the message revealed a chilling yet exhilarating truth: "Dear Dr Fray, by the time you read this, I will be dead and buried. You and I made a pact. I believe you kept yours by burying me, and now it's time for me to keep mine." The instructions continued, guiding him to the Yesmin Bank, where a safe awaited his discovery. The note assured him, "Whatever you find in the safe is yours to keep. You deserve this reward for your kindness and support to others."

Emotions surged within them, dumbfounded, yet filled with hope and determination. Despite the uncertainties that lingered, they decided to heed the instructions and ventured to the bank. That moment marked a profound shift in their destinies. With the financial support from Madam Feli, Dr Fray was finally equipped to establish the practice he had always envisioned. The chance to make a meaningful impact on the lives of his future patients was finally here. The dream he had nurtured for so long was now within reach, promising not only personal fulfillment but also a brighter path for those he would serve. The lessons learned from his past fueled his passion, and he vowed to prioritize compassion and care in every interaction. As he envisioned the welcoming space where healing would take place, he felt a profound sense of excitement. He understood that this new chapter wasn't only for his fulfillment but also a chance to uplift his community, providing them with the health and support they deserved.

He opened his private practice, quickly establishing himself as the go-to physician in town. With his warm demeanor and keen diagnostic skills, patients flocked to his office, trusting him with their health concerns. His reputation for compassionate care spread, leading to word-of-mouth recommendations that further solidified his standing in the community. Each patient received not just medical attention but also a listening ear, as he took the time to understand their needs beyond their symptoms. His professional expertise, combined with a genuine interest in patient well-being, made him not only the best doctor in town but also a cherished pillar of the community. As he continued to build his practice, Dr Fray remained committed to elevating the standard of care while fostering lasting relationships with his patients, making a positive impact in their lives.

Dr Fray had finally turned his dreams into reality, embracing a life he once thought unattainable. He purchased a magnificent mansion that boasted exquisite architecture and sprawling gardens, offering his family the comfort and luxury they deserved. With the addition of sleek, high-end cars parked in the driveway, every aspect of his life radiated success and opulence. As he navigated the glitzy social circles of the elite, he felt a sense of belonging that had long eluded him. The vibrant events and lavish parties opened doors to new opportunities, allowing him to reconnect with influential figures in society. He celebrated the new chapter of his life, grateful for the journey that had led him to this point, where he could share his good fortune with loved ones and savor the fruits of his hard work.

Betsy was far from the typical housewife; she thrived in a world of sophistication and luxury, surrounded by high-class friends who appreciated the finer things in life. With a passion for culinary arts and an eye for detail, she successfully launched her own catering service, quickly establishing a reputation for excellence. Betsy's clientele consisted of the wealthy elite, who sought her expertise for their extravagant events and gatherings. Each dish she crafted was a testament to her creativity and dedication. As she navigated the demands of her flourishing business, she found fulfillment not only in her culinary creations but also in the friendships she forged with her upscale customers, all while confidently embodying the essence of modern entrepreneurship.

Njeri squinted, her heart racing as she peered through the dim light. "Am I seeing right?" her voice a mix of disbelief and wonder. Or was it her imagination? The air felt charged with a strange energy, and she couldn't help but feel that she was on the verge of uncovering a hidden truth. As she drew closer to the mysterious figure, her mind raced with possibilities. Ayanda, also a new comer on campus stood on the sidelines, feeling a swirl of uncertainty and apprehension as she observed the bustling crowd around her. The other girls, engrossed in their conversations, occasionally glanced in her direction; it was evident that Ayanda was an outsider, and the unspoken bond among the others only heightened her sense of isolation. Despite her initial fears, she could sense the possibility of new friendships on the horizon, if only she could muster the courage to step forward and join the vibrant social scene that unfolded before her. They had all been in her shoes at some point, navigating the complexities of a new environment filled with unknowns. Ayanda hesitated, feeling the weight of their gazes. She yearned to be part of the circle of friends, but first, she had to find her voice amidst the quiet storm brewing within her.

"Is there something wrong?" she asked, concern evident in her voice. Njeri shook her head, disbelief clouding her thoughts. "No, not at all," she murmured quietly to herself, trying to dismiss the fleeting shadow of familiarity that had darted past her vision. She could have sworn she glimpsed a familiar face in the bustling crowd, a hint of recognition tugging at her mind. But was it truly someone she knew, or merely a trick of her imagination playing games with her senses? The more she pondered, the more the lines between reality and illusion blurred. Perhaps she was just seeing things, or the chaos that surrounded her. Nonetheless, the fleeting moment lingered, making her heart race, determined to uncover the truth behind that fleeting glimpse.

Njeri stood a few steps away from Ayanda, her gaze fixed on the figure before them. Abeba's back was turned, obscuring her face, but there was an unmistakable familiarity in the way she held herself. Despite the distance that separated them, Njeri felt a surge of certainty - this was Abeba; She had spent countless years studying her best friend's mannerisms and quirks, and even from behind, Abeba's soul shone through. The slight slouch in her shoulders and the telltale way she tucked her hair behind her ear were unmistakable indicators, speaking volumes about her emotions. Njeri shared a knowing glance with Ayanda, who looked puzzled; she could sense that Njeri recognized Abeba even in the shadows. Just then, Njeri's heart swelled with a rush of affection, ready to bridge the distance and remind Abeba she was never truly alone. As Njeri approached the figure that had caught her attention, it became clearer with each step, and soon it was unmistakable - it was Abeba, her long-separated friend. Memories flooded back, memories of laughter shared and secrets whispered.

Abeba stood there, seemingly unchanged by the passage of time, yet there was an air of mystery about her. Questions bubbled up in Njeri's mind: Where had Abeba been? Why had they lost touch? As she closed the distance between them, Njeri's heart raced, hoping for answers and a rekindling of their friendship, all while the world around them faded into the background. "Oh my gosh!" screamed Njeri, her excitement bubbling over. "So I wasn't seeing things after all! I knew I could recognize you anywhere, from any angle!" Njeri's voice, a mix of disbelief and joy as she rushed forward to embrace her long-separated friend. Memories flooded back, each moment filled with laughter and countless shared adventures. The warmth of their reunion felt electric, igniting a spark that had been dormant for months. They exchanged stories, catching up on everything from life's ups and downs to the small details that made their friendship unique. Nothing else mattered; it was just the two of them, reconnecting as if no time had passed at all. Njeri couldn't help but smile, feeling grateful for this unexpected yet perfect reunion.

Abeba raised an eyebrow, her surprise evident as she watched Njeri's euphoric behavior. It was almost comical how she tried to play it cool, despite knowing that Abeba would be on campus too. The air between them felt charged, as if the knowledge of their impending meeting was a secret they were both trying to keep under wraps. Njeri's nervous laughter echoed in Abeba's ears, a blend of excitement and apprehension that was almost contagious. Abeba couldn't help but smile at Njeri's antics, reminded of their countless shared moments and the unspoken bond that always seemed to draw them together. As she took a step closer, Abeba wondered what adventures this day might hold for them, both ready to embrace the surprises it had in store.

"Girl, you knew I would be here, so drop the act," Abeba warned, her tone a mix of frustration and amusement. The tension in the air crackled as the two friends stood there, memories of their countless shared moments flashing through Abeba's mind. Abeba's challenge hung in the air, compelling Njeri to either dismiss her facade or confront the reality of their friendship head-on. Abeba felt a mix of frustration and confusion as she reflected on her communication with Njeri. She questioned herself, recalling the moment she had reached out to her to announce her enrollment. It had been a straightforward message, meant to keep Njeri informed, yet the silence that followed was heavy. She had hoped for a response, perhaps some acknowledgment of her news, but instead, her words drifted unanswered into the void. Abeba's feelings deepened into scorn as she remembered how important this was to her. The lack of reply from Njeri felt like a dismissal, leaving her wondering if their friendship still mattered when such essential updates went unrecognized. In her mind, the weight of unspoken words hung between them, and she couldn't shake the disappointment that lingered on the edges of their relationship.

Njeri looked perplexed as she faced Abeba, her voice tinged with confusion. "How was I supposed to know?" she questioned, recalling the silence that lingered between them. "It seems there might have been a misunderstanding." She took a breath, trying to make sense of it all. "I didn't receive any updates from you, but I remember writing to tell you that my aunt finally got a job offer in the city, which prompted my move here. Yet, I was equally surprised that I never got a response from you." Njeri's words a blend of frustration and longing for connection, as she hoped to bridge the gap that had formed over their missed communications, yearning for clarity amidst the uncertainty. "It's been quite a transition for all of us, adjusting to the new environment and settling in. I'm eager to catch up and hear what you've been up to since we parted ways. Let me know if you received my earlier message about the move; it would be great to stay connected and share our experiences in this new chapter of our lives."

"Really?" Abeba asked with excitement, her eyes sparkling with joy. "Anyway, I am so glad to see you! I was worried I wasn't going to see you again." She felt an overwhelming sense of gratitude; the thought of losing that connection had weighed heavily on her, but now, with the warmth of their friendship rekindled, all her worries melted away. Abeba couldn't help but smile, eager to catch up and make new memories together. It was a moment she had longed for, and now it was finally here. After a long time apart, the two were finally reunited, their hearts overflowing with joy. Each moment spent in each other's presence felt like a cherished blessing. They shared stories, reminiscing about the past and catching up on everything that had happened during their time apart. Laughter filled the air as they recalled fond memories, and their connection grew even stronger with each passing minute. The warmth in their eyes spoke volumes, reflecting the deep affection they held for one another. It was not just a meeting; it was a celebration of their friendship, a reaffirmation that no distance could diminish the bond they shared. As they sat together, the world around them faded away, leaving only the bliss of companionship and the promise of many more moments to come.

Abeba jubilantly hopped into her small car, a gift from her dad for her 21st birthday. The compact vehicle, a symbol of newfound freedom, was perfect for navigating the bustling streets. She had promised her friend Njeri a ride home, and as they drove, the two friends chatted animatedly, sharing dreams and laughter. The car's interior was cozy, filled with their favorite tunes playing softly in the background. Abeba felt a sense of joy and pride every time she turned the key in the ignition, knowing that this car represented both the generosity of her dad and the adventures that lay ahead. As they approached Njeri's house, Abeba glanced at her friend, grateful for moments of friendship that made every journey worthwhile. Even though they lived miles away from each other, the distance did not dampen their spirits. They found comfort in their busy campus lives, spending eight to ten hours a day immersed in their studies and activities.

Abeba and Njeri's journey took an exciting turn. It was a moment filled with joy and anticipation, as they had dreamt of this day for months. With shared classes and mutual friends, their bond deepened as they explored the campus together. They attended orientation, discovering the myriad opportunities the university offered, from vibrant clubs to academic resources. Late-night study sessions in the library became their routine, filled with laughter and late-night snacks. They navigated the challenges of university life side by side, supporting each other through stressful exams and celebrating small victories. As they embraced this new chapter, Abeba and Njeri knew that their friendship would thrive in this bustling academic environment, making unforgettable memories along the way. Their college experience was not just about education; it was about the journey they shared and the dreams they would pursue together. The rigorous schedule allowed them to focus on their goals while strengthening their bond. Each weekend became a cherished opportunity as they eagerly anticipated their visits. They were filled with laughter, stories, and the warmth of being together, allowing them to reconnect and share in each other's experiences.

For Njeri, college presented a formidable challenge that weighed heavily on her both financially and academically. Each semester, the burden of tuition fees loomed over her, forcing her to juggle part-time jobs while striving to keep her grades up. The constant stress of financial strain often clouded her focus in classes, making it difficult to absorb complex concepts or participate actively in discussions. Late nights spent studying often turned into early mornings at work, leaving her exhausted and overwhelmed. Despite the difficulties, her determination to succeed never wavered. She sought help from professors, formed study groups, and meticulously planned her budget to make ends meet. This relentless struggle taught her resilience and time management, ultimately shaping her into a stronger individual. She joined the school sports team and quickly made a name for herself with her remarkable skills in volleyball. Her natural athleticism and dedication to practice set her apart from her teammates. Each game showcased her impressive serve and strategic plays, earning her not only points for the team but also admiration from coaches and classmates alike. Njeri's enthusiasm for the sport was infectious, inspiring others to push their limits and improve. Her passion for volleyball not only made her a standout player but also created lasting memories and friendships throughout her school years. Whether playing in a packed arena or during casual practices, she thrived in the world of sports, showcasing her talent and love for the game.

Njeri was a striking figure, standing tall with an athletic build that turned heads wherever she went. Her graceful posture and confident demeanor exuded an undeniable charm, captivating those around her. With her radiant smile and sparkling eyes, she effortlessly drew people in, leaving an impression that lasted long after she had left the room. Njeri was not merely beautiful; her charm lay in her ability to engage in conversations with kindness and wit, making everyone feel valued. Whether she was playing sports or socializing at a gathering, her presence was magnetic; it reflected her vibrant personality and zest for life. In every way, Njeri was a remarkable blend of strength, a woman who inspired admiration and affection in equal measure.

The campus was bustled with life, and among the vibrant student population were numerous young men who were just as striking as they were friendly. Their diverse styles and confident demeanor created an inviting atmosphere, making the environment feel alive with energy and friendship. Those young men contributed to the overall charm of the campus. With their approachable smiles and genuine conversations, they formed connections that enhanced the college experience for everyone. It wasn't just their looks that caught the eye, but also their passion for learning and commitment to building a vibrant campus

Amidst the energetic atmosphere surrounding the men's volleyball team, one player consistently drew Njeri's gaze. While the others exchanged playful winks and laughter, this particular athlete stood apart, exuding a magnetic charm that was hard to ignore. With his confident appearance and radiant smile, he created a sense of intrigue that piqued Njeri's curiosity. Each time their eyes met, she felt a spark, an unspoken connection that lingered longer than a fleeting moment. It was as if he understood her thoughts, mirroring her excitement with a knowing glance. Concentrating on the game around them, she couldn't shake the feeling that something special was unfolding, waiting for the right moment to be recognized. In the bustling crowd, he was the beacon of light, drawing her closer into a world where sports and romance beautifully intertwined.

Standing tall and imposing, he exuded an aura of confidence that immediately drew attention. His dark features, complemented by strikingly handsome looks, made him the center of admiration wherever he went. As the captain of his team, he balanced charm and authority effortlessly, inspiring his teammates with both his skill on the field and his magnetic presence off it. His athletic build and delightful good looks were enhanced by a playful smile that hinted at a deeper charisma. As the days turned into weeks, the connection between Njeri and Ojo deepened, starting with casual conversations that flowed effortlessly. Their initial chats blossomed into a series of enchanting dates, each one more meaningful than the last. From cozy cafes to weekend strolls in the park, they shared stories and dreams, forging a bond that felt both thrilling and comforting. Laughter echoed on every outing, and inside jokes began to form, adding a lightheartedness to their bickering affection. With every moment spent together, it became increasingly clear that this was the beginning of something special, two hearts discovering the joy of companionship amidst the excitement of newfound love. Njeri had a sense that this time it could be different.

The cautious optimism in her heart urged her to pay attention to Ojo, who seemed to embody a genuine charm that she hadn't encountered before. Unlike others who had come before him, he carried himself with an authenticity that piqued her interest. She found herself drawn to his easy smile and warmth eyes, both of which hinted at something deeper. As she observed him from a distance, she couldn't shake the feeling that perhaps this connection was worth exploring. Even though she held her guard up, there was a flicker of hope that maybe, just maybe, this would lead her to a meaningful relationship after all. Njeri and Ojo hit it off and momentarily, the whole school knew they were an item. Ojo's study block was just across from Njeri's and break-time never came early enough. All eyes were on the duo as weekends never passed without them going unnoticed.

One muggy Saturday afternoon, Njeri settled into her study space, determined to tackle her final exam preparations, knowing that her future depended on the effort she put in. Surrounded by textbooks and notes, she could feel the weight of the upcoming exams looming over her. Each equation and concept she reviewed brought her a step closer to her goal. Despite the heat in the study room, her focus was unwavering; she was committed to making the most of her time that day. As the hours passed, the quiet hum of her thoughts blended with the distant sounds of weekend life outside. After hours of intense studying, she felt her mind swirling with information and restlessness. Seeking a break, she stepped outside into the crisp air, hoping to rejuvenate her spirit.

The sun began to set as she walked, the gentle rustle of leaves and the distant chirping of birds provided a soothing backdrop. Each breath she took filled her lungs with freshness, washing away the fatigue of her studies. Njeri glanced around, taking in the beauty of nature that surrounded her - vibrant flowers swaying in the breeze. The brief escape from her books offered her clarity, allowing her to gather her thoughts and prepare for the next round of her academic journey. She cherished those moments, knowing that balance was essential for a successful study life. As she strolled leisurely across the college campus, the familiar routes and vibrant atmosphere filled her with a sense of wistfulness guiding her steps towards Ojo's residence. With each step, her heart raced in anticipation, as memories of laughter and shared dreams flooded her mind. She could almost envision him waiting at the door, a warm smile lighting up his face, ready to pull her into an adventure.

Njeri's stroll wasn't just a walk; it was a journey into the heart of her sweet dreams, where love, laughter, and endless possibilities awaited her just beyond the next corner. Her stroll was a delightful escapade, weaving through the vibrant campus filled with the joyful sounds of student life. With each step, she felt her heart race, a blend of excitement and nerves coursing through her as she approached Ojo's dorm. Just as she rounded a corner, she unexpectedly bumped into Jack, one of Ojo's friends. He stood casually against the wall, absorbed in his phone, but upon seeing her, his face brightened with a warm smile. "Hey, Njeri! What brings you here?" he asked, his friendly tone melting away her apprehensions. They exchanged pleasantries.

As Njeri stood amidst the swirling conversation, the overly pleasantries felt strangely out of place. What appeared to be genuine friendliness masked an underlying tension that set her instincts on high alert. As she observed Jack's overly cheerful demeanor, a sense of unease crept in. His incessant smiles and animated gestures seemed more like a mask than a reflection of genuine happiness. Njeri couldn't shake off the feeling that beneath his bright facade lay a deeper meaning, perhaps a hidden or unspoken secret was brewing. Each laugh and smile seemed to echo with unspoken implications, casting a shadow over the otherwise light-hearted exchange. The more she engaged, the more the air thickened with uncertainty, making her pulse race.

Torn between the allure of friendliness and the creeping suspicion clawing at her thoughts, her anxiety boiled beneath the surface. In a moment of defiance, she pushed past Jack, her heart pounding as she struggled to navigate the complex emotions brewing within her. The encounter was far from innocent, and she was ready to confront whatever lay ahead. The atmosphere felt thick with tension as she climbed the stairs, her resolve hardening with every step. She burst into Ojo's room, her breath pulling in her throat at the sight before her. There, nestled under the covers, lay Ojo, intertwined with another girl, a scene that shattered her heart in an instant. Disbelief washed over her, followed by a wave of betrayal that gushed through her veins. This was not the love she had thought they shared; it was a desolate reality that left her wobbling with the painful truth of a shattered trust. What stung even more was the realization that this girl, who had feigned friendship, had been plotting all along - not to forge a bond, but to win over Ojo's heart.

Njeri grappled with her shattered trust as the weight of her heartbreak settled in. She stood on the brink of losing not just a love, but a friend she had never truly known. The realization struck her like a lightning bolt, leaving her to grapple with the duplicity of someone she had considered close. It was painful to acknowledge that what she perceived as friendship was merely a facade, masking jealousy and ulterior motives. As she reflected on past interactions, she felt a deep sense of betrayal, realizing that trust had been broken. Njeri sat quietly, reflecting on the turmoil that had unfolded around her. Disappointment lingered in the air, but it was merely a shadow of the far more significant issues she faced.

Heartbreak had never truly taken root in her chest; she had always maintained a cautious distance, knowing deep down that trust was a fragile thing. Friends had let her down, and she had witnessed the betrayal of loyalty too many times to risk her heart on hollow promises. Instead of wallowing in sadness, she resolved to forge a stronger path forward, one built on self-reliance and resilience. She understood that her worth did not hinge on the love of others and that true love emerges from within.

Embracing her independence, Njeri prepared to navigate the complexities of life, armed with the lessons of the past and an unwavering commitment to herself. She was profoundly aware of the myriad of scum-bags and fake people surrounding her. With a mix of determination and wariness, she quietly left the residence, clutching her books tightly against her chest. They were her refuge, the only companions she truly trusted in a world that often felt deceiving and superficial. Each subject represented knowledge, adventure, and the comfort of familiarity amidst chaos. As she stepped out into the world, she felt a sense of liberation; with her precious books in hand, she was ready to navigate the challenges ahead, shielded by the wisdom they contained. In a society fraught with insincerity, her loyalty to literature provided solace and strength, reminding her that not all was lost.

CHAPTER NINE

"A Merchant Who Is Willing to Give
Credit Will Get the Trade"

◆ ◆ ◆

For a long while after Njeri's disappointing experience on campus, she decided to take a step back from romantic relationships. The emotional turmoil from that time made her wary of opening herself up to new connections. Instead, she focused on her personal growth, dedicating her energy to her studies and self-discovery. She found solace in Abeba and Ayanda, a supportive circle that helped her heal. The period of contemplation allowed her to understand her feelings better and reassess what she truly wanted in a partner. Although the memories of disappointment dissipated, she clung to a deep-seated sense of mistrust. She had learned to guard her heart. While the echoes of betrayal lingered in her mind, she waited for the day when someone would prove her wrong, believing that true love would eventually find its way to her, but only at the right time.

Njeri held on to the belief that true love was merely a mirage, an elaborate illusion crafted from the intricacies of human emotion. To her, love was just another game played in the grand theater of life, where every action demanded a price, and nothing was ever given without expectation. She watched as relationships blossomed and wilted around her, each one reinforcing her conviction that genuine connection was unattainable. In her mind, love was an intricate web spun from desires and deceptions, a fleeting pleasure that ultimately lead to disappointment. Njeri's heart became a fortress, fortified by skepticism, as she wandered through a world that danced to the rhythm of give and take, convinced that no one could ever truly connect without the sting of loss or the burden of unfulfilled promises. Her journey of self-discovery not only strengthened her resilience but also prepared her for a future filled with possibilities and hope.

She found herself increasingly consumed by her work, her once casual approach evolving into a fervent obsession. Late nights became the norm, as she poured her energy into projects, driven by an insatiable desire for excellence. Colleagues began to notice the change; she was always the last to leave the office, her creativity flowing like never before. The thrill of deadlines and the satisfaction of completing tasks gave her an adrenaline rush she hadn't anticipated. Each success only deepened her commitment, pushing her to take on more responsibilities.

While the pursuit of her career was exhilarating, it also blurred the lines between dedication and addiction. Friends worried about her well-being, but Njeri was unapologetic; she had found something that ignited her passion, fulfilling her in ways she never thought possible. In her eyes, she wasn't simply working; she was building her future, one project at a time. Her social life became decidedly uneventful; it was simply nonexistent. She often found herself alone on weekends, scrolling through upcoming projects and past projects. While others filled their calendars with events and activities, Njeri's invitations were few and far between. The loneliness was perceptible, yet she remained an observer.

The sun shone brightly in the sky, stretching endlessly above; dotted with the occasional fluffy white cloud that floated lazily by. The vibrant colors of nature seemed to come alive, and Njeri felt a wave of relief that there were no imminent signs of rain. The day felt perfect, promising an uninterrupted adventure ahead. It was the perfect day for her bi-weekly grocery shopping, and although the heat and humidity was intense, she was determined to make the most of it; a ritual she cherished despite the sun's oppressive grip. This time of day was ideal, as the roads were relatively quiet and the grocery store promised fewer crowds. With a shopping list in hand and a sense of purpose, she set out to navigate the aisles, eager to gather fresh produce and essentials. The warmth outside contrasted with the chilled air within the store, creating a comfortable refuge as she meticulously filled her cart, anticipating delicious meals ahead. As she unloaded her groceries onto the checkout table, her attention was suddenly drawn to the dark clouds gathering terrifyingly above. Panic surged through her as she realized the rain was imminent. She quickly gathered her bags, glancing anxiously at the sky, and hurried towards her car parked a few blocks away.

As the dark clouds gathered threateningly above, a tall man in his mid-forties sprinted from his maroon Audi, the tires of his vehicle crunching gravel as he abandoned it. He glanced over his shoulder, feeling the first droplets of rain begin to splatter against the pavement. The wind howled through the streets, urging him to move faster. With each hurried step, he could sense the storm's fury building behind him, a relentless force that threatened to interrupt the day's activities. He raced toward the store's entrance, hoping to find refuge and shelter from the tempest that loomed. In his panic, he brushed past Njeri who was equally driven by the urgency of the storm, unaware of each other's struggles against the unpredictable weather. The air was thick with tension as the drops of rain began to intensify spurring them into action as they sought shelter from nature's impending fury. The man's careless maneuver sent Njeri's groceries tumbling to the ground, a chaotic mix of fruits, vegetables, and other items scattering everywhere. Despite her anger, Njeri managed to keep her composure, aware that accidents happen. He quickly stepped in to assist, apologizing for the disruption and helping her gather the salvageable items. He offered to replace anything that was damaged, but Njeri firmly declined, prioritizing a swift escape before the impending rain worsened.

They hurried to her car, the sky darkened, and just as the last grocery item was secured in the trunk, the rain began to pour heavily, drenching everything in its path. Njeri watched as the rain fell heavily, each drop seeming to soak the earth beneath. She knew that finding shelter for him meant he would have to walk blocks from the parking lot, and the thought of him getting drenched was hard to bear. With a warm smile, she offered him a place in her car, hoping to keep him dry while they waited for the storm to pass.

While they were settled in Njeri's car, an oppressive silence surrounded them, punctuated only by the howling wind and lashing rain of the storm. The strange man decided to break the ice to disrupt the stillness.

"Hi, my name is Orji, and I'm really sorry for causing the delay and messing up your shopping gig," he introduced himself, his tone a curious blend of warmth and unease. Njeri's heart raced, caught between relief at the break in silence and the unsettling feeling that his presence, while polite, held an air of unpredictability. She glanced at him, her thoughts racing as she tried to gauge his intentions amidst the chaos of the storm outside, unsure if she should feel reassured or on guard.

Njeri responded with a reassuring smile. "That's fine, I'm sure it was an accident, no malice intended. By the way, my name is also Njeri." The similarity in their names sparked an unexpected conversation between them, easing the tension that lingered after the mishap. In a light-hearted moment, Orji greeted Njeri with a warm smile, marking the beginning of a friendly exchange. "Njeri, nice to meet you." Orji nice to meet you as well." Orji quick to reciprocate, playfully asked if there was any way to make amends for the mishap earlier. Njeri inquired about what needed remedying, prompting a humorous recollection of the unfortunate accident that had caused a minor disaster with Njeris groceries. With the initial awkwardness behind them, their laughter filled the air. They began to chat more freely, finding common ground and laughter amidst the remnants of a disrupted day. What started as an uncomfortable encounter transformed into a delightful conversation filled with understanding and friendship. As they sat together, the rhythm of the rain against the windshield created an unexpected sense of comfort, transforming an inconvenient situation into a moment of connection.

With the world outside drenched, they shared stories and laughter, finding warmth not just from the car's interior, but from each other's company.

Orji was a dynamic and ambitious young CEO, who had returned from the States to take leadership of his family empire. With a fresh perspective and innovative ideas, he was determined to revitalize the business and steer it toward a prosperous future. Orji's journey was marked by rigorous education and invaluable experiences in one of the world's most competitive markets. As he stepped into his role, he blended traditional values with modern strategies, aiming to honor his family's legacy while also embracing change. His vision was clear: to expand the empire's reach, attract new talent, and foster sustainable growth. With his youthful energy and commitment to excellence, he was poised to become a transformative leader in the refinery industry, inspiring those around him and setting a new standard for success within the family enterprise.

After an unexpectedly awkward incident in the car park, Orji and Njeri found themselves forging an impressive connection. What began as a clumsy moment, filled with embarrassed laughter and shared apologies, quickly transformed into an opportunity for them to discover common interests and spark intriguing conversations. They realized that the incident served as an unlikely icebreaker, allowing them to open up to each other in ways they had not anticipated. As they exchanged stories and laughter, a bond began to form, one that promised to flourish beyond the confines of that parking lot. The initial awkwardness faded, replaced by an undeniable chemistry that left both of them excited to see where this newfound connection might lead.

Njeri's well-paying job was conveniently located just a short drive away from Orji's home. Every morning, she would set off early to avoid the morning rush, enjoying the peaceful drive through the city's scenic routes. Her position at a reputable company came with its own challenges, but Njeri found fulfillment in her work, thriving in a fast-paced environment. The distance, though manageable, allowed her to reflect on her day ahead and unwind during the journey back home. She often appreciated this time for herself, using it to listen to her favorite radio or music. The job not only provided financial stability but also enriched her life with new experiences and connections. Njeri felt fortunate to have such a professional aspirations, making the commute worthwhile. She found immense joy in her role as an advertising artist, where her creativity increased and her talent shone brightly. With each project, she brought fresh ideas and innovative designs that captivated audiences and left a lasting impression. Her keen eye for detail and understanding of market trends allowed her to craft compelling advertisements that effectively conveyed messages and attracted clients' attention.

Colleagues often marveled at her ability to transform concepts into visually stunning art that told a story. For Njeri, work wasn't just a job; it was a passion that inspired her every day. The satisfaction of seeing her designs come to life and resonate with people was unparalleled, fueling her dedication and enthusiasm for her craft. Njeri was not just proficient; she truly excelled in her field, establishing herself as a remarkable talent in the world of advertising. Several months into her relationship with Orji, she sensed that a significant step was approaching. Orji always thoughtful and considerate decided it was time to share their love story with his family. This decision brought a mix of excitement and nervousness for both of them. Njeri wondered how his family would react to the news, hoping they would embrace her warmly.

As Orji prepared to reveal their relationship, he reminded Njeri of the strength of their bond, assuring her that love often finds a way to triumph over doubts. Together, they envisioned a future where his family would not only accept her but also celebrate their connection, marking a new chapter in their journey. The moment was pivotal, a blend of vulnerability and hope, as they stood on the brink of a deeper commitment to each other and to the families that would soon be woven into their lives. Orji was excited as he prepared for the family dinner one weekend, inviting Njeri over to meet his loved ones for the first time. He had spoken about her fondly, and now it was time to let his family experience the warmth and charm he adored in her. Njeri exuded elegance as she entered the room, her stunning dark skin illuminated by the warm glow of the evening light. The red dress she wore hugged her curves perfectly, a bold choice that not only highlighted her figure but also reflected her vibrant personality. As she prepared to meet Orji's family, a mix of excitement and nervousness swirled within her. She held her head high, confident in her beauty and grace, ready to make a lasting impression. The fabric of her dress flowed elegantly with each step, capturing the attention of everyone present.

Njeri's radiant smile and the lovely aura she carried made her the undeniable center of attention, setting the stage for a memorable evening filled with hopes and new beginnings. As she arrived, Orji felt a mix of nerves and anticipation, hoping that his family would embrace her as he had. The aroma of homemade dishes filled the air, setting a cozy atmosphere for the evening. His family welcomed Njeri with open arms, eager to learn more about the woman who had captured his heart. Laughter and conversation flowed throughout the dinner, and Orji quietly observed, feeling a sense of joy as he watched the connections being forged. He hoped the dinner would mark the beginning of a beautiful bond between Njeri and his family.

During the family dinner, Orji's mother was openly critical of Njeri, a fact that became increasingly apparent as the evening progressed. With each probing question directed at Njeri, Orji's mother seemed to unearth more reasons to express her disapproval. The tension at the table was obvious as Njeri attempted to redirect the conversation with smiles and laughter, but

Orji's mother was relentless, her tone sharp and her questions pointed. The atmosphere grew heavy with discomfort as the other family members exchanged uneasy glances, unsure how to mitigate the situation. Njeri's bright demeanor began to wane under the weight of scrutiny, leaving Orji in a dilemma; torn between loyalty to his family and his desire to defend the person he cared about.

The indistinct sniff of disdain betrayed a silent judgment. What was intended to be a pleasant gathering quickly transformed into an interrogation strained by unspoken judgments. Njeri's only crime was her humble origins. Without a family name steeped in wealth and prestige, she felt the sting of societal judgment. In a world where lineage and status dictated worth, her lack of a prominent last name became a barrier against acceptance. Orji's mother, a staunch believer in hierarchies, remarked that Njeri "did not smell rich enough," using her words to convey disdain. This narrow view overshadowed

Njeri's true essence, her character, and the profound love she poured into her son's life. In the eyes of his elite mother, she was deemed unworthy; yet, in the heart of Orji, she was the embodiment of strength and resilience.

Njeri understood that her worth was more than material wealth, but navigating a society obsessed with status proved an ongoing challenge, leaving her to fight for her place in a world that prioritized titles over talent. Her lack of a well-known family name became a silent barrier. While those around her benefited from their illustrious connections, she fought against the tide. Determined to carve out her own path, her spirit remained unbroken, fueled by a fierce resolve to prove that identity is shaped by actions rather than ancestry. Every rejection she faced only strengthened her resolve.

However, Orji's mother believed that she lacked a surname that would adequately reflect the wealth and prominence necessary for her son. She felt that a name carried significant weight in society, suggesting status and lineage, and Njeri's absence of a distinguished last name became a point of concern. In her eyes, a worthy last name was more than just a label; it was a symbol of success and legacy that would elevate her son's standing in the world. Her longing for a bright future for her son overshadowed her ability to appreciate Njeri for who she truly was; a judgment clouded by aspiration leading her to view Njeri through a lens of skepticism. To her, Njeri felt disappointingly plain, devoid of the splendid aroma that crowned the truly privileged. This belief significantly influenced her perspective on her, fundamentally altering how she perceived their relationship.

Orji, caught in the tension between family expectations and friendship, felt a growing unease, torn between loyalty to Njeri and the weight of his mother's lofty standards. As he navigated these conflicting emotions, the rift between social status and genuine connection loomed larger, leaving him questioning what truly defined worth. Despite his mother's objections, he continued to see Njeri, drawn to her in a way that he found hard to explain. Each secret meeting felt like a stolen moment, filled with laughter and whispers that echoed in the corners of their favorite spots. Orji was fully aware of his mother's concerns; she believed that Njeri was not the right influence for him. Yet, the more he heard her disapproval, the more determined he felt to prove them wrong. He saw a future with her that surpassed the superficial markers of prestige and elitism, a future where their dreams could intertwine despite the hurdles. With every encounter, he realized that love often comes with challenges, but he remained steadfast, willing to face the world for a chance at happiness with the one he adored.

It was a calm day, with no signs of the impending disruption and Njeri went about her routines, blissfully unaware of the change that was about to unfold. Suddenly, in an instant, her life shifted; a sense of frustration filled the air as events spiraled beyond her control. Her life altered in ways that none could have foreseen, and in frustrations, lessons would be learned about the fragility of certainty in life. The moment served as a reminder that change often arrives unannounced, challenging her perceptions and encouraging resilience in her unexpected circumstance. Njeri had always believed she was prepared for any situation life threw her way. However, on that fateful afternoon, as she sat in her favorite spot, the inevitable unfolded unexpectedly. The sounds of laughter and clinking cups faded into a dull hum as a wave of realization washed over her. A message on her phone illuminated the screen, and her heart raced as she deciphered its contents. The news was jolting, something she had feared yet hoped would never come. In that moment of shock, time seemed to freeze; the bustling world around her blurred, and the weight of the revelation held her captive. It was a wake-up call, reminding her how life can shift in an instant and how unprepared she truly was for the twists that awaited her.

Reflecting on the message, Njeri couldn't help but acknowledge the unpredictability of life, where the unforeseen can redefine one's paths in extraordinary ways. She had always been cautious about the choices she made, particularly when it came to her health and relationships. Despite her best efforts she found herself in a situation she hadn't planned for. Overwhelmed and unsure, the weight of her news pressed heavily upon her. The untold emotions coursing through her - fear, confusion, and a flicker of hope left her feeling lost. She pondered her options, grappling with thoughts of her future and the implications of this unexpected turn of events. In the solitude of her mind, Njeri sought clarity and support, hoping to navigate through the uncertainty that lay ahead. With each passing moment, she realized that understanding her own feelings would be paramount in making the decisions that could change her life forever.

In her moment of hardship, she felt an overwhelming absence as she longed for the comforting presence of her mother. The world around her felt cold and distant, a sharp contrast to the warmth she once felt. Memories of her mother flooded her mind, each recollection a bittersweet reminder of love and guidance now detached. With her mother out of reach, Njeri was left to navigate her struggles alone, feeling like a ship adrift in a vast ocean.

The ache of loneliness weighed heavily on her heart, and she yearned for the familiar voice that could soothe her fears and provide the wisdom she so desperately needed in her trying times. Later, while sitting alone in her room, the weight of her thoughts pressed heavily upon her heart. Her best friend, Abeba, the one person she could always count on for comfort and sage advice, was inexplicably absent. It felt as though a vital piece of her support system had vanished into thin air, leaving behind a void that was both unsettling and mysterious. She pondered over whether Abeba was facing her own battles or if her absence was simply a fleeting moment. The silence around her deepened the uncertainty, igniting a flicker of anxiety within her. Without Abeba's familiar presence, she was left to navigate her feelings alone, yearning for the warmth of their conversations and the reassurance that everything would be alright. The mystery of Abeba's whereabouts lingered in her mind, a puzzle she desperately wished to solve, as the last she heard of her was at the welcoming party of Malik and Jabari.

Njeri had always valued her friendship with Ayanda, but she knew there were certain boundaries that should not be crossed. Although Ayanda was part of their close-knit circle, Njeri hesitated to share her personal struggles with her. It wasn't that she lacked trust; rather, she felt that their relationship, while warm and supportive, didn't have the depth required for intimate revelations. She preferred to keep her challenges private, believing that some vulnerabilities were best held close to the heart. She cherished their friendship for what it was, enjoying lighthearted conversations and shared laughter, but she understood that not every friend needed to be privy to her innermost thoughts. As much as Ayanda cared, Njeri felt that revealing her circumstances might complicate their bond, and she was not ready for that.

CHAPTER TEN

"Do Not Learn to Swim Where the River
Enters the Sea"
(Know Your Own Limitations)

At a crossroads in their lives, Jabari and Malik found themselves grappling with uncertainty unsure of the future. Questions lingered in their minds, would staying close to family provide support they needed or would the allure of new opportunities in the States lead to greater fulfilment? They explored various pathways, weighing the pros and cons of their choices. After much deliberation, they embraced the idea of returning to their roots, hopeful that the journey back would lead them to clarity and a renewed sense of purpose. The prospects of settling down with their family was far more rewarding than pursuing their dreams in the United States. As they parked their belongings a mix of nostalgia and uncertainty washed over them. With their hearts full of hope and minds racing with possibilities, they took a deep breath and headed home ready to weigh their options and reconnect with the cord that had shaped them.

In Prof and Jada's world, life remained a beautiful shared journey, filled with laughter and love at every turn. To celebrate the arrival of their two sons, Malik and Jabari, the family decided to host a warm welcoming party that would bring together friends and relatives. They envisioned a lively atmosphere filled with laughter, music, and joy, where everyone could come together to share in their excitement. As the day of the welcoming party approached, Prof and Jada poured their hearts into the planning, determined to create an unforgettable experience for their children. Recognizing their family's legacy of hosting remarkable celebrations, they decided to hire a live band, knowing that the vibrant music would infuse the event with energy and joy. Colorful decorations transformed the venue into a festive haven, where every detail was carefully planned to enhance the mood. With the sound of music providing the perfect backdrop, the scene was set for a joyous reunion. Prof and Jada's meticulous planning and attention to details truly brought the event to life, showcasing their love for their children and the importance of family gathering in their lives. It was a celebration that would be remembered by all who attended. Malik and Jabari felt an overwhelming sense of gratitude and happiness as they basked in the warmth of their homecoming.

Abeba could hardly contain her excitement as the welcoming party approached. She excitedly shared with her friends, Njeri and Ayanda all the details. "You won't believe the decorations they're setting up! It's going to be so warm and inviting," she exclaimed, her eyes sparkling. Her mother, Betsy, was in charge of the food, and Abeba couldn't stop raving about her cooking. "She's even reserved catering from her amazing restaurant, so we're in for a feast! I can already imagine the flavors," she said eagerly. Abeba mentioned that guests could expect a delightful mix of traditional favorites alongside some innovative new dishes, stirring their anticipation further.

Ayanda shared a close bond with her college mates, Abeba and Njeri, forming a friendship that blossomed during their years on campus. Beyond academics, Ayanda was also a familiar face in the neighborhood, living next door to the Simpsons. Prof had known her since she was born, and had watched her grow up, witnessing her journey from a curious child to a bright college student. Touched by the invitation, Ayanda considered how much joy and warmth such gatherings brought to the community, making her eager to join and contribute to the festive atmosphere. As the date drew nearer, Ayanda's anticipation grew, and a smile lit up her face at the thought of the upcoming party. She could already envision the joy that would fill the air as friends and family gathered at the Simpson household. The laughter, heartfelt conversations, and the clinking of glasses would set the tone for a delightful evening surrounded by loved ones. She looked forward to forging new connections and strengthening old ones, knowing that the gathering would be a memorable highlight filled with genuine happiness. As the three friends chatted about the details of the party, Abeba reminded them "Don't forget, the dress code." Ayanda nodded eagerly, already imagining the stylish outfits they would wear and the delightful conversations they would share. This gathering promised to be unforgettable, and she couldn't wait to have a second celebration with her friends by her side after their college graduation celebration.

Njeri graduated together with Abeba and

Ayanda. Despite Njeri's struggles juggling school and a part-time job, she graduated with first-class honors. Her determination and perseverance were evident as she balanced her responsibilities, often sacrificing personal time to meet her academic goals. Each late-night study session and early morning class contributed to her success. Support from Abeba and family uplifted her spirits during challenging times, reminding her of the importance of her educational journey. Graduating with such distinction reflected her resilience in the face of adversity. Abeba's graduation with honors a remarkable achievement, came as no surprise to those who knew her. Her intelligence was often compared to that of a weasel. With her sharp mind and relentless determination, she navigated her academic journey with finesse, excelling in every subject she tackled. Friends and teachers alike admired her ability to grasp complex concepts swiftly, often leaving them in awe of her analytical skills. As she donned her cap and gown on graduation day, it was evident that her hard work had paid off, and a bright future awaited her.

The day everyone had been eagerly anticipating finally arrived, and the excitement in the air was unforgettable. It was a beautiful Saturday with clear skies and perfect weather, making it an ideal setting for the much-anticipated party. While the trio eagerly awaited the much-anticipated party, an atmosphere of joy surrounded them as their recent graduation had left them buzzing with happiness. Brainstorming ideas for the upcoming celebration, laughter and aspirations flowed effortlessly among them. Each suggestion ignited a spark of excitement, as they pictured a gathering brimming with unforgettable memories. With gleaming smiles lighting up their faces and hope guiding their hearts, they decided to embark on a shopping adventure in Abeba's car, excited to find the perfect outfits for the upcoming party. The drive was filled with laughter and playful banter, with each of them sharing their fashion preferences and ideas. As they arrived at the clothe shop, the anticipation of finding stunning dresses and accessories heightened their spirits. They eagerly explored the latest trends, helping one another pick out the best styles while enjoying their time together.

As the clock struck six on Saturday evening, the atmosphere at the Simpson family mansion buzzed with excitement and anticipation. Guests began to arrive: the grand halls came alive with a vibrant atmosphere and elegant decorations shimmering under the warm glow of chandeliers. Laughter and lively chatter echoed off the fancy walls, creating a symphony of excitement. Each guest, dressed in their finest attire, added to the festive ambiance, navigating through clusters of conversation and clinking glasses. The scent of exquisite cuisine wafted through the air, teasing the senses and enticing everyone to indulge in the culinary delights that awaited. Caterers dashed about, ensuring that every detail was perfect - from the exquisite appetizer artfully arranged on platters to the soft lighting, mingling with the sounds of laughter and music that set the mood for an enchanting evening. Friends and family gathered, dressed to impress, each eager to celebrate and create unforgettable memories. It was clear that the Simpsons had pulled out all the stops for this event, making it one of the most talked-about gatherings of the season. The evening promised to be a splendid blend of warmth, joy, and celebration, setting the stage for lasting connections.

The atmosphere was alive with excitement and anticipation. The bandstand, beautifully decorated, stood proudly on the spacious lawn, ready to host an evening of music and joy. Tables were adorned with colorful tablecloths. Refreshing drinks were chilling nearby, ready to quench the thirst of partygoers. The stage was set not only for a fantastic performance from the band but also for memories, marking the occasion as a night to remember. By eight, guests began to arrive at the grand Simpson mansion, their excited chatter filled the air. Two hours later, the lavish halls were brimmed with dignitaries from all walks of life, each adding to the vibrant atmosphere of the gathering. Elegant gowns and tailored suits adorned the attendees, as they mingled and exchanged pleasantries underneath the sparkling chandeliers. Laughter and music intertwined, creating an enchanting mood. As the evening unfolded, conversations flowed freely, drawing people together in a celebration of friendship, connection, and shared moments. The Simpson mansion, with its lavish decor and warm hospitality, transformed into a hub of joy.

That night, Abeba, Ayanda, and Njeri captured everyone's attention with their magnificent appearances. Each of them, in their unique way, brought joy and light to the evening. Ayanda, in her stunning dress, moved with an elegance that enchanted onlookers, while Njeri's lively spirit and charm filled the atmosphere with joy. Together, they created an unforgettable sight, exuding confidence and grace as they mingled with friends and danced the night away. Their presence illuminated the room, making it a night to remember for everyone in attendance. It was a celebration of beauty, friendship, and the captivating energy that only such moments can bring. However, Abeba's elegant dress and pretty smile made her stand out among the crowd leaving a lasting impression on everyone. Her radiant beauty mesmerized all who crossed her path. The soft glow of the chandelier light accentuated her features, giving her an elegant quality. Conversations paused and laughter floated in the air as eyes were drawn to her, making it clear that Abeba was the highlight of the night.

Soon after, her beauty and vibrant spirit transformed the ordinary evening into something truly memorable. As Abeba made her way through the lively crowd at the party, she balanced her empty glass in one hand and a plate of snacks in the other. The laughter and chatter immersed her; lost in thought, she didn't notice Joe standing in front of her until it was too late. With a sudden jolt, she accidentally bumped into him, causing her drink to splash across his shirt. "Oh, I'm so sorry!" she exclaimed, her cheeks flushing with embarrassment. Joe grinned, his eyes sparkling with amusement. "No harm done," he replied, helping her steady her glass. This unexpected encounter sparked a charming exchange, and amidst the party's chaos, a new connection began to blossom.

Joe, the son of a prominent minister of state, often found himself utterly captivated by Abeba's beauty. Each time their paths crossed, he experienced a whirlwind of emotions, his heart racing at the mere sight of her. She seemed to embody grace and charm, leaving him speechless. Despite his usual confidence, their encounters turned him into a bundle of nerves, making it difficult for him to muster the courage to speak. However, fate had a way of bringing them together, and each bump into her presented a golden opportunity for him to start a conversation. Joe longed to break the ice, to share thoughts and laughter, and perhaps discover the person behind the enchanting exterior. With every encounter, he couldn't shake the spark of hope igniting within him - a yearning to transcend his awe and genuinely connect with her. Their chemistry was evident from the very first moment, an unspoken understanding passing between them as they exchanged brief greetings. Each "hi" felt charged with potential, a fleeting glimpse of what could be, yet no deeper conversation unfolded. As they parted ways, the warmth of their interaction lingered in his mind, haunting him with the possibilities of what could have happened if only he had found the courage to bridge the gap between admiration and connection. Each meeting left him yearning for more, wondering if the next time would finally bring him closer to the connection he craved.

Kevin, Joe's best friend equally watched Abeba from a distance, his heart racing but his feet rooted to the ground, hesitating to approach her. Meanwhile, Joe shared his own experience with him about Abeba, animatedly recounting their encounters. "You have no idea how she gets under my skin," he confessed, revealing a vulnerability that surprised Kevin. "She makes me shiver," Joe added, a mix of admiration and frustration in his voice. Kevin couldn't help but feel a qualm of envy. Abeba had a way of captivating those around her, leaving a trail of mixed emotions in her wake. While Joe seemed entranced, Kevin wrestled with his own fear of rejection, contemplating whether he would ever muster the courage to bridge the distance between them. The unspoken feelings swirled in the air, a tension that lingered as both friends navigated their complicated crush on the same girl.

The band renowned as one of the top band at the time created an unforgettable atmosphere. They played with incredible energy and skill, captivating the audience with their powerful performances and infectious melodies. Every note resonated with the crowd, fueling an exuberant sense of joy and celebration. People danced and sang along, fully immersed in the moment, as the band's mix of classics and original tracks kept spirits high. The combination of their talent and charisma transformed the gathering into a remarkable experience, making it an event to remember long after the last song was played.

As the crowd buzzed with excitement at the party, Abeba felt a mix of curiosity and anticipation. It was the first time she would meet her brother, Jabari, who had been away for so long. When their father, Dr Fray, raised his glass to toast, the room fell silent, all eyes on him. With a warm smile, he introduced Jabari and Malik, welcoming them back into the country with heartfelt words. Abeba's heart raced as she took in the sight of Jabari for the first time - his demeanor, his familiar features, and the sense of family she longed for. The atmosphere was filled with love and hope, and at that point, Abeba knew that this was the beginning of a beautiful new chapter in their lives, connecting the pieces of their family story once more.

Prof proudly introduced his son Malik to the lively crowd, ensuring to highlight the accomplishments of both Malik and his adopted son Jabari. With enthusiasm, he shared stories about their recent achievements in the United States, celebrating their hard work and dedication. The audience listened intently, captivated by tales of Malik's innovative projects and Jabari's remarkable academic success. It was a moment of family pride, as Prof emphasized the importance of perseverance and ambition. The warm atmosphere of the gathering encouraged conversations about aspirations and dreams, with many eager to congratulate the young men on their notable milestones.

Joe excitedly requested his favorite songs, his anticipation building with each track that played. Amidst the music, he found the courage to ask Abeba if she would do him the honor of dancing with him. To his delight, Abeba obliged, her smile radiating joy as she stepped onto the dance floor beside him. The atmosphere was charged with a delightful energy as they moved together with laughter and music intertwining. Abeba seemed to relish the moment, basking in the attention Joe showered upon her. The dance brought them closer, the evening felt magical, a perfect blend of rhythm, connection, and the thrill of shared moments. Joe understood that his feelings for Abeba were not just a momentary crush; they were genuine and profound. The connection they shared was unlike anything he had experienced before, tugging at his heart with an intensity he couldn't ignore. Every moment spent together only deepened his affection, and the way she laughed and smiled made his heart race. Joe realized that delaying any acknowledgment of his emotions would only lead to regrets. He recognized the undeniable truth that love, when it feels this authentic, should never be put off. It was time to embrace his feelings and let Abeba know just how much she meant to him, for he feared missing out on a chance at something truly special. With determination, Joe decided he would express his heart, knowing that the risk was worth the potential reward of finding true love.

Later that night, Abeba and Joe found themselves deep in conversation, discussing everything from their dreams and aspirations to their favorite books and movies. Their words flowed effortlessly, revealing layers of understanding and connection they hadn't realized they shared. Laughter punctuated their discussions, making the atmosphere vibrant and lively. They explored deeper topics, challenging each other's viewpoints while cultivating respect for their differences.

Growing up as the son of a minister, Joe experienced a unique blend of privilege and pressure that shaped his identity. He shared with Abeba the intricacies of living in a household where money and power was paramount, yet personal struggles often loomed large. He recounted the expectations placed on him by his family, especially his father, which at times felt burdensome. He reflected on the complexities of balancing his own political beliefs with those of his father and the country. Through heartfelt narrative, Joe unveiled not just the challenges he faced, but also the profound lessons learned about empathy, resilience, and the importance of authenticity in a world where appearances often overshadow reality. Abeba shared with him that much of her childhood was spent in the village, shaped significantly by her father's career. She fondly recalled those days, reminiscing about the simplicity and beauty of village life. As she transitioned into college and city living, she embraced every moment, especially cherishing the experiences shared with her best friend Njeri, who she had known since their days in the village. Their friendship deepened over the years, filled with laughter and shared dreams. Abeba expressed her excitement for the future, eager to embark on her upcoming career while hoping to create more cherished memories with Njeri by her side. The sense of remembrance blended with anticipation for new adventures fueled her aspirations, reminding her that the roots of her past would always be a part of her journey ahead.

Before parting ways, they decided to exchange phone numbers, marking the beginning of a potential new chapter in their lives. With the music still echoing in her ears, Abeba couldn't help but feel grateful for such a memorable night surrounded by sophisticated people. It was a night that would linger in her memory, capturing the beauty of new connections and the joy of unforgettable experiences. As the hours slipped by, they both felt a sense of fulfillment, knowing they were not just sharing words, but also building a meaningful relationship grounded in mutual respect and genuine interest. The night ended with a promise to continue their conversations, signaling a new chapter in their lives.

As the evening unfolded, Prof's introduction not only honored his sons but also inspired those around him to pursue their own goals with vigor and enthusiasm. The vibrant party began to wind down, the lively music softened and gradually faded into the stillness of the night. One by one, guests, who had been dancing and celebrating throughout the evening, started to take their leave, satisfied and weary from the festivities. Conversations turned into whispers, and laughter lingered in the air as tired smiles were exchanged. Although the party was intended to last until dawn, fatigue had taken its toll on many, leading them to bid farewell before the first light of day broke. The atmosphere shifted, embodying a bittersweet mix of joy and exhaustion, as the once-bustling gathering transitioned into a quiet echo of memories shared.

Jabari was in the midst of a chaotic night, his senses tangled in a web of confusion. The vibrant lights of the mansion flickered in his vision, making him feel as though he were seeing double. Each clink of a glass echoed in his ears, but among the normal sounds, there were whispers and laughter that seemed to arise from nowhere. The weight of the alcohol run down his veins blurred the line between reality and illusion, leaving him stranded in a dizzying swirl of noise. He grasped the edge of the banisters for balance, reminding himself to stay grounded as the world around him spun wildly. It was a moment of recklessness, but deep down, the realization loomed that he had crossed a line into a haze where clarity was lost and shadows of voices lingered.

That night, Jabari experienced the

intoxicating effects of alcohol for the very first time. The world around him blurred as he consumed drink after drink, each sip pulling him deeper into a haze of confusion and ecstasy. In the state of intoxication, his senses dulled, and reality slipped away, leaving only a fog where clear memories should have resided. Laughter echoed around him, faces became indistinct, and the line between enjoyment and chaos began to blur. What transpired in those hours became a patchwork of fragments - moments he would struggle to recall in the times that followed. The aftermath of that night haunted him for a long time, a reminder of how one choice can lead to an avalanche of unforeseen consequences, forever marking the beginning of his abstention relationship with alcohol.

As the sun began to rise, the Simpsons' mansion stood glimmering with remnants of the previous night's extravagant party. The cleaning crew, diligently and efficiently cleaned through the halls. With every sweep they transformed the mansion ensuring that both the grandeur and elegance of the halls were impeccably maintained. The crew's hard work was evident as they polished the banisters and vacuumed up the last bits of festive debris, transforming the once chaotic space back into a stainless masterpiece. Laughter and music still echoed faintly in the air, remnants of joyful memories made under the chandelier. Prof was seen gracefully making his way down the stairs. The exhaustion from the previous night's party was evident in his demeanor. As he reached the bottom, Mr Cole, eager to catch a glimpse of the esteemed figure, warmly greeted him with a cheerful "Good morning!" It was well-known among those who crossed paths with Prof that, despite his immense wealth and the layers of fame that surrounded him, he maintained a demeanor of genuine humility. He treated everyone he met with the utmost respect and kindness, effortlessly breaking the barriers that often come with status. Whether he was engaged in conversation with a fellow millionaire or sharing a jovial moment with a service staff member, Prof's polite and approachable nature left a lasting impression on all who encountered him. "Good morning Mr Cole," replied Prof with a warm smile. It was a beautiful Sunday morning, the sun casting a golden hue over the neighborhood while a gentle breeze danced through the trees. "You must be exhausted from yesterday," Mr Cole continued, knowing how hard his team had worked to ensure everything was spotless.

As the manager of the cleaning company, he took pride in the efforts of his employees and understood the demands of their job. Mr Cole felt a sense of fellowship with his team, grateful for their dedication and resilience. Although he usually preferred to stay behind the scenes and allow his cleaning staff to handle their assignments independently, he occasionally made exceptions for certain clients. Prof, a person of great significance, was one such client. Understanding the weight of his reputation and the respect he commanded, Mr Cole chose to accompany his team during the cleaning session. This decision was not only a gesture of appreciation for Prof's status and his respect for him, but also a way to ensure that the service met his high standards. The cleaning staff appreciated his involvement, as it showcased the importance of their work.

Prof acknowledged his exhaustion but expressed his excitement about welcoming his sons home. Despite the fatigue from the previous night's party, he cherished the opportunity for one-on-one time with them. The anticipation of their arrival filled him with joy. He understood that moments spent with loved ones were precious, and he was determined to make the most of this occasion. His weariness seemed insignificant compared to the happiness that awaited him as he prepared to reconnect with his sons and create lasting memories together. As he readied himself to reunite with them after so many long years, a surge of anticipation filled his heart. He was determined not to miss another moment of their lives, each memory, each laugh shared, would serve as a thread weaving them back together, filling the gaps left by years of separation. His mind raced with thoughts of all the small details he had longed to be a part of, from school events to everyday victories.

"Have you seen them up around here?" he asked hopefully, his eyes searching for clues that would lead him to the family he had missed so dearly. The time was finally near, and he was ready to embrace the happiness that waited just around the corner. "I think I might have seen one of them," he confessed, his voice low and careful. Mr Cole recalled his encounter with one of the Simpsons early in the morning. The meeting was unexpected and fleeting, the man appeared to be in a hurry, his eyes wide with a mixture of urgency and fear, as if he were being pursued by something unseen. The brief moment provided no opportunity for conversation; before Mr Cole could register what was happening, he had vanished into the back garden leaving behind an unsettling impression. It was as though he had evaporated into thin air, disappearing like a ghost into the gray mist of the garden. The urgency of the encounter lingered in his mind, prompting him to wonder what had driven the young man to flee so recklessly. Memories of shadowy figures darting between the bushes later flooded his mind, igniting a mixture of curiosity and apprehension. Although he prided himself on minding his own business, the thought of what, or why compelled him to ponder the mysteries that lay just beyond the back of the garden. The back garden, once a simple entryway, now seemed to hold untold stories, waiting patiently to be uncovered.

Jabari, however, was back in his room, still lost in a deep sleep. As it was his first experience with alcohol, the thrill of the celebration felt delightful at the time, but now the harsh reality of a throbbing headache served as a painful reminder of his excess. He longed to escape the discomfort and drift back into a peaceful slumber, where he could momentarily forget the consequences of his merrymaking. Sunlight filtered softly through the curtains, hinting at the promise of a new day, yet every ray felt like a burden, intensifying his struggle to shake off the remnants of a night filled with too much fun and perhaps too little caution. While it had seemed like a fun adventure at the time, the harsh reality of his pounding headache was now a painful reminder of his overindulgence.

Jabari felt overwhelmed by his father's incessant calls, seeking refuge in the men's room to escape the pressure. The muffled sound of Prof's voice echoed through the door, each insistence heightening Jabari's tension. He paced the tiled floor, wrestling with the urge to respond and the desire to remain unseen. After a few moments, curiosity got the better of him, and he decided to break the silence. Mustering his courage, he called out from the confines of the men's room, letting his father know he was nearby but not ready to face him just yet. Jabari sighed, as he heard his father's persistent calls from the other room.

"Dad, I will be right with you," he shouted back, trying to reassure him. "Just give me a few minutes, please!" he added, feeling the weight of his father's expectation pressing down. He knew that his dad was waiting patiently, but he couldn't shake the feeling of urgency in his voice. All at once, he took a deep breath, focused on the task at hand, and promised himself that he would make it to his father as soon as he could. After all, those moments with family were precious, and he did not want to keep his dad waiting any longer than necessary.

Prof smiled warmly as he leaned against the bathroom door, offering reassurance in the quiet of the early morning. "Take your time, son," he called gently, knowing the first day back in dissociative surroundings could feel overwhelming. "I have all day." The comforting words were meant to ease any anxiety Jabari might have felt after returning home. All he wanted was to share a simple morning greeting and check in on his sons' well-being. The familiar sounds of the house brought a sense of normalcy, and Prof felt grateful for this moment together. It was a small gesture, but in the warmth of their home, it meant the world. While he was waiting he spotted the picture flashing on the screen of his cell phone located on his bed. He got curious and took a look at them. He shook his head and smiled. He remembered when he first met Jada; it was love at first sight. He knew from the very beginning that would be his long life friend and indeed she was.

Jabari stepped out of the bathroom. He noticed his dad sitting at the kitchen table with a cup of coffee, the aroma filling the space. "Hi Dad, you up early," he remarked with a hint of surprise. "I thought you should still be sleeping." His dad grinned, looking up from the newspaper spread out in front of him. "Can't miss a beautiful morning, can I?" he replied, clearly enjoying the tranquility of the hour. Jabari shrugged, moving to grab a glass of orange juice as he settled into the familiar rhythm of his morning routine, feeling a mix of comfort and curiosity about the day ahead. After taking a refreshing sip of orange juice, he turned to his father with a thoughtful expression. "I wanted to come and say hi to you and Mom," he began, his voice a mix of excitement and consideration. "But I didn't want to disrupt your sleep either." Glancing around the room, he added, "Is Mom up?"

The morning felt brighter, infused with the sweetness of juice and the warmth of family bond. Prof turned to Jabari with a slight smile playing on his lips, "don't you think my being here should earn me some favorable treatment?" he asked, raising an eyebrow playfully. It was a light-hearted moment between father and son, filled with warmth and a touch of humor. Jabari glanced up, a mischievous grin spreading across his face. "Well, Dad," he replied, "if you promise to let me win sometimes, I might consider it!" The playful banter highlighted the easy rapport they shared. Prof chuckled, appreciating the bond rekindled, knowing that moments like these were just as important as any grand lesson, as love and laughter were the true foundations of their relationship. Prof continued the conversation with a hint of sarcasm. He looked at Jabari with a playful tone of amusement and slightly exasperation in his voice and said, "well, since your mom is clearly your top priority, let me remind you that your favorite person is still hitting the hay."

Jabari, feeling a mixture of embarrassment and affection, could only chuckle in response. He knew his dad was right; his mother had always been a source of comfort and joy in his life. Yet, this casual banter reminded him that it was also essential to appreciate those around him while keeping a lighthearted approach to family dynamics. After all, family was all about sharing moments of laughter, love, and a little teasing every now and then. He looked at his father with a playful grin, teasingly challenging the seriousness of the moment. "Come on, Dad," he said, trying to read his father's expression. "Don't tell me you're jealous of Mom, are you?" He added with sincerity. "Of course, I love you both equally!" His father's frown began to soften as Jabari continued, "it's just that she's a lady and ladies deserve a little preferential treatment, don't you think?"

As Prof sat comfortably in his armchair, sipping his steaming coffee, the aroma wrapping around him, Jabari savored his bright, refreshing orange juice, the tangy sweetness dancing on his taste buds. The air between them was filled with a playful energy, a bond evident in their laughter as they engaged in a lighthearted teasing exchange. Jabari couldn't resist poking fun at his father's old-fashioned taste, while Prof retorted with witty comments about Jabari's latest fashion choices. Each jab was delivered with a smile, underscoring the affection that underpinned their banter. It was a moment that perfectly cemented their relationship, one built on love, humor, and the shared joy of being together. Prof was happy, as he realized how much he cherished the special moments spent with his sons. He looked around the house, a hint of worry etched on his face. "By the way, where is your older brother Malik?" he asked, glancing toward Jabari. "I checked in his room first, but he wasn't there." "Did he mention if he was going out?" Jabari shook his head, feeling a mix of concern and curiosity.

Malik often had his own plans, but it was unusual for him to vanish without telling anyone. The silence in the house felt heavier, prompting Jabari to wonder where his brother might be and if he was okay. As they both considered their options, Jabari decided he would try calling Malik's phone, hoping to get a response that would ease their worries. "No dad, maybe he is outside." They both headed downstairs.

Later, Jabari strolled into the cozy, sunlit room, eager to see if his mom was awake. "Hi, Mom!" he called out cheerfully, his voice filling the space with warmth. "I came to see if you were up and how your night was." He leaned against the doorframe, a smile spreading across his face as he remembered the sweet moments they shared over breakfast. Jabari's heart swelled with love and concern as he awaited her response, hoping for a bright and lively start to their day together. Jada smiled, feeling a sense of warmth. "My night was fine," she responded. "I'm so glad you're home. We finally get to share our family together," she said. As she reminisced about their shared memories, there was an unmistakable feeling of joy and relief; the long- awaited reunion had finally arrived. With a heart full of gratitude, Jada felt the bonds of friendship and family growing stronger, promising new adventures and cherished times ahead. Her heart was filled with love, anticipation, and the simple happiness of being together once more. "I will be right down to join you, your dad and Malik, let me freshen up."

Later, the three settled down in the family room. As soon as Prof, Jada, and Jabari settled into the cozy family lounge, Malik burst in with excitement, eager to share tales of his adventures from the early hours of the morning. His animated storytelling filled the room with laughter and curiosity, as he described everything from the mysterious noises he heard outside to the fleeting shadows that danced in the dim light. Meanwhile, Mr Cole had previously assured Prof Simpson that he had seen one of his sons that morning, although he conveniently skipped mentioning Malik. As the family listened intently, they found themselves captivated by Malik's whimsical ramblings, eager to piece together the puzzle of his escapades while pondering the significance of Mr Cole's vague assurance. It was a delightful day filled with chatter, intrigue, and the warmth of family togetherness.

Malik woke up before dawn, in the stillness of the early morning. Eager to seize the tranquility of the morning, he slipped quietly out of the house and ventured into the garden. The dew on the grass sparkled in the soft light, and the air was fresh with the scent of blooming flowers. As he walked along the path, lost in thought, he unexpectedly encountered Mr Cole, who was overseeing the cleaning crew. The scene was a blend of bustling energy and calm serenity, and Malik felt a sense of connection to the world around him, making him appreciate the beauty of early mornings even more.

While exploring the garden, he wandered under the shade of the milk bush, a vibrant green shrub known for its unique texture and appearance. As he crouched down, something caught his eye, a glimmering object partially hidden amongst the fallen leaves. He cautiously approached, wondering what it might be; was it a lost toy, a shiny pebble, or perhaps something more mysterious? With each step closer, the anticipation grew, and he felt excited and unease about uncovering the secret that lay beneath the bush. As he approached the object concealed beneath the leaves, an unsettling chill ran down his spine, igniting a series of questions.

"Who could have left a gun here, and for what reason?" The tranquil beauty of the milk bush, usually a calming sanctuary, transformed into a shadowy mystery as he grappled with the implications of his discovery. Each rustle of the leaves seemed to whisper untold stories, blending fascination with a growing sense of dread. Driven by curiosity yet paralyzed by fear, he found himself entranced by the possibilities threaded within this unexpected encounter. The fear of what lay underneath the surface of the serene landscape made his heart race, as he stood at the crossroads of intrigue and dread. What was meant to be a refreshing morning quickly transformed into an experience filled with unexpected twists, as series of events unfolded hinting at deeper secrets waiting to be uncovered. Malik examined the gun closely, to his surprise, it was his own weapon. Confusion mingled with a sense of urgency as to how the gun got outside. He remembered the last time he had seen it - it was safely tucked away in Jabari's bag. The weight of the discovery settled heavily on his shoulders; he couldn't help but wonder how it had ended up in the bush. What were the implications of this turn of events? Malik's mind raced with questions as he analyzed the situation. The hidden gun now represented not only a potential risk but also a tangled web of trust and betrayal. He knew he had to confront Jabari and uncover the truth behind this unexpected revelation before it spiraled out of control. Time was of the essence, and Malik felt the urgency creeping in.

Later that morning, Dr Fray and his wife, Betsy, found themselves waking up late following a lively night at the party. The sun was already high in the sky, marking mid-day as the perfect moment to go and greet their son, Jabari. Excitement buzzed in the air as they hurriedly got ready to leave. With a sense of urgency, they reached out to the Simpsons, letting them know they were on their way. The anticipation of reuniting with Jabari filled their hearts with joy, and they could hardly wait to see his smiling face once again. As they made their way to the Simpsons' home, they reflected on the night's festivities, feeling grateful for the vibrant community that had surrounded them.

The day's adventures were just beginning, and they were eager to create new memories together. Laughter and joy filled the air as the two families came together to properly welcome Jabari and Malik home. With the initial celebration being a whirlwind of excitement, they felt they had missed the chance to give them the reception they deserved. Now, with heartfelt smiles and open arms, everyone gathered in the warm glow of the living room, sharing stories and reminiscing about old times.

The mood buzzed with the promise of new memories to be made, as both families reaffirmed their bonds and celebrated the return of their sons. It was a moment to cherish, filled with warmth, love, and the undeniable connection that brought them all together. Jabari was eagerly waiting for his sister Abeba to arrive with his parent, but as time passed, he began to wonder where she could be. Concerned, he reached out to ask about her whereabouts. Dr Fray and Betsy exchanged puzzled glances, each trying to decipher the unexpected situation unfolding before them. Both were under the impression that Abeba had chosen to spend the night at the Simpsons' house. The cozy ambiance of the living room seemed to amplify their confusion, as whispers of concern danced in the air, their minds racing through possibilities while an unsettling silence enveloped the room. With a shared sense of urgency, they resolved to uncover Abeba's whereabout. As they shared their confusion, Jabari felt a a hint of apprehension, realizing that he might need to investigate further to ensure his sister was safe and sound.

The day took an unexpected turn as they navigated through their assumptions, each waiting for news that would finally bring clarity to the unfolding mystery. The Frays were in a state of panic as they hurriedly contacted Njeri to confirm Abeba's whereabouts. Njeri's voice was calm but brewed with concern as she relayed the news that struck the Frays with a mix of anxiety and disbelief. "I saw Abeba leave the party with Joe," she said, referring to the charming son of the minister of state, whose presence had captivated everyone at the party. The two had shared more than just casual conversations;

they had danced closely, igniting whispers among the guests.

As Njeri recounted the moment, the Frays couldn't shake their worries about Abeba's sudden departure with Joe, a young man who carried the weight of his father's influence. They exchanged worried glances, realizing that their daughter was missing, and questions filled their minds about the intentions behind this unexpected pairing. The party was a night filled with laughter and dancing, but for Njeri, it marked the last time she would hear Abeba's vibrant voice. After that fateful night, Abeba vanished, leaving a void that no one could fill. The investigation dragged on, with detectives scrutinising every detail, yet days turned into weeks with no leads.

CHAPTER ELEVEN

"A Disobedient Child must Eat the Bread of Sorrow"

◆ ◆ ◆

Njeri felt the weight of her friend's disappearance pressing heavily on her heart. Each passing moment was a reminder of the laughter they shared, now replaced by an agonizing silence. With Abeba gone, she found herself carrying the burden of uncertainty alone, desperately wishing she had someone to confide in. The memories replayed in her mind like a haunting melody, and as she navigated through the shadows of worry and despair, she realized that the journey ahead would be one of solitude, until Abeba was found. In the quiet sanctuary of her apartment, Njeri found herself engulfed by a wave of confusion that left her trembling. For years, she had devoted herself to her career, believing that her relentless effort and unfaltering commitment would ultimately earn her the recognition she craved. Yet, the universe had other plans; the shocking news of her unexpected pregnancy turned her world upside down.

The responsibilities of impending motherhood stood in stark contrast to her professional aspirations, leaving her to grapple with the uncertainty of her future. What once seemed clear now felt like a complicated web of decisions, where the stakes had never been higher. As she sat alone, she wrestled with the duality of joy and apprehension, realizing that her life would never be the same again, and the path ahead filled with both promise and ambiguity. As she gazed out her window, the weight of her discontentment bore down heavily, and the heavy uncertainty about her future loomed like a threatening stormy cloud. What had once promised a bright future, now felt like a path leading to a hole of uncertainty leaving her to ponder her next steps in a world that seemed all too unforgiving.

With every tick of the clock, the gravity of her situation sunk in deeper. For Njeri, the decision to continue a pregnancy was deeply personal and non-negotiable. The idea of terminating the pregnancy was simply off the table; it was a decision that had been made with careful consideration and emotional clarity. The thought of ending a life, regardless of the circumstances, felt unacceptable. Emphasizing the importance of support and resources, her focus shifted to nurturing the pregnancy and preparing for new challenges. The journey ahead would be filled with unpredictabilities but the unwavering commitment to embrace this path made it clear that fulfilling this role was not just a responsibility, but a profound calling that would shape her life forever.

After days of wresting with her emotions,

Njeri finally found the courage to pick up the phone and dial Orji's number. Her heart raced as she waited for him to answer, each ring heightening her anxiety. When Orji finally picked up, she could hear the warmth in his voice, but the weight of her news made her feel like time had stopped. "Orji," she began, her voice trembling slightly, "I have something important to tell you." With a deep breath, she shared the news of her pregnancy, seconds felt like hours as she awaited his reaction, wondering how surprised he must look at that moment. Njeri felt a surge of relief as she finally expressed what had been on her heart.

Orji felt a profound sense of fear and frustration at the prospect of the impending pregnancy. While Njeri seemed to approach the situation with a mixture of hope and acceptance, Orji was aware of the daunting challenges that lay ahead. The overwhelming responsibility of bringing a new life into the world weighed heavily on his shoulders, amplifying his anxiety. He wrestled with the uncertainty of their future, knowing that the journey would be filled with obstacles that could test their relationship and resolve. To add to Njeri's frustrations, Orji lashed out; "how could you let this happen?" he found himself at a crossroads, grappling with the weight of family expectations and his feelings for Njeri. His mother had voiced her concerns, warning him that his relationship with her could jeopardize not only his standing within the family but also the long-established values they held dear.

Despite his mother's objection, Ola cherished his connection with Njeri, viewing her as more than just a romantic partner; she symbolized freedom and happiness in a world that felt constrictive. Torn between loyalty to his family and the pursuit of his own happiness, he faced the daunting possibility of losing everything he had worked for. As he wrestled with these conflicting emotions, he realized that the choices to be made in the coming days would shape not only his future but also the dynamics of his family relationships in profound ways. He found himself at a crossroads, torn between his deep love for Njeri and the weighty expectations of his family. Despite his feelings of inadequacy, he yearned to find a way to navigate this new chapter, hoping that together they could overcome the impossible hurdles that awaited them. In his heart, he recognized the gravity of their circumstances urging him to believe that, despite the daunting journey, they could find solace in one another and navigate the uncharted waters hand in hand. Njeri, with her vibrant spirit and unwavering support, represented everything Orji cherished outside the confines of family pressure. Yet, turning his back on the family's legacy felt like a betrayal to those who had sacrificed for his future.

Late nights spent in turmoil left him questioning where his true happiness lay. Orji stood at a pivotal juncture in his life, his heart caught in the agony of conflict; on one side lay his profound love for Njeri, a beacon of hope and happiness that filled his days with joy, on the other, the suffocating expectations of his family's empire loomed large, casting a shadow over his dreams. He grappled with the realization that adhering to his family's ambitions would mean sacrificing the love that invigorated his soul. However the thought of a life dictated by necessity and want was unbearable; it stripped away the essence of who he was. He yearned to blend his passion and duty, but the path before him remained agonizingly unclear, he knew he had to make a choice, one that would forever alter the course of his life and the hearts intertwined with his own. He could not imagine a reality where every decision was made out of desperation rather than desire, where survival overshadowed passion.

The mere notion felt like a slow suffocation, draining him of hope and individuality. He recognized that many had succumbed to this fate, their vibrant spirits dimmed by the weight of unfulfilled needs and relentless struggles. He felt an instinctive resistance to this worse reality, a life where aspirations were snuffed out and dreams remained unspoken. He was not ready to taste the other side of life, at least not willingly, as he clung tenaciously to the fragments of joy and freedom that defined him. In his heart, he yearned for a different path, one where choice reigned over compulsion, and life could still be a beautiful adventure. Amidst the turmoil, he turned to Njeri, attempting to persuade her to consider the unimaginable - terminating the pregnancy. In his mind, he believed that this drastic decision might free them both from the shackles of their current reality and open the door to a future filled with possibility. Yet, the burden of such a choice loomed heavily upon them, threatening to overshadow the very adventure he longed for.

The struggle within him mirrored the struggle around them, revealing the complexity of love, fear, and hope intertwined in their uncertain journey. Orji grappling with the weight of his own desires and the shadows of past joy, found himself increasingly drawn to Njeri. His affection for her deepened, manifesting in extravagant gestures that he believed would sway her. The latest car gleaming and promises, was his attempt to weave a spell of happiness, a distraction from the turbulent emotions surrounding the unplanned pregnancy. In his mind, this sacrifice might conjure a shared sense of freedom, a chance to rewrite their story. Yet, beneath the surface of his attempts, there lingered a profound sense of dilemmas - of love, control, and the dangerous balance between holding on and letting go. With every sweet moment they shared, he clung tenaciously to the hope that they could find joy together, even as the future loomed uncertain and complex.

Njeri stood firm in her convictions, unwilling to consider Orji's suggestion of terminating the pregnancy. To her, it was not just a matter of choice; it encompassed her deepest beliefs about life, hope, and the potential of each new being carried within. She felt an overwhelming sense of responsibility, believing that every child deserved a chance to experience the world, regardless of the circumstances surrounding their conception. Orji's arguments fell on deaf ears as Njeri pondered the moral implications of their conversation. This was not merely a decision about her body, but about a future she was determined to protect, one that she envisioned filled with love and possibility. Her heart whispered to her that nurturing this new life was her calling, and she was unyielding in her resolve to follow that path. She felt a profound sense of purpose as her heart urged her to embrace the journey of nurturing this new life. This calling became her guiding light, illuminating the way forward despite the challenges that lay ahead. However, as her focus shifted towards this new endeavor, the once warm and respectful bond she shared with Orji began to fray. Small disagreements escalated into larger misunderstandings, creating an embitteredness that neither of them had anticipated.

Orji's mother was beside herself with fury after learning of Njeri's pregnancy and her resolute decision to keep the child. The news hit her like a bolt from the blue, igniting a firestorm of emotions - anger, disbelief, and frustration. She could not fathom why Njeri would choose to embrace motherhood under such circumstances. In a desperate attempt to regain control of the situation, Orji's mother boldly approached Njeri with a staggering offer: a significant sum of money to persuade her to reconsider her choice. The proposition was laced with a mix of intent and manipulation. The tension between the two women escalated, revealing the depths of fear, and the complexities of family dynamics in the face of unexpected life changes.

The laughter and companionship that

once filled Njeri and Orji gave way to silence and resentment, leaving Njeri to navigate her path while grappling with the emotional distance that had developed. Yet, she remained resolute in her commitment to her calling, determined to bring forth the new life she had been entrusted with, even as the shadows of her deteriorating relationship loomed larger. Njeri sat quietly, lost in her thoughts, memories of her mother flooded her mind, vivid and clear. It felt as if she were whispering directly to her, sharing the wisdom that had shaped her life. The warmth of her mother's voice wrapped around her like a cord around a finger, reminding her of the lessons learned through shared laughter and heartfelt conversations. Njeri could almost see Maa-me, her mother's gentle smile, hear the softness of her tone, and feel the strength behind every word.

Suddenly, the world around her faded, leaving only the profound connection to her past and a reminder of the enduring bond they shared and the impact those cherished memories had on her journey. Njeri realized that Maa-me's words were not just echoes of the past, but a guiding lights that could illuminate her path forward. As the evening light gently faded, she continued to reflect on Maa-me's insightful words. They had served as a comforting presence throughout her turbulent teenage years, often echoing during moments of doubt and uncertainty. She remembered the night of her high school graduation, after the celebrations had concluded and the house was quite in a peaceful hush, Maa-me summoned her with a soft invitation. It was a moment of intimacy and connection, a chance to share not just advice but also heartfelt dreams and hopes for the future. Njeri felt a surge of gratitude, recognizing that Maa-me's wisdom was not just advice from the past, but a roadmap guiding her toward her next adventures.

"Njeri, as you stand on the edge of this new journey, there is something crucial I want you to carry with you," Maa-me started, her voice, a blend of warmth and wisdom. "Life will present you with countless choices and challenges, but always remember to stay true to yourself. Listen to your heart, seek knowledge, and embrace every experience, both good and bad. Each step you take will contribute to the incredible person you are destined to become. While the path may not always be straightforward, trust in your ability to navigate it. Surround yourself with love, kindness, and positivity, and you'll find that the journey itself holds as much beauty as the destination. Cherish every moment, learn from every stumble, and never forget that I will always be here cheering you on." While Maa-me was speaking, Njeri nodded, feeling the weight of her mother's words, ready to embrace whatever lay ahead.

Gazing intently into Njeri's eyes, Maa-me gently reminded her, "the older you get, the tougher life's choices become. With each passing year, decisions that once seemed simple will grow more complex, filled with consequences that could alter the course of future. One thing that has stood the test of time," her voice steady and firm, "is to never forget or break the chain of your umbilical cord." It was a metaphor that trumped the physical bond of life, serving as a reminder of the connections that is definitive. Njeri pondered this profound wisdom, understanding that the ties to her roots, her family, and her heritage were eternal. This unbreakable bond would shape her identity and would guide her through the complexities of life. As she listened, she felt a sense of comfort, knowing that no matter the challenges ahead, the love and legacy of her family would always be with her, intertwined like an unbreakable thread in the fabric of her existence.

Maa-me gazed intently at her, a blend of tenderness and gravity evident in her expression, "never forget where the link is buried," she urged, her voice carrying the weight of wisdom. Njeri contracted her brow in deep thought: "what does that even mean Maa-me?" she asked, trying to make sense of her mother's cryptic words. It was as if the phrase held a secret, something vital that she needed to grasp. Was it about family, roots, or perhaps a hidden truth waiting to be uncovered? Njeri sensed that this piece of advice was more than just words - it was an invitation to explore her identity and the connection she had with her past. As the moments stretched, she realized that sometimes understanding comes not from clarity but from the journey of seeking and discovering one's own link to the world. She pondered the weight of Maa-me's words, realizing that the innocence of childhood had slipped away, making space for a world that demanded more thoughtfulness and responsibility. "The city is just supposed to be a quick money finding place. It is not a place to be made home." Maa-me continued to warn her about the allure of the city, emphasizing the transitory nature of urban life. It was a hub of opportunities, but also a trap for those who forgot their roots. Maa-me imparted timeless wisdom, her voice echoing with the teachings of the past. "This is what was done in ancient times," she explained, her look steady and filled with warmth.

"In a world that often pulls you in many directions, it is essential to return home, to the core of who you are. Finding oneself amidst the chaos is not just an act; it is a journey of discovery. Home is where your true essence resides, a sanctuary that nurtures your spirit and aligns your thoughts. As you navigate life's challenges, remember that no matter how far you wander, there will always be a place to which you can return - a place that reminds you of your roots and guides you towards your authentic self." Njeri understood her concerns; the bright lights and bustling streets could easily entice someone to settle down, forgetting that true comfort lies in the familiarity of home. While the city promised riches and excitement, Maa-me believed it lacked the warmth and security that a real home provided.

Njeri felt a pull between adventure and stability, realizing that the city, despite its opportunities, was not meant to be a permanent residence but rather a fleeting chapter in one's life's journey. According to Maa-me, as soon as one makes a little start-up in the city, they are to return home where family ties and cultural heritage await. This simple yet profound statement resonated deeply with Njeri, who often felt torn between her ambitious dreams and the comforting familiarity of home. Her mother's words reminded her that while pursuing her aspirations was essential, it was equally important to stay connected to her origins. She listened intently, understanding that her mother's wisdom was a treasure she would carry with her always. Maa-me gently reassured her, "the oldest cord will always stay with you and will never break from you." This comforting notion filled Njeri's heart with warmth and security. She imagined the wise, ancient cord, gliding gracefully through the water, an eternal companion in her life's journey. Each ripple in the pond mirrored the deep bond she felt, reminding her that some connections are unbreakable. The cord, with its glittering scales and gentle presence, became a symbol of loyalty and love, embodying the idea that true link endure the test of time.

"I don't even know why people forsake their countryside for the city," Maa-me murmured. Her voice carried a hint of regret as she stared at the window, watching the sun set over the rolling hills and vast fields that had cradled her since childhood. "There's a certain peace here that the hustle and bustle of the city can never replicate. The fresh air, the sound of rustling leaves, and the gentle flow of the nearby stream - these are the things that nourish the soul," she added wistfully. Njeri absorbing those words, made her feel the depth of her connection to the land. The city might glitter with lights and opportunities, but to Maa-me, the countryside was a treasure trove of beauty and serenity that, once abandoned, could never truly be replaced. "But Maa-me, there is nothing here," interjected Njeri, her voice laced with frustration. She stood in the center of the empty room, her arms crossed tightly over her chest as if to shield herself from the overwhelming sense of desolation that surrounded her. The walls seemed to echo her words, amplifying the emptiness that hung in the air. Njeri's heart ached as she tried to grasp the memories that danced just beyond reach. She longed for warmth, for laughter, and for the vibrant energy that had faded into silence.

"Why do we have to stay here?" she pondered, wishing to break free from the void that had enveloped them since she was born. Maa-me replied gently, "Yes, my daughter, there is nothing here because no one has placed anything here." Her words carrying a sense of emptiness and the realization that sometimes, the absence of things can speak volumes. Njeri looked around, her eyes scanning the barren space, contemplating the significance of presence and absence. At that instance, she understood that the void could represent possibilities yet to be explored, dreams yet to be realized. Maame sighed, reflecting on the harsh realities of life. "Everyone abandons the countryside for the allure of the city, chasing dreams that often lead to disappointment. Few truly succeed, and among those, many resort to desperate measures that compromise their very essence. They forget the beauty of their roots, sacrificing their peace for a relentless struggle in a concrete jungle. It saddens me to see so many lose themselves in this pursuit, as if the city holds all the answers, while the simple joys of life in the countryside are left behind. We must remind ourselves that true fulfillment doesn't always lie in riches or recognition, but in staying true to who you are. Those who leave, never come back, and those who do return often fail to contribute anything meaningful to the betterment of their own home."

She paused for a moment, her gaze drifting out the window as memories flooded her mind. "Let me leave you with this mystery to ponder over," she said, her voice soft yet firm. "You young ones today don't understand the profound impact that meddling with nature can have on both body and soul. The world once thrived on a delicate balance, where every action had its consequences. Experiencing the vastness of the natural world teaches wisdom, patience, and humility. In seeking to control and manipulate, you may lose sight of what truly matters - connection to the earth and to each other. Embrace the wild, respect its rhythms, and you might just unlock secrets that have been whispered through generations. Those of us who do seek, experience that which defies explanation: which make us know the true beauty of life. The moments we spend in nature, surrounded by its serenity, bring us a joy and tranquility that cannot be matched by the bustling city life. While you may be captivated by flashy cars and well-furnished homes, it is in the gentle whisper of the wind and the rustling leaves where we find solace and deeper connections. The sights and sounds of nature resonate in ways that urban living cannot replicate. Until you step away from the chaos and immerse yourself in the natural world, you will never truly understand the profound peace it can offer.

Life is not just about circumstances but about one's perspective; It's how you make it." Njeri, was encouraged and urged to find joy in the little things. "Brighten the corner where you are. You see, in the countryside, knowing your herbs is essential for every aspect of life. Just like those before me, I take pride in the freshness that surrounds us - fresh food, fresh air, and that deep connection to nature from which we all originate. Here, every meal bursts with vitality, and the scents of the herbs create a harmony that nourishes both body and soul. The crispness of the morning dew serves as constant reminders of nature's bounty. When you cultivate a relationship with the earth, you learn to appreciate the simple pleasures and the gifts it offers. It's not just about sustenance; it's about understanding the cycles of life and the magic that unfolds in our gardens. In this way, we honor our roots while embracing the present.

One wonders why humanity has strayed completely from the ways of the source from which they came. In recent times, especially in rural areas, our approach to healthcare has shifted dramatically. The simplicity and wisdom of age-old practices are often overlooked. People have begun to rely heavily on modern technology and pharmaceuticals, losing touch with natural remedies and holistic methods that once bloomed in these communities. This change has left many feeling disconnected from their roots, as the essence of caring for one another through traditional means seems to be fading. We must reflect on the importance of integrating the old with the new, finding a balance that honors our heritage while still embracing progress." Maa-me leaned closer, her voice tinged with wisdom. "You know, most people are oblivious to how easy it is to prevent ailments and imbalances from escalating into serious issues by simply incorporating herbs into their lives. The natural world has so much to offer us, from soothing remedies to nutritional support. Truth be told, the best place anyone could live in this universe is out in the countryside, where the air is clean and free from synthetic pollutants. Here, you can reconnect with nature and embrace the gifts it provides, cultivating wellness in a much more organic way. It's a simpler, healthier lifestyle that many have yet to recognize, but those who do, find a profound sense of peace and vitality.

You see, this small house belongs to me. Papa built it before he passed away at the age of ninety-five, but his spirit was vibrant and full of dreams. He crafted this home with his own hands, designing it exactly how he envisioned it. Every corner of this place holds a memory, a story of our lives together." she smiled gently as she spoke, her voice filled with encouragement. "I know this house isn't as big or as modern as you might prefer," she said, glancing around at the familiar yet humble surroundings. "But think of it as a blank canvas - filled with potential. You can always transform it into something that reflects your own taste and standard. It's not just about the size or the latest design; it's about creating a space that feels like home. With a little creativity and effort, you can make this house truly yours, filled with memories and personal touches that tell your unique story." Maa-me's eyes glistened as she spoke, a testament to the love and dedication that filled those walls. Njeri could sense the deep connection her mother had with the house, a living symbol of their family heritage and the lasting bond that exceeded time. Soon after, the house felt less like a mere structure and more like a cherished chapter of their shared history. Njeri listened intently, feeling a spark of inspiration growing within her as she imagined the possibilities. Maa-me sighed, her eyes filled with concern as she spoke.

"My dear Njeri, I've seen so many people chase dreams in the city, but often they rush in without a plan and end up lost. They think the city holds all the answers, yet they find themselves stranded, sometimes even homeless, with no way back. It's heartbreaking to witness how some refuse to acknowledge their need to return home. Home is where love resides, where we are grounded and understood. No matter how far we travel, it's essential to remember where we truly belong. It's not just a place; it's the support, warmth, and familiarity that provide solace in a world full of chaos. Always cherish this, my precious child for resilience is born from facing challenges head-on and that self- belief is the first step toward any success." Her words carried a weight of experience, echoing the stories of countless families torn apart by the need to seek opportunities elsewhere. Reflecting on the bittersweet nature of returning home. Njeri listened, absorbing the wisdom in Maa-me's lamentation, recognizing the complexities of longing and belonging.

Maa-me's words rekindled a sense of strength within her, empowering her to confront her fears. With renewed determination, she resolved to honor her mother's legacy by embracing her own journey, ready to make choices that would shape her future. Each step she takes would be infused with the love and guidance her mother had instilled in her, reminding her that she was never truly alone. Njeri sat on her bed, staring at the walls that felt too cold and empty without her mother's comforting presence. She longed for the warmth of her mother's embrace and the gentle wisdom in her words that had always guided her through life's difficulties. Whenever Njeri faced a dilemma, her mother seemed to have an uncanny ability to know just what to say, turning confusion into clarity. Today, as she wrestled with feelings of loneliness and uncertainty, her heart ached for that familiar voice that offered solace and strength. She wished she could hear her mother tell her everything would be alright, reminding her that even in tough times, she was never truly alone. Soon after, Njeri promised herself to carry her mother's lessons in her heart, determined to navigate her challenges with the courage and love she had always received.

Orji's mother, steadfast in her beliefs, relentlessly pressured Njeri to consider terminating her pregnancy, believing it was the only viable option for a future she envisioned for her son. Each conversation was fraught with emotion, as Njeri grappled with her own desires and fears. She felt torn between her love for the unborn child and the heavy burden of her expectations. Amidst the throbbing ache of uncertainty, she yearned for understanding and support, desperately seeking a way to reclaim her voice in a situation that felt increasingly beyond her control.

The clock was ticking, and she knew she had to find clarity soon, but the path ahead was shrouded in doubt and confusion. After enduring numerous challenges and heated exchanges with Orji's mother, Njeri found herself cornered and vulnerable as Orji's mother made veiled threats, pulling the rug from beneath her feet, instilling fear and uncertainty about her future. With each encounter, she felt the weight of her situation grow heavier, her resolve weakening under the strain. The mounting pressure was relentless. Doubts and fears clawed at her mind, but she knew that avoidance was no longer an option. With every heartbeat, the reality of her circumstances became clearer, demanding acknowledgment and action. Summoning her courage, she took a deep breath, bracing herself for the inevitable confrontation with both her fears and the decisions that awaited her.

The termination of her employment from a company she had dedicated her all to uplift marked a profound turning point in her life. For years, she poured her heart and soul into her work, nurturing projects and fostering a sense of community among her colleagues. When the unexpected news came, it felt as though the ground beneath her feet had vanished. The termination did not merely signify a loss of income; it felt like a calculated personal attack, orchestrated by Orji's mother, who wielded her connections with ruthless precision. With just a few strategic phone calls to key board members, she skillfully applied pressure on the human resources department, turning the workplace into a battleground.

This hostile environment left her feeling cornered and vulnerable, particularly for standing firm against unreasonable demands that struck her as not just unfair, but inhumane. The experience was not merely about losing a job; it was a painful reminder of the power dynamics that could devastate a person's life, amplifying her sense of isolation and betrayal. With her dignity slipping away alongside her position, she resolved to rise from this ordeal stronger, despite the heavy toll it would take on her life.

Njeri's decision to keep her pregnancy had become a point of contention, igniting a fierce battle against a formidable force whose authority was deeply challenged. As she navigated the aftermath of this betrayal, she realized that her fight was not only for her job but for her dignity and the right to make choices about her own life. This moment, though filled with uncertainty, ignited a flame of resilience within her. As she reminisced over her mother's words of advice, she felt a wave of comfort; cherishing her mother's gentle reminders that echoed in her mind, each piece of wisdom, and shared love, became a guiding light. Njeri recognized the simple life that country living offered, a richness that bustling cities often overlooked. It was in the gentle rhythm of country life that she learned to appreciate the blend of nature, family, and optimism.

With those echoing words of wisdom, she felt a longing to explore the mysteries awaiting her, eager to discover the relationships shaped by the natural world that her mother so cherished. As she pondered those profound thoughts, she felt a sense of responsibility to her roots, understanding that true home was not just a place, but a legacy that demanded care and investment. Maa-me's voice echoed in her mind, reminding her that every empty space has the potential to be filled, not just with material things, but with love, laughter, and moments that create memories. Njeri felt a spark of hope ignite within her, a sense of excitement for what might come next. From then on, she understood that though life may change and challenges may arise, the essence of deep family relationship remains constant, just like the steadfast cord by her side. With a mix of apprehension and excitement, she embraced the journey ahead, knowing that each decision was a step toward becoming the person she aspired to be. Life was no longer a carefree adventure; it was a series of crossroads, each leading her closer to her true self. The notion of returning home, a safe haven filled with love and support, brightened the path she needed to navigate. With a heart full of hope and determination, Njeri realized that her journey would not be just about personal success but also about honoring her past and the relationships that shaped her. It was a balance of ambition and tradition, a dual journey that would ultimately define her future.

In the firmness of purpose, she stepped into the unknown. Each step was fueled by courage as she navigated her path, leaving behind the familiar city life that had once defined her. She had made the bold decision to return to her roots in the countryside, a place filled with memories and the promises of tranquility. The bustling city streets had been her home for years, but the allure of wide-open spaces, fresh air, and the comforting embrace of nature called to her soul. Njeri envisioned mornings spent wandering through meadows and evenings filled with the golden hues of sunset. As she prepared for this new chapter in her life, she carried with her the hope that the countryside would not only rejuvenate her spirit but also provide the fulfillment she longed for. Although she had been robbed of a thriving career in the city, going back to the countryside came as a complete shock to everyone. Acknowledged for her talent and dedication, Njeri seemed to have it all in the bustling urban landscape. Yet, the allure of a simpler, quieter existence drew her in, prompting her to pack her belongings and drain her savings to embark on this new chapter.

As she set off for home, she felt a mixture of excitement and uncertainty, leaving behind

the familiar high-rises and fast-paced life for the rolling hills and serene surroundings of the countryside. It was a bold move, one that signaled her desire for change and a deeper connection to herself and her roots. Only time would tell if this leap of faith would lead to the fulfillment she sought. Njeri felt a heavy heart as she prepared to leave the city behind, grappling with
the pain of unresolved goodbyes.

CHAPTER TWELVE

"A Sheep That Bites off its Own Tail
Shames the Entire Family"
(The Misdeeds of One Affect All)

◆ ◆ ◆

Two years had passed since Abeba's mysterious disappearance, leaving an ache that was almost unbearable, especially now that Jabari was struggling with his own demons. Njeri believed too much had changed, that too many bridges had been burned, and it wasn't the right moment to stir the pot. With a deep breath and a weary spirit, she chose to let sleeping dogs lie, at least for now. The countryside called to her, a refuge where she hoped to find solace in the familiarity of rolling hills and quiet fields. As she set off on her journey home, she contemplated the weight of the past but also the hope that perhaps someday, peace could be found amidst the chaos of her life.

The familiar sounds of urban life faded away, replaced by the gentle rustle of leaves and the occasional whispers of creatures. Each twist and turn of the winding path seemed to hold secrets of the night, the darkness alive with whispers of the world beyond the city she had left behind. Njeri arrived in the countryside under the cloak of night. It was a journey into solitude, a moment of reflection as she navigated the curves. With every passing mile, she felt a growing connection to the vastness of the universe, the stars twinkling like distant memories, guiding her forward on this quiet adventure beneath the night sky. The journey had been anything but smooth; the road was rough and uneven, riddled with potholes that jostled her vehicle and tested her patience. Yet, despite the discomfort, she felt a sense of relief as the city lights faded into the distance. The tranquility of the countryside beckoned her with its promise of peace and solitude, an obvious contrast to the bustling urban life. She inhaled the fresh, crisp air, an intoxicating blend of earth and nature that reminded her of simpler times. Tonight, she was ready to welcome the calming embrace of the countryside, where the chaos of city life would finally feel like a distant memory.

Maa-me felt an overwhelming sense of relief and joy as she embraced her tightly. The warmth of their reunion filled the room, erasing the distance that had separated them for so long. Without uttering a single question, she could see the telltale signs of struggle etched on her daughter's face. The shadows in her eyes spoke volumes about the crises she had endured. Instantly, the bond between them overshadowed words; her mother's heart ached for her, knowing she would do anything to help heal the wounds that had brought her back home. Love, intuition, and an unbreakable connection united them, as they silently began to navigate the path toward understanding and healing together.

The morning sun spilled through the curtains, stirring her from a peaceful slumber. As she stood at the doorstep of her home, a wave of disbelief washed over her. The familiar sights and sounds surrounded her like a warm embrace, yet a lingering doubt gnawed at her heart; had she truly made it back? Memories of her journey flooded her mind, each hardship endured, every moment of longing for this very place. The door creaked open, revealing the comforting chaos of her childhood. The faint scent of her mother's cooking wafted through the air, and laughter echoed softly from within, rekindling feelings she thought had faded. It was surreal, yet here she was, standing in the place that held the fragments of her past. She took a deep breath, allowing hope to replace uncertainty. Perhaps this was not just a return; it was a chance to rebuild, to reconnect, and to find herself amid the beloved chaos of home.

Njeri stepped out, everywhere she turned, familiar faces greeted her with smiles and warm embraces - old school friends, caring relatives, neighbors who had watched her grow up. Even 'jones', the family's matriarch sheep came around her to welcome her. "Oh my gosh, Maa-me, 'jones' is still around?" she asked. "Well as you can see, she is well and healthy. Many buyers have tried on many occasions to buy her but I said no, I will not sell her nor kill her; 'jones' deserves to leave this earth at her own pace, on her own terms." The air was filled with laughter and stories of the past, echoing the joy of her long-awaited return. She could hear snippets of conversations, each one a reminder of her roots and the bonds that had shaped her. Indeed, home sweet home, Njeri whispered to herself, a smile spreading across her face. This place, filled with memories and love, was not just where she had left her childhood; it was where her heart belonged.

As she walked down the street, she felt a profound sense of belonging, knowing she was finally back where she was always meant to be. She reflected on her time in the countryside, recalling her mother's words with a pang of regret. "Not much has changed here," she mused, observing the familiar sights that had remained steadfast amidst the passage of time. The fields still stretched endlessly under the sun, and the small homes whispered stories of generations past. Yet, a certain emptiness lingered in the air; people had come and gone, leaving behind echoes of laughter and memories. Though the landscape looked the same, Njeri felt the subtle shift that comes with loss - the absence of friends and loved ones who had ventured into the wider world. It dawned on her that while nature was tough, the heart of the countryside pulsed differently. The unchanged scenery stood in stark contrast to the fleeting presence of those who had once breathed life into it, leaving her to ponder the truths of home and departure.

Njeri felt a mix of relief and apprehension as she sat down with her mother, ready to share the news of her unexpected pregnancy. To her surprise, her mother listened without anger or rebuke, though the disappointment was evident in her eyes. She had always been taught to steer clear of such situations, and she felt the weight of her actions heavy upon her. As she confided in Maa-me about Orji and his family's relentless pressure for her to terminate the pregnancy, she could see her mother's heart ache for her. "Abomination!" Maa-me screamed. "Im glad you did not listen to the idiot because if you had done that, you would not have lived to tell your tale."

"How?" inquired Njeri. "Well, for starters, it's a taboo in our land to do such," "oh mother, enough with the 'superstition' already," Njeri interjected. "Superstition you said my dear daughter? I wish it was just that, 'superstition'. Do you remember Auntie Emma's daughter? The dark and beautiful with bright eyes and curly hair?" "What happened and why ask Maa-me?" "Well you were in the city and you mean you did not hear?" "Heard what mother?" As reported, sorry to say, we lost her, the whole community lost a great and amazing daughter. Till this day, her poor mother still mourns her loss," "What happened to her?" "Apparently, she thought out of sight, out of disaster. She got pregnant just like you, in the city. Whispers that circulated was that she sought the expertise of top-tier doctors, and underwent a dilation and curettage (D&C) procedure at a highly reputable hospital known for its specialization in such matters. The attending physician himself was taken aback, grappling with the shocking turn of events for months. Despite the successful completion of the procedure, the unthinkable occurred - she passed away on the operating table. This unforeseen outcome left her family and friends in mourning, while the whole community was left to ponder how flouting a taboo could lead to such a tragic end. Her story remains an enduring puzzle, a haunting reminder of traditions and customs."

"But mother, what has that got to do with taboo?" Although Njeri knew in her heart that in that quaint hometown of theirs, where whispers of the past mingled with the breeze, deep down, she understood that everything and anything was possible, a place cloaked in shadows and secrets. She and her best friend Abeba had experienced their fair share of mysteries - strange happenings that defied explanation. "My dear child, what an adult sees sitting down, a child can climb the tallest mountain but will never see it. Its forbidden, like I said earlier, in our land for any child to do that, either here or outside the land; as long as the child is from this soil the repercussions will get to you wherever you are. Anyways, Im glad you stood your ground if not you will not be here today with your questions."

As Maa-me imparted invaluable lessons to Njeri about the rich customs and traditions of their land, a dark cloud loomed over the Simpson family's affluent neighborhood as neighbors exchanged worried glances and whispers, casting anxious glances at each other. Abeba's mysterious disappearance sent shockwaves through the community, sparking fear and concern among residents who had previously enjoyed a sense of security. Months turned into years, yet no clues emerged about her whereabouts. The Fray family found themselves engulfed in despair and hopelessness. Initially, they had clung to the hope that the police would uncover the truth and bring their beloved Abeba back home. However, as days turned into months, and months into years, the family's trust in the investigation began to wane. Endless assurances and promises of updates gave way to silence, leading the Frays to the painful realization that they could no longer rely on law enforcement for answers. Instead, they turned inward, searching their own hearts for closure while grappling with the unanswered questions that haunted their minds. Each passing day was a reminder of the void Abeba's absence had created in their lives, a wound that time could not heal. From the day they realized she was missing, the Fray family's life was consumed by desperation and heartache. Each morning, they found themselves running to the police headquarters, hoping for any news that might bring their beloved daughter back.

Initially, suspicions fell on Joe, the last person seen with her, casting a shadow of doubt over his innocence. The tension escalated as his father, pulling strings, worked tirelessly to disentangle his son from the mounting accusations. Despite the pressure, Joe vehemently proclaimed his innocence, swearing with every fiber of his being that he had no involvement in her disappearance. The Fray family clung to hope, navigating the heavy burden of uncertainty, haunted by the question of what truly happened to their daughter. In the wake of Abeba's disappearance, some members of the community, from all corners, united by their desire to help offered practical advice, with some advocating for spiritual intervention. A few unconventional thinkers even proposed the use of magical powers, believing in the unseen forces that might reveal Abeba's whereabouts. As they collaborated, the air buzzed with a mix of hope and urgency, all driven by the shared goal of bringing Abeba back home safely. Dr Fray and Betsy, once hesitant about seeking spiritual help, finally succumbed to the overwhelming advice from friends and family.

The tales of a renowned seer had spread far and wide, and the prospect of uncovering hidden truths about Abeba's whereabout was both thrilling and daunting. As the sun began to rise, they set out towards the neighboring town, excitement intertwining with a hint of anxiety. Each step felt heavy with the weight of their expectations, and whispers of what might be revealed. The journey seemed to stretch endlessly, yet they pressed on, fueled by curiosity and hopeful anticipation. Just when they arrived, the seer instructed them to enter her space barefoot, symbolizing a cleansing of their spirits and a direct connection to the earth. This unique request both intrigued and unsettled them, adding to the gravity of the situation. With hope and tension, they stepped forward, eager to uncover any insights that might lead them closer to Abeba, fully aware that this could be a critical moment in their quest.

The seer, a figure cloaked in mystery, welcomed the Frays into her dimly lit chamber, a space thick with the scent of incense and anticipation. With a swift motion, she cast three cowrie shells to the floor, their clanging echoing the weight of the moment. As the shells settled, the seer's eyes danced with an uncanny light, revealing the interpretations whispered by the spirit. She spoke with a voice both soothing and urgent, conveying a singular truth: the one they sought was still alive. Yet, amidst the haze of revelation, the seer knew her gift had limits; this was the only privilege granted to her in the vast tapestry of fate. The Frays, a mix of hope and dread, clung to her words, each feeling the electric pulse of possibility that lingered in their minds, as the boundary between the seen and the unseen blurred ever more.

They journeyed back home with heavy hearts filled with frustration more profound than before. After much deliberation, they concluded that their last chance to finding Abeba lay in seeking the wisdom of the most celebrated shrink known to them - the master of compassion and understanding, 'Jesus'. With a sense of renewed determination, they prepared themselves to embrace whatever guidance might unfold, hoping that the insights they would gain could mend the frayed threads of their hearts. The unwavering faith of the Fray family in the power of fasting and prayers from their church came at a significant cost, yet it was a sacrifice they were more than willing to make. As they gathered with fellow church members to seek divine intervention, the burden of worry for their beloved daughter, Abeba, weighed heavily on their hearts. While days turned into anxious nights, the bond between the Frays and the Simpsons and support for one another became unbreakable. Through thick and thin, they stood by each other like true blood brothers, sharing in both joyous moments and hardships alike. Their connection outshone mere friendship, becoming a deep-rooted alliance forged through shared experiences and mutual respect.

As Malik immersed himself in the demanding world of his top-rated clothing firm, a nagging anxiety tugged at his thoughts. The gun that was meant to be securely concealed in Jabari's locked suitcase had inexplicably ended up in the garden, raising unsettling questions in his mind. How had this dangerous item escaped its intended confines? The absence of clarity made the situation even more troubling - who had taken the gun outside, and for what purpose? With every passing moment, Malik felt the weight of uncertainty growing heavier. The stakes were higher than ever, as he grappled with the implications of this reckless oversight. As he juggled the pressures of his career with the haunting mystery of the misplaced weapon, he realized he had to find answers quickly before his life, and that of others became irrevocably altered. Lives hung in the balance urging him to uncover the truth before it was too late. A bullet had been fired, but questions lingered: who had pulled the trigger, and how? For two long years, he bore the weight of this gun saga alone, never daring to ask Jabari about it. Despite the absence of blood in the vicinity and no reports of gunfire, the mystery remained unsolved, deepening its grip on his psyche. Each passing day intensified the urgency to unravel the threads of this mystery, compelling him to confront the shadows that threatened to engulf him. The stakes were rising, and he knew he had to act before it was too late.

Ayanda's life was a tapestry woven from the vibrant threads of urban existence, where the pulse of the city resonated with her every thought and action. Unlike her friends Abeba and Njeri, who found themselves at crossroads filled with uncertainty, Ayanda flourished amid the familiar chaos that surrounded her. Abeba's unexpected disappearance sent ripples of sorrow through their once-tight-knit circle, leaving Ayanda to confront the haunting silence of their shared moments. Njeri's retreat to her village, seeking refuge and yearning for a fresh start, an escape from the ceaseless rhythm of city life. Yet, for Ayanda, the city was not merely a setting; it was the very essence of who she was, a place where dreams danced amidst the noise and every street corner held the promise of possibility. The bustling streets, the lively chatter, and the razzle-dazzle lights shaking with energy that fueled her dreams and aspirations. As her friends pursued new paths, she embraced her urban life, finding beauty and inspiration in the vibrant contrasts that defined her world.

Born to a single mother, a woman who navigated the treacherous waters of high society by exchanging her charms for survival. Her mother skillfully navigated the intricate web of social connections, hosting lavish dinners that dazzled the corrupt government officials designed to forge powerful alliances to secure influence and protection for her family's prosperity. Ayanda grew up amidst the glitter and grit of urban life. Her mother's lifestyle provided her with opportunities, but it also exposed her to life's darker realities. She grew up in a world that revolved around her every whim, a product of being the sole focus of her single mother. She developed a sense of entitlement, believing that her needs should be met without any effort on her part. This mindset made her appear spoiled and brutish, as she often resisted any responsibility or obligation to contribute to her own well-being. While her mother struggled to provide for them both, Ayanda's refusal to engage with the realities of life left her ill-prepared for the challenges that awaited her outside their home.

After graduating college, Ayanda found herself at a boiling point. Instead of embracing independence and stepping into the challenges of adulthood, she chose a path of ease and convenience. The ambitions that once fueled her academic journey seemed to fade as she settled into a comfortable routine; living off the support of her mother. She drifted through life, clinging to the safety net that shielded her from the struggles of adult life while many of her peers ventured into careers and took on responsibilities. The allure of a simple existence was powerful, but as time passed, she began to wonder if the easy life she had chosen was truly fulfilling or merely a way to avoid the inevitable challenges that awaited her in the real world. Consequently, Ayanda's journey became a reflection of the struggles between parental sacrifice and the consequences of unearned privilege. Her focus gradually shifted from living a high life filled with excitement to the more conventional desire of settling down.

As a stunning beauty, she believed that marrying a wealthy man would bring her the security and comfort that would alleviate the struggles life had so often presented. The attraction of a glamorous lifestyle dimmed as she contemplated the joys and stability that could come with a committed relationship. In her mind, love intertwined with wealth could provide a sanctuary from the chaos she had seen her mother experience, allowing her to trade the unpredictability of her past for the promise of a more dazzling future. Ultimately, she was convinced that marrying someone prosperous would not only fulfill her dreams but also shield her from the harsh realities that awaited outside the confines of marital bliss.

While many women attended social gatherings with the primary goal of mingling and seeking love, Ayanda took a different approach she proudly referred to as a "more classy way." Every Wednesday, she eagerly picked up the mid-week edition of the newspaper, its pages filled with obituaries that detailed the lives of those recently departed. Her eye was drawn to the profiles of wealthy and influential men, particularly those mourning the loss of their wives or partners. The idea of weaving her way into the life of a grieving man was both tempting and tantalizing, setting the stage for what she believed could be a lucrative opportunity.

At first she thought Jabari was going to be an eligible target, a man she initially deemed promising, with his upbringing in the United States and a father who held a prestigious position as a medical doctor with his own practice. Ayanda couldn't help but feel a surge of excitement at the thought of Jabari. He seemed to perfectly embody the qualities she had always imagined in a partner, qualities that her friend Abeba had shared during their conversations in school. Memories of childhood tales of her brother and her enthusiastic descriptions of him and Malik painted a picture of handsome siblings who seemed almost like characters from a movie, leaving her eager to learn more about him. Even though years had passed since she last saw him in person. Ayanda's mind was filled with images of his good looks and magnetic personality. The allure of the unknown intrigued her further and her anticipation only grew. Each detail she recalled deepened her curiosity and desire, making her hopeful about what could unfold when their paths finally crossed.

Although she repeatedly insisted that her feelings for Jabari were strictly platonic, the fluttering in her stomach told a different story. Each time she saw his picture, Ayanda found herself daydreaming about him, even as she tried to convince herself that it was nothing serious. "What is wrong with liking a guy anyway?" she questioned, her passion evident in her tone. He is handsome, undeniably charming, and comes from a wealthy background, highlighting his success and stability. Beyond these attributes, Ayanda admired his education and to her, he represented everything she admired in a partner, leaving her puzzled as to why anyone would criticize her affection for him. After all, love should be based on appreciation, not public opinion.

Ayanda was notorious for her outspoken nature, often voicing her opinions without a filter. She couldn't understand why people judged her for liking a guy who ticked all the right boxes. She found herself caught in a whirlwind of emotions. While Jabari didn't make any grand gestures, the mere act of mentioning her in one of his letters to Abeba felt significant to her. It was a moment that stirred feelings she had been reluctant to acknowledge, even to her closest friends. Watching Jabari struggle with his own demons, she grappled with her desire for a deeper connection with him, yet the weight of his turmoil felt overwhelming. She believed the situation was more complicated than Malik claimed. Despite his insistence that Jabari wasn't involved in drugs, perhaps only God truly understood. In a world where her own life demanded attention, the thought of babysitting those lost in their struggles was a heavy burden she wasn't prepared to carry.

For two long years, Ayanda diligently combed through the newspaper, searching for a promising prospect to marry. Each day brought a flurry of articles and announcements, but none seemed to spark her interest. Just when her hope was dwindling, fate intervened. She read the startling news that a distinguished Supreme Court judge had recently lost his wife. This unexpected development of 'romancing the old', ignited a spark of excitement within her. With newfound determination, she envisioned the possibility of companionship with someone of such age and stature. The judge, grieving yet renowned, could be the partner she had been longing for, offering not just love, but also the prestige of his position. As she pondered this unanticipated turn, her heart raced at the thought of the life she might create alongside him in this chapter of her life.

Ayanda stood at the threshold of the judge's imposing home, her heart pounding with a mix of sorrow and determination. The air was heavy with grief, yet the atmosphere remained tightly guarded, a reflection of the strict privacy surrounding the burial service. Despite the objectionable barriers, Ayanda's resolve drove her to navigate through the sea of solemn faces and muted whispers. As she entered the home, she braced herself for the emotional weight of the moment, knowing that her presence, though uninvited, came from a place of genuine care. The shadows of loss enveloped her, but so did the hope of offering solace in a time when words felt inadequate. Despite the judgmental glances and snide remarks from those around her,

Ayanda remained unfazed. She believed that within the depths of his sorrow lay a glimmer of something precious, something that went beyond the whispers; and she was willing to defy social norms for a chance at happiness.

Ayanda found herself at the center of town gossip, as whispers spread about her secret romance with the widowed judge, who was navigating life after losing his wife. Her secret relationship with the widowed judge transformed from a hidden affair into a significant chapter of her life. However, after months of secret meetings and whispered conversations, she found herself at a crossroads, grappling with a sense of isolation and the weight of her choices.

The first night of their intimacy, Ayanda felt an unease settle in her chest. There was something off in the way he made love to her, a predicament that sent shivers down her spine. While his charming facade captivated her, a nagging suspicion whispered that there was more beneath the surface. Despite the unusual feelings stirring within her, she brushed them aside; her ambitions clouded her judgment. She was determined to secure his commitment, to weave herself into the fabric of his life. Yet, as the night deepened, shadows danced around her thoughts, hinting that perhaps the path she was so eager to forge was fraught with hidden complexities, and her heart hesitated, questioning whether she truly knew the man she was so desperately trying to claim.

Seeking solace and understanding, Ayanda began to look for someone to share her predicament with, yearning for connection and support. It was a painful realization that she could no longer rely on her mother's judgment, which had been clouded by ambition. Her mother, had become ensnared in a web of greed, trading her values for the fleeting charms of wealth and influence. Her desires overshadowed any semblance of guidance. In a decisive moment of courage, she chose to marry the judge, despite her misfortune, a step that not only cemented their relationship but also marked the beginning of a transformative chapter in her life. The union was not a romantic endeavor but a brave step towards a future where she could seek relief and strength from someone who held the power to change her destiny.

As Ayanda walked down the aisle, her heart raced not just with excitement and anticipation for the future, but from the disdainful glances cast her way by her soon-to-be husband's older children, remnants of his late wife's legacy. The echoes of whispered judgments and silent accusations hung heavy in the air, making her aware of the complexities lurking beneath the surface of their family dynamic. Did these children harbor suspicions regarding their father's peculiar intimate behaviors, the nuances of which remained shrouded in secrecy? Perhaps their late mother had dropped subtle hints, cautionary tales woven into the fabric of their upbringing. With every step she took, Ayanda felt the weight of their scrutiny, prompting a whirlwind of insecurities and questions about her impending role in a family fraught with hidden histories and unspoken truths.

Despite her fervent desire to embrace her new role as the mistress of the house, she found herself tormented by the unsettling shadows of the judge's concealed existence. The thought of his secret life clung to her, casting doubt on the future she longed to embrace. Each face that stared at her brought an uneasy feeling that settled in her stomach. It was as if their eyes bore into her soul, scrutinizing her every move and thought. She could feel their judgment hanging in the air, thick and oppressive, casting a shadow over her confidence. Determined to forge ahead, she clung to her dreams of happily ever after, yet the specters of uncertainty loomed large, forcing her to question the very foundation of the life she was about to commit to. His hidden life that cast a shadow over her dreams, prompting her to question the choices she had made and the price of her commitment. She ultimately realized that the journey ahead would be fraught with challenges reminding her of the complexities and sacrifices that love often demands. As she navigated her new reality, the remnants of their hidden romance served as both a reminder of their unique journey together and the challenges that lay ahead.

One night, Ayanda found herself reflecting on her past experiences with a new found clarity. It was a night when she decided to confront the feelings that had been bubbling beneath the surface for too long. With a mixture of nervousness and determination, she called her husband, seeking an honest discussion about their intimate moments together. "Do you even know what you do during intimacy?" Her voice steady yet tinged with vulnerability.

Judge Ayoley leaned forward, intrigued by the escalating tension. "Why, do you have a problem with it?" he inquired, his eyes fixed on Ayanda, who seemed desperate to make her point. However, before she could fully articulate her thoughts, her husband interrupted with a mocking tone "or what? you gonna sue me? Good luck with that in this part of the universe," he said, a smirk playing on his lips. He waved his hand dismissively as if to brush aside her concerns. "Nobody will even listen to you, let alone believe you. If you want to ridicule yourself, be my guest." With that, he turned away from the conversation, cocooning himself in an air of indifference and promptly drifting off to sleep, leaving Ayanda feeling frustrated and unheard as she observed the scene unfold with a mix of disappointment and contemplation.

In a moment of revelation, she realized that her husband was fully aware of his actions and desires. Despite her initial confusion, it became clear that he had crafted a reality where each woman he had been with was not just a participant but a conscious choice. They understood the unique dynamics of their relationships and the complexities that came with being married to him. For her, this was a bittersweet realization; while she felt a sense of betrayal, she also recognized that the allure of their life together came with both enchantment and burden. Knowing that he had intentionally chosen this path left her grappling with her own feelings. Caught between high society marriage and the unsettling knowledge of her husband's fantasy, Ayanda wondered if she could embrace this truth or if it would drive them apart. She felt the weight of her decisions pressing heavily on her conscience. She understood the deeper implications of intimacy, and the thought of someone else finding solace to ease themselves within her body felt like a betrayal, an act that reduced her essence to something disposable and meaningless.

This inner turmoil stirred a fierce determination within her, prompting her to reclaim her sense of worth. She knew that embracing wealth and power should not come at the expense of her humanity. Ayanda stood resolute, vowing to preserve the sanctity of her own body and soul, understanding the importance of preserving her own dignity and the sanctity of her being, amidst the encroaching tide of another's desire. With each passing moment, she felt the pressure to conform, to surrender her essence to the fervor that threatened to engulf her. She knew what was at stake and she equally knew that allowing another to ease themselves inside of her during intercourse was inhumane.

As she reflected on her marital situation, she vowed to take decisive action. Considering the many facets of her life - her age, her new social standing, and the current economy, weighed heavily on her mind. Each factor seemed to inter twine, creating a complex web of choices that left her feeling vulnerable yet resolute. As she sat in her cozy living room, sipping on her favorite herbaceous tea, she couldn't shake the persisting doubts that clouded her mind. Was she truly ready to risk the financial stability she was enjoying? The safety net she had carefully woven felt incredibly comforting. The fear of losing what she had found appeared grimly in the background. She pondered the consequences of stepping into the unknown; a potential for both reward and regret. Balancing her self-respect against her current comforts proved to be a delicate dance, one that required clarity and courage. The question loomed over her like a shadow, urging her to confront her fears and desires. She understood that change was inevitable, but the path she would choose remained uncertain. She recognized that to reclaim her happiness, she might have to let go of the familiar, embracing the unknown for the prospect of a brighter future.

Decisions and wonders became the true elements that propelled the Frays and the Simpsons. They devoted themselves to fervent prayer and exchanged updates at the police station. However, Joe, the only son of the state minister, felt a rising urgency to act differently. His bond with Abeba was deep, nearly romantic, and her absence ignited a fierce determination within him. With resources at his disposal, he hired private detectives across every city in the country, investing significant funds into their search. He refused to let bureaucracy hinder his quest; each update he received only fueled his resolve. Joe was determined to pierce through the veil of uncertainty, convinced that somewhere, someone held the key to Abeba's whereabouts.

Despite being the eldest son, Joe found himself at a crossroads between duty and desire. His father harbored grand political ambitions, envisioning a legacy that Joe could never embrace. Instead, his heart beat for the world of technology, a realm where he could innovate and create. The tension between his father's expectations and his own dreams became noticeable. When his father announced a project in a nearby village, Joe felt the weight of obligation. Reluctantly, he agreed to accompany his father, hoping that the journey might provide clarity amidst the chaos of conflicting aspirations. As they set off, Joe couldn't shake the mix of anxiety and excitement - this could be a step toward reconciling his own identity with the burden of his father's legacy.

The village organized a durbar for the commissioning of a senior center. The atmosphere was filled with joy as the once overlooked members of the community began to receive the care and attention they deserved. The elderly residents, who had tirelessly contributed to the vibrancy of the countryside, were finally being recognized and appreciated for their unwavering commitment. A beautiful ceremony unfolded, during which blessings and praises rained down upon the minister and his dedicated team. They were celebrated for their efforts in revitalizing the community and honoring its roots. As the day drew to a close, the local kings offered their heartfelt farewells while the government officials prepared to return to the city, their hearts light with the joy of the occasion. The moment marked not just a celebration of the past, but a hopeful step toward a brighter future for all involved.

The drive back to the city was painstakingly slow due to the deplorable road conditions. About a mile away, a young woman collided with a car carrying the deputy minister, prompting an urgent rush to the nearby hospital for her treatment. The incident unfolded before the crew's camera, capturing every moment. The injured lady was detained for observation after sustaining head injuries.

The next day, Joe was tasked with reviewing the footage to select appropriate clips for a press release regarding the project commissioned. As he sifted through the recordings, a sense of recognition poked at him, urging him to pay closer attention - he thought he recognized the woman who had been struck by the deputy's vehicle; he leaned closer to the screen. The revelation left him both concerned and intrigued, Despite his uncertainty, Joe felt compelled to investigate further and ensure that his eyes were not deceiving him. He grabbed his keys and headed to the hospital, eager to learn more about the lady he had seen. However, upon arrival, he discovered that her name was not Abeba, leaving him perplexed.

The confusion deepened as he realized he could not identify her due to her head and part of her face being obscured by bandages. Nevertheless, Joe refused to give up. He rushed to inform the Frays about his findings, and they quickly hopped into their cars and sped to the hospital. Once there, both the Frays and the Simpsons were cautioned by the medical staff to refrain from doing anything that might jeopardize her recovery, heightening the tension surrounding the mystery of her identity and condition. They were asked to come the next day when she might have recovered and safe to speak.

The following day, Joe, the Frays, and the Simpson families returned to the hospital, filled with anticipation and hope. As the light filtered into the room, they were finally permitted to see the woman who had been in a deep slumber, now slowly awakening and regaining her strength. To their astonishment, the woman was Abeba. The moment her eyes met Betsy's, a spark of recognition ignited within her, and the emotional reunion they had prayed for became a beautiful reality. With tears of joy streaming down her face, Betsy rushed to Abeba's side, her heart swelling with gratitude. In that moment, all the pain of uncertainty and longing was washed away, replaced by an overwhelming sense of relief and love.

The room filled with laughter and joyous tears as mother and daughter embraced, their bond stronger than ever, celebrating the miracle of life that had brought them back together. Their gratitude extended to the hospital staff, and soon, Abeba was transferred to a top facility for continued care.

Discharged and on the mend, she had the unwavering support of her family and Joe by her side, ensuring her recovery journey was filled with love and encouragement. Together, they embraced the new chapter ahead, grateful for every moment together. Fragmented pieces of amnesia clung to her mind refusing to fade as she still could not remember what happened to her despite her desperate attempts to recall the events that had led her to this point. Jabari was over the moon to see her sister found sound and in good health. His episodes of mental breakdown somehow intensified, he kept having heavy migraine as if something was clogging his brain that needed purging.

In one of his episodes, it came to him how he was served his first alcohol drink - a rite of passage that changed everything. The taste danced on his tongue, igniting a sense of excitement, however, as the night wore on, a wave of anxiety crashed over him, and he felt his heart racing uncontrollably. In a whirlwind of confusion and fear, he dashed to his room, frantically emptying his bag in search of his sleep-wear. Amidst the familiar clothes and scattered belongings, he stumbled upon something unexpected - a gun he had never seen before. Confused and oblivious: how did a gun end up in his bag? The weight of the discovery sent chills down his spine, and from then, he felt a blend of fear and curiosity. Questions flooded his mind: Was it his? Did someone plant it there?

As he stared at the cold metal glinting under the light, he knew he had to uncover the truth behind this shocking find, even if it meant delving into secrets he wasn't prepared to face. The quest for answers had just begun, and he could feel the air around him charged with uncertainty. What had he unwittingly gotten himself into? He stumbled outside, gripping the cold metal of the gun tightly in his hands. The world around him swayed as he leaned against the rough bark of a large tree, struggling to steady his thoughts amidst the haze of alcohol. The night air was crisp, but his mind was clouded; he squinted at the weapon, its surface gleaming under the pale moonlight. Each part seemed to take on a life of its own as he twisted it in his grasp, pondering its purpose. Questions filled his foggy brain, but clarity eluded him like a shadow in the dark. The adrenaline of the moment mixed dangerously with his intoxication, creating an unsettling emotions. Here, in his fragile state, he found both fascination and fear, caught in the dangerous balance of his choices.

Abeba spotted Jabari from a distance, she could hardly contain her excitement. Her heart raced as she began to rush towards him, each step filled with anticipation, igniting a spark of joy that propelled her forward. The world around her faded as she focused solely on him. Her quickened pace mirrored her eagerness to connect, to share stories and laughter once again. In that moment, nothing else mattered; it was just her and Jabari, ready to create new memories together. However, in Jabari's intoxicated haze, he misinterpreted her approach. When he noticed movement coming toward him, his instinct kicked in - clouded by alcohol and a sense of danger.

Soon after, he pulled the trigger, despite the stillness of the night, there was no sound from the shot fired. Abeba's enthusiastic intention turned into a heart-stopping moment of fear, as she realized the split-second misunderstanding that had escalated into chaos. The air thick with tension, both their fates coiled tightly together in an unforeseen twist of events. Jabari still did not comprehend the gravity of what he had just done. The chaos around him blurred his thoughts, but he couldn't shake the image of Abeba, her face pale and purple-stricken, as she staggered toward the street. Each labored breath she took seemed to echo in his mind, a haunting reminder of the accident that had unfolded in an instant.

Time seemed to slow as he watched her move, his heart racing with fear and guilt. He wanted to reach out, to help, but felt paralyzed by the weight of his actions. The world around him faded into a distant hum, but the urgent reality of the moment pierced through the fog. In that critical juncture, Jabari realized that some choices had irrevocable consequences, and he was left grappling with the overwhelming sorrow of what had transpired; one moment forever changing the course of their lives. He staggered back inside the house, his mind clouded and weary.

As he shuffled toward his bedroom, the weight of the night pressed heavily on his shoulders, yet he remained blissfully unaware of the terrible act he had just committed. The moonlight spilled through the window, illuminating the trail of chaos he left behind, but he couldn't grasp the magnitude of his actions. In his stupor, he collapsed onto the bed, the soft sheets cradling him into a false sense of security. Sleep enveloped him quickly, shielding him from the darkness that loomed just outside his dreams. Though, he rested peacefully, oblivious to the storm brewing just beneath the surface. Little did he know, the reality of what he had done would awaken him later, shattering his calm and plunging him into a whirlwind of guilt and horror.

CHAPTER THIRTEEN

"Never Despise the Old Hoe, Before You
Have Tried out the New One"

Njeri faced a significant dilemma as she prepared for the arrival of her child. Although she had previously been delivered by a home midwife, she felt uneasy about repeating the experience for her own baby. To ensure the best care, she decided to adopt a more integrated approach. Njeri opted to combine home therapy with visits to a traditional midwife, believing that the wisdom of traditional practices could complement her needs. Additionally, she arranged for regular check-ups at a modern hospital nearby, valuing the advancements in medical care and technology. This holistic strategy allowed her to blend the comforts of home with the expertise and safety that a hospital provided, reassuring her as she embarked on this new chapter of motherhood. By preparing in this way, she hoped to create a nurturing environment for her child while also addressing her own anxieties.

To her pleasant surprise, the information she received from the traditional midwife aligned perfectly with what the hospital had conveyed about her pregnancy. This uncanny consistency between the two sources of advice filled her with assurance and hope. It reinforced her belief in the wisdom of traditional practices, prompting her to seek the midwife's guidance more often. She appreciated the personal touch and the nurturing environment the midwife provided, which conformed with the more clinical approach of the hospital. This newfound trust not only deepened her connection to her pregnancy but also made her feel more empowered as she navigated this significant chapter of her life. Embracing both modern and traditional wisdom, she found a harmonious balance that gave her confidence in her journey toward motherhood.

The traditional midwife reassured her, emphasizing the numerous benefits of the old-fashioned way of birthing. She explained that this method not only prioritized the safety of both mother and child but also created a more conducive and natural environment for delivery. By allowing for greater intimacy and connection during the birthing process, the traditional approach mitigated potential complications associated with modern medical interventions. The midwife illustrated how this timeless practice nurtured the bond between mother and unborn, providing a familiar and comforting atmosphere that could ease anxiety and stress. She felt a renewed sense of confidence as she listened to the midwife, recognizing that the wisdom of past generations could still offer valuable insights into a safe and fulfilling birthing experience. From then on, she began to embrace the idea of a natural birth, trusting in the age-old knowledge that had supported countless mothers before her.

Njeri's first experience of motherhood was nothing short of miraculous. She had planned to deliver at the hospital, but nature had other ideas, delivering a surprising twist to her expectations. One quiet night, as she immersed herself in the pages of her favorite book, an unexpected urge washed over her. "Could this be? oh dear," she said, her heart racing with anticipation. The reality of impending birth encircled her, blending excitement with a touch of anxiety. Soon after, Njeri realized that life often follows its own script, and she was about to embark on the most profound journey of her life. The comfort of her book was soon replaced by the thrilling unknown of motherhood, a chapter she had long awaited and was now ready to embrace. Realizing the reality of impending birth, a whirlwind of emotions surged within her. She quickly called her mother, hoping for some reassurance, but before she could articulate her fears, she felt the unmistakable signs that the baby was already halfway into the world.

"No way, no how!" she screamed in disbelief, her voice echoing through the room. The urgency of the moment prompted her mother to signal their neighbor, who dashed off to fetch the traditional midwife. In those frantic minutes, Njeri found herself caught between panic and anticipation, her heart racing at the thought of welcoming a new life while grappling with the suddenness of it all. As the minutes ticked away, she prepared herself for the extraordinary journey that lay ahead. The midwife shouted with joy, "It's a boy!" Njeri felt an overwhelming rush of emotions, she had anticipated a long and painful process, having heard countless tales of childbirth that painted a daunting picture.

Yet, her experience was utterly different: no complicated procedures - just a handful of herbs gently rubbed on her tummy, and suddenly, the delivery was complete. While she cradled her bouncy baby boy in her arms, tears of joy streamed down her cheeks. The moment, so filled with love and wonder, was everything she had hoped for. She gazed at her precious bundle of joy, realizing that all the fears she had held were washed away in the bliss of welcoming her child into the world.

Living in the countryside and close to family and friends came with its own perks. Njeri was never stranded with child care. In fact she had lots of rest from new mom burdens which city mothers go through. Family and neighbors took turns caring for her new born. Maa-me, although old, was the main caretaker of her grandchild coupled with the community support.

A year after the arrival of the new addition into Njeri's life, she thought it was time to put all her plans she had been working on into action. Whilst on it, she remembered one of her mother's sayings "you will be surprised what opportunities lie in the countryside waiting to be explored and captured." Her heart soared with determination as she exclaimed a resounding "yes!" Her face illuminated with a warmth that filled the room, reflecting her unwavering optimism. "Now is the time," she said, resolving to uncover the truth in her mother's words. Despite the dwindling funds that weighed on her mind, she felt a fierce urgency; failure was not an option. The thought of returning to the harsh and unforgiving city haunted her, compelling her to press on. "This is a do or die affair for me, come what may," she vowed, a fire igniting within her spirit. She knew that the path ahead would be fraught with challenges, but the promise of discovering her own destiny fueled her resolve. With each heartbeat, she steeled her determination, ready to embrace whatever lay ahead.

Njeri had meticulously planned her

agricultural venture, and now it was time to put her strategies into action. She first employed local labor to dig a borehole, ensuring her crops would thrive during the dry season. She reminded the workers that harnessing the abundant water from the rainy season was crucial for sustainability. This lesson, passed down from her parents, resonated deeply with her. Within few years, she managed to cultivate thirty acres of palm nut trees, sweet potatoes, and other profitable crops. Living in the countryside, she recognized the multitude of blessings that nature offered to those who are willing to engage with it thoughtfully.

As luck would have it, Njeri's son was fortunate to attend school in their local community, allowing him to benefit from education without the challenges she once faced. In her time, she had to brave the treacherous waters in a canoe for hours just to reach the nearest school. The journey was not only physically demanding but also filled with risks. Now, seeing her son walk to school brought her immense joy and relief. She reflected on her own sacrifices and the hurdles she overcame, grateful that her child has the opportunity to learn and grow in a safer and more accessible environment. For Njeri, the change signified hope and progress, marking a new chapter in their community. This progress marked not just a personal achievement but a generational shift towards a brighter future.

Whilst in the city, her community underwent a transformative shift in basic education that profoundly impacted the lives of the children. Young students paddling canoes for miles to attend school, risking their safety and missing valuable learning opportunities, became a thing of the past. Now, with the establishment of primary, vocational, and technical schools right within their neighborhood, education became a readily accessible resource for all. This transformation was made possible by a kind-hearted individual, a native of the town and the leader of the community youth. His dedication and efforts opened doors for the younger generation, allowing them to pursue their education without the obstacles that once hindered them. Thanks to his vision and commitment, children could now focus on their studies and aspire to a brighter future without the hardships that previously defined their educational journey.

Njeri's plantations thrived, captivating the entire community with her unexpected success. The villagers watched in awe as this well-educated woman made the bold decision to abandon the bustling, glamorous city life for the tranquil simplicity of rural living. Her choice to embrace farming not only transformed her own life but also inspired others to rethink their own aspirations. As her crops began to thrive, Njeri's financial situation improved significantly, allowing her to sell produce and achieve a level of prosperity she had never experienced before.

With her newfound success, she could now afford anything she desired, including luxuries that once seemed unattainable during her urban life. Her accomplishments filled her mother with immense pride, showcasing the rewarding journey of a woman who dared to follow her passion and make a difference in her community through agriculture.

Njeri transformed her life and the lives of those around her by building a magnificent mansion on the hill for herself and her son. With a generous spirit, she also supported her relative and ensured her mother lived comfortably. Recognizing the importance of family heritage, she redesigned the family house built by her father, bringing it up to modern standards while maintaining its sentimental value. Her employees thrived under her leadership, as she prioritized their well-being by offering competitive wages. Additionally, her contributions to her community were significant; she invested in local projects and initiatives that fostered development and growth. Her dedication not only elevated her own lifestyle but also uplifted her community, making her a beloved figure among neighbors and family alike.

After a long and exhausting day tending to the fields, Njeri found herself on the side of the road, stranded due to her broken-down car. Just as she began to feel disheartened, Ato Kwame, a familiar figure from Tsetsebo, whizzed by in his vehicle. He had just returned from the city, where he had been chasing a business deal for six months, and had never crossed paths with Njeri. However, as he glanced into his rear-view mirror, he noticed her car had come to a halt. Recognizing the need for assistance, he quickly made a U-turn, his heart racing with a mix of eagerness and concern. Kwame sat in Njeri's car, his fingers nervously tapping against the steering wheel as he fidgeted with the ignition. After a few tense moments, the engine sputtered back to life, filling the air with a reassuring hum.

Although the car desperately needed serious attention, Kwame felt a rush of relief. He glanced at Njeri, assuring her that she could manage an hour's drive despite the vehicle's questionable state. Njeri smiled as she thanked Kwame for his help, feeling a sense of relief from the support he had offered. "Oh, I'm only about ten minutes' drive from home," she mentioned, her voice light with gratitude. "My name is Kwame, and it was a pleasure to assist you. Good luck with everything, and drive safely." Njeri appreciated his kind words, hopeful for a smooth journey ahead. "You as well," wishing him well in return. With that, they exchanged friendly smiles and parted ways, each carrying a bit of warmth from their brief encounter.

Njeri took a bold step by introducing the "Bounty Festival," into the community; an event that attracted numerous farmers from the surrounding villages. The festival served as a platform for farmers to showcase their produce, share best practices, and learn about preservation techniques that could enhance the longevity of their crops. By facilitating connections among growers and encouraging collaboration, she not only helped increase their profits but also fostered a sense of community among the farmers.

The Bounty Festival quickly became a much-anticipated event, bringing together not just agricultural expertise but also a celebration of local culture and resilience. Originally, many farmers were unable to secure fair prices from buyers, leading to significant losses as their fresh bananas spoiled quickly. To address this issue, Njeri introduced the idea of processing bananas into various products which would extend their longevity and contribute to sustainable income for the farmers. This innovative approach not only aimed to improve the farmers' earnings but also provided consumers with diverse banana-based products, creating a valuable exchange within the community.

The Bounty Festival became a platform for education, collaboration, and a brighter economic future for the farmers involved. This innovative idea sparked excitement, and soon, people began transforming bananas into an array of products, including banana flour for baking, delicious banana pudding, crispy banana chips, and so much more. The festival not only celebrated the harvest but also opened new avenues for economic sustainability in the community.

The Bounty Festival, brilliantly organized by Njeri, became a vibrant platform for local talents to shine. Residents poured their hearts into showcasing their unique skills, from traditional dance performances that captivated attendees to home-made crafts that highlighted their creativity. The festival not only celebrated their talents but also fostered a sense of community, drawing families and friends together to enjoy the festive atmosphere. Food stalls offered a delightful array of local cuisine, adding to the rich cultural tapestry of the event. As music and laughter filled the air, it became clear that Njeri's vision had transformed the festival into more than just an event; it was a heartfelt celebration of the community's spirit and creative prowess, leaving everyone looking forward to each year's celebration.

At that year's festival, the air was filled with laughter and vibrant colors, but for Njeri, everything else faded into the background the moment she laid eyes on Kwame. Memories of her desperate hour rushed back, reminding her of his unwavering support when she felt utterly stranded. As Kwame approached, Njeri's heart raced, and a smile danced across her lips. She felt a powerful gratitude for the providence that had brought them together again. The occasion once just an array of festivities, now transformed into a celebration of not only the culture but also the unexpected bonds of support and friendship that can arise even in life's most challenging moments.

Njeri eagerly called her family over, proudly introducing Kwame with a twinkle of gratitude in her voice. "Oh, that was you!?" Maa-me exclaimed, a warm smile spreading across her face. "My daughter spoke highly of you when she got home that evening." Kwame chuckled, responding teasingly, "I hope they were good things!" Maa-me placed a reassuring hand on his shoulder, declaring, "My son, what you did was honorable and commendable, and you deserve all the accolades." Kwame, feeling a swell of appreciation, replied humbly, "thank you, Maa-me, your words are far too kind." Before long, the air was filled with warmth and admiration as the bond of gratitude and respect between them deepened amidst the festive atmosphere. Njeri felt a sense of achievement as she listened to her folks praise the festivities. "Nice one by the way, well organized and planned," one of them commented. "Thanks, I think," Njeri replied with a hint of pride.

She excused herself to attend to other guests, but her thoughts lingered on their exchange. After mingling for a while, she spotted Kwame across the room and decided to return to his side. Their previous conversation had sparked something intriguing, and she felt drawn to him. With a warm smile, she handed him another glass of drink, ready to dive back into their engaging conversation. The atmosphere buzzed with laughter and chatter, but for Njeri and Kwame, it was as if they were the only two people in the world. Kwame turned to Njeri with a curious smile, eager to learn more about her life in the countryside. "Tell me, what is a beautiful charming lady ,and I heard you are very intelligent as well, doing in the countryside, engaging in farming?" he asked in a playful tone. Njeri, always quick with her wit, replied, "The word is agriculture." Their laughter filled the air, lightening the mood as Kwame playfully mocked, "ok, agriculture," still chuckling at his own misunderstanding. Suddenly, their cordiality shone through, highlighting the joy of friendship amidst the serene rural backdrop. It was a simple exchange, yet it reflected the beauty of connection and the shared humor that enriched their conversations, making the countryside feel all the more welcoming and vibrant.

Njeri turned to Kwame, her expression thoughtful. "Well, I think it's about time we all looked back and assessed what works for us as a people and what does not. I believe it's essential for us to reflect on our past choices and their impacts on our community," she explained thoughtfully. "We have to understand our challenges and recognize what has been effective in bringing us together." Kwame listened intently, intrigued by her perspective. "So, you're suggesting we evaluate both our successes and our failures?" Njeri nodded, her eyes brightening with conviction. "Exactly, by learning from our experiences, we can forge a path forward that truly resonates with our values and aspirations." The conversation deepened as they began to explore the possibilities of change and growth, realizing the importance of collective contemplation in shaping their future.

"The essence of our community lies in our responsibility to one another, a duty we have unfortunately overlooked. This land nurtures us, allowing us to thrive and blossom into individuals of promise. However, when the time comes to reciprocate, we often abandon our roots in favor of city life, leaving behind the elders who once tended the fields. These older generations, now unable to cultivate the land, become forgotten while we turn to them in our moments of need. When crops fail and food become scarce, we raise our voices in discontent, forgetting that we are the ones who have strayed from our fundamental obligations. It is crucial to recognize that our survival depends on the bonds we forge and the responsibilities we uphold toward each other and our environment. Only by honoring these connections can we hope to thrive together."

Njeri's passionate outcry highlighted a critical oversight in their community: the urban drift that has disconnected them from agriculture and food production. "As we chase the allure of city life, we forget that cities do not cultivate crops, leaving the responsibility of farming to an aging population who can no longer sustain it. When the time comes for us to take over, we abandon rural life in pursuit of industrialization and urbanization, neglecting our fundamental need for food. This shift has left us unprepared, eroding the knowledge and practices of older generations without developing or refining the raw materials they once mastered. As we commemorate the conveniences of modernity, it is essential to reflect on the roots of our sustenance and recognize the pitfall of overlooking the agricultural foundations that nourish our very existence." Kwame couldn't help but admire Njeri's dedication to the community and the country. "Wow!," he exclaimed, "for the first time in a long while, I'm witnessing someone who truly cares for her people, just like my father did." Kwame felt a deep respect for her passion and wished his father were present to appreciate Njeri's spirit. "You would have won him over immediately," he added, beaming with pride.

Curiosity sparked in him as he probed further, "So, does that mean you've never liked city life? Are you really never going back?" Kwame's questions reflected his own struggle with the pull between urban excitement and the tranquility of deep-rooted connections. In Njeri, he saw a vision of purpose that stirred something within him, urging him to reflect on his own life's choices.

Njeri looked at Kwame with a hint of defiance in her eyes, responding to his question, "Who said I didn't?" With a voice of both sentiment and strength, she began to recount her life experiences in the bustling city. Each story she shared reflected the trials and triumphs that had shaped her into the person she had become. Although the tales were familiar to many in their community, each retelling carried new layers of meaning, resonating with shared struggles and dreams. As Njeri spoke, Kwame listened intently, understanding that the snippet of her past were not just a history of hardships, but also a testament to resilience and hope that connected all who lived in their vibrant neighborhood.

"Enough about me, what about you? What draws you to this tranquil setting?" Kwame smiled, a glimmer of mystery in his eyes, and replied, "Trust me, my story is better told another day. For now, would you do me the honor and dance with me?" With a nod, Njeri accepted, and together they swept onto the dance floor. The lively music consumed them, and the world around faded away as they lost themselves in the rhythm. Njeri's family watched from the sidelines, their gazes filled with a mix of surprise and joy, as the pair danced with unrestrained passion, the evening festivities transforming into a magical moment where time stood still.

Kwame's heart brimmed with emotion as he whispered, "I wish this night will stand still for me." Njeri's laughter filled the air, her teasing spirit igniting a spark between them. "Why, are you on a battlefield like Joshua?" she quipped, lightening the mood. "No, not like Joshua, but I want to savor this enchanting moment with you," he replied earnestly. They both understood that every beautiful encounter must eventually fade. Yet, Kwame couldn't help but ask, "Do you promise we'll continue this someday?" Njeri's playful banter turned serious as she teased, "Are you asking me out?" With a hopeful smile, he asked, "Would you honor me with a date? I still have stories to share." "Sure, I would love to," she answered, and as they wished each other goodnight, the promise of tomorrow lingered in the air, full of possibilities and unspoken words.

CHAPTER FOURTEEN

"When the Eye Is Filled with Tears, the
Nose Also Gets Moist"
(My Sorrow Also Affects My Brother)

◆ ◆ ◆

Abeba was thriving, her health blossoming as each day passed. After a long, arduous journey, she found her memory returning, piece by piece, like a puzzle coming together. Vivid images began surfacing from the depths of her mind, illuminating the dark corners of the night where fear and confusion had once resided. The weight of her ordeal started to lift as she recalled the moments that had shaped her experience, bringing both relief and a sense of closure. Abeba embraced her newfound clarity, ready to move forward and build a brighter future, one filled with hope and the promise of healing.

She recalled, after parting ways with Joe, she stepped outside, seeking solace in the cool evening air. The music boomed from the Simpson's mansion, its relentless beat echoing in her ears and drowning out her thoughts. She took a deep breath, the crispness of the night air filling her lungs. She closed her eyes for a moment, letting the chaos fade away. The vibrant energy of the party was substantial, yet she longed for a moment of peace amidst the celebration. The chatter and laughter from inside continued to swirl, but out in the open, under the starlit sky, she found a brief reprieve. Abeba leaned against the tree, allowing the gentle breeze to calm her racing mind, hoping to gather her thoughts before rejoining the lively crowd. In that perfect stillness, she felt a sense of clarity, a reminder of the importance of balance between noise and quiet in her life.

While Abeba stepped into the vibrant

outdoors to seek freshness outside, Njeri and Ayanda discovered a charming group of new friends who instantly captivated them with engaging stories and laughter. As the music played in the background, the two friends found themselves in deep conversations, exchanging ideas, and sharing personal shaggy-dog stories. Njeri, with her infectious enthusiasm, animatedly recounted a recent adventure, while Ayanda chimed in with witty remarks that kept everyone laughing. The atmosphere buzzed with excitement as more guests joined the circle, creating a sense of togetherness that complemented the evening's festivities. Njeri and Ayanda left the party feeling grateful for the connections they had forged, looking forward to new adventures together with their newfound companions.

Abeba's heart raced as she recalled the shot that had narrowly missed her, a chilling reminder of her close brush with death. In a moment of panic, she stumbled and fell into the drainage right in front of the Simpson's house, her head striking the ground with a hard thump. Dazed but determined, she quickly pushed herself up, desperately seeking help. However, in her confusion, she turned the wrong way, heading toward the road. Just as she regained her bearings, she froze at the sight of an oncoming car dashing toward her. Time seemed to slow as she realized the danger she had put herself in, the world around her spinning with the echoes of her near-miss and the urgency of the situation escalating. As the headlights of the oncoming vehicle illuminated the dark road, Abeba's injuries became painfully visible.

The impact had left her disoriented and bleeding, and the sight of her injury struck a chord of fear in the driver. Overcome by panic, he quickly exited his car, his hands trembling as he approached her. Without hesitation, he carefully lifted Abeba and placed her in the passenger seat. The urgency of the situation ignited a surge of adrenaline, and he sped towards the hospital, driving through the night with a fervent hope that every second counted. As the city lights blurred past, his thoughts raced alongside, praying for her recovery and reflecting on the fragility of life in that harrowing moment. As he sped towards the hospital, the night blurred around him, each passing moment heavy with urgency. Memories flooded his mind, stark and painful; he remembered his neighbor, a man of courage, who had tried to intervene when tragedy struck - a child torn away by a hit-and-run driver. The world had not understood his intentions, and justice had been twisted, leading the neighbor to prison for his acts of kindness.

Now, as the driver maneuvered through the streets, his heart raced not just for the life he raced to save, but also for the haunting reminder of how swiftly good intentions could be misconstrued. Fueled by fear, he grasped the steering wheel tightly, determined that this time, fate would not snatch away another chance. Instead of speeding towards the hospital, he made a sudden decision and veered off the main road, heading into the dense bush. The smell of earth and foliage filled the air as anxiety coursed through his veins. He knew this was a risky move, but desperation clouded his judgment. Abeba's life hung in the balance, and he had to believe that somehow, the wild unknown held answers. With each twist and turn, he prayed for a miracle, willing the universe to align in her favor. Time seemed to stretch endlessly as he navigated through the undergrowth, hoping against hope that his unconventional detour would yield the salvation she so desperately needed. As the chilling wind run through the trees, he pulled Abeba from the backseat of his car, her body limp and motionless. The night was dark and silent, yet without constrained he placed her on the cold, damp ground.

Abandoned in the shadows, she lay alone among the underbrush, vulnerable to the frigid air that surrounded her. The stark reality of her situation began to sink in as the cold grasp of the night crept closer. Unbeknownst to her, time was slipping away, and with each passing moment, the danger grew. In the stillness of the bush, a sense of foreboding loomed the world around her unaware of the turmoil that had led to this heart-stopping moment. When dawn approached, an elderly woman found her unresponsive as she was later told. The woman brought her into her small house and nursed her back to life. She was not able to recall who she was and what her name was. The hit on the ground was pretty severe. The woman had helped her in more than one way. She fed and clothed her. She gave her a new name - Lilly for she was found among lilies she said.

This remarkable woman known for her healing abilities dedicated her life to helping those in need. With a steady stream of patients, she offered not just remedies but also a warm home, inviting many to stay until they regained their health. Among them was Abeba, a young woman whose prolonged presence had become a topic of conversation among the neighbors. While Abeba was seen as merely one of the healer's numerous patients, her bond with the healer grew deeper over time. The healer's home became a sanctuary, where each recovery was celebrated, transforming lives and fostering a sense of community. Abeba found not only healing but also a sense of belonging, forever grateful to the woman who had opened her heart and home to her in time of need.

The Frays and the Simpson scheduled a visit back to the old woman who had helped nursed Abeba back to life. They wanted to pay her a visit of gratitude and to provide her with gifts. The visit was well thought through. Joe had become an integral part of the family, shadowing Abeba wherever she went. His presence was reassuring, especially during the gratitude trip, which carried a weight of emotion for everyone involved. Knowing the location of the accident where Abeba was discovered, he felt a sense of responsibility to be there. As they approached the town in their fleet of flashy, elaborate cars, a sense of unease settled over Dr Fray and Betsy. They exchanged glances, a flicker of recognition passing between them - was this town familiar? Despite the unsettling feeling, they maintained their composure.

As they arrived in the town, Abeba guided them down a path that felt strikingly familiar to the Frays. Eventually, she stopped in front of a house that had been her refuge. With anticipation, she knocked on the door, and a warm voice called them inside. "Mama!" Abeba exclaimed, her face lighting up as she embraced the woman who had welcomed her with open arms. Dr Fray and Betsy exchanged bewildered glances, realizing they stood in the same house they had visited nearly a year prior in search of Abeba. It was the seer who had confirmed her survival, yet her exact location had remained a mystery. Overwhelmed with emotions, Dr Fray began to lose his composure, but Betsy intervened gently, reminding him of their purpose: to express their gratitude.

The Seer received them warmly and explained to Dr Fray that things of the spirit, no human has control over; messages are 'as is basis.' Dr Fray was astounded that, despite his extensive education and knowledge, he fell victim to an illiterate con artist who claimed to communicate with spirits while his beloved daughter suffered in her care. This experience opened his eyes to the hypocrisy around him. He began to see the church in a similar light, questioning its practices as they charged for prayer warriors, fasting keepers, and mediators, all while promising to bind demons and grant salvation. It struck him that in this world, anyone could be manipulated and swayed by the promise of hope or the fear of despair. The realization left him disillusioned, grappling with the fragility of trust and the vulnerability that comes with love. Ultimately, he understood that no one, not even the well-educated, was immune to deception. Only time will tell. They presented the seer with the accompanying gift and they parted ways.

Abeba's determination to piece her life back together was inspiring, and with each breakthrough, she grew stronger and more resilient. Through therapy and patience, she learned not only about her past but also about the beauty of living in the present, reminding herself that while memories may fade, the essence of who she was remained intact. After weeks of grappling with the revelation of the shooting, Abeba and Jabari gathered with their family to confront the harrowing events that had unfolded. The atmosphere was thick with tension as they exchanged heavy glances, each one burdened with their own emotions. Abeba and Jabari, sat down with the rest of the family to discuss the harrowing events. Through tearful conversations and shared memories, they slowly began to piece together what had transpired that fateful night. As they recounted each moment, it became clear that the chaos that erupted was not born from malice but rather a tragic accident - a series of unfortunate circumstances that spiraled out of control. This realization brought a flicker of comfort amidst the pain, as they understood that dwelling on blame would only deepen their wounds. The family united in their grief, found strength in one another and embraced the hope that, although scars would remain, healing was possible only by accepting the truth of that night.

In the midst of their profound grief, the family found solace in one another, weaving together a tapestry of shared memories and unspoken understanding. Despite the weight of their individual struggles, they found strength in one another, embracing the hope that healing could emerge from their pain. In a quiet ceremony, they laid their past to rest, burying it deep, vowing that it would never again be unearthed. Through this collective act of remembrance and release, they discovered the powerful bond of love that overstepped sorrow, allowing them to look toward the future with cautious optimism, united in their journey toward healing.

A year after Abeba's emergence from the fog of amnesia, she found herself ready to reclaim her life. With each day, she pieced together fragments of who she was, rediscovering her passions and reestablishing connections with friends and family. Her unwavering determination to pursue a career in medicine fueled her journey as she celebrated her acceptance into one of the prestigious universities in the United States. With dreams of becoming a doctor, she embraced the challenges that awaited her, knowing that each step on this path would bring her closer to her goal. As she prepared for her study abroad adventure, excitement coursed through her veins. She prudently packed her bags, eager to explore new cultures and embrace the challenges that lay ahead.

This journey symbolized not just a physical departure, but a profound leap into the future, a chance to further define herself beyond the shadows of her past. Armed with her newfound confidence, Abeba stepped into this next chapter with an open heart and boundless curiosity, ready to learn not just about the world, but about herself. With Joe and her family by her side, she embarked on an exciting new chapter in her life. Abeba's journey toward becoming a medical doctor was marked by determination and resilience. From a young age, she was captivated by the intricacies of the human body and the profound impact that healthcare professionals have on people's lives. Her unwavering commitment to her studies and relentless pursuit of knowledge propelled her through rigorous years of education.

Her family, thrilled and proud, celebrated her success with heartfelt hugs and joyful tears, knowing the challenges that lay ahead. She felt empowered to embrace the rigorous journey of medical education, ready to face the demands and responsibilities that would ultimately prepare her for a bright future in healthcare. The bustling campus, filled with ambitious students from around the world, became a new home for her aspirations. Abeba immersed herself in her studies, inspired by the rich resources and supportive faculty that surrounded her. Every lecture, every late-night study session, brought her one step closer to wearing that white coat and making a difference in the lives of her patients. She was not just pursuing a degree; she was chasing her dream with passion and purpose, determined to leave her mark on the world of medicine.

In the meantime, Jabari embarked on a transformative journey through a series of therapy sessions focused on deliverance, aiming to confront and expel the haunting mental demons that tormented him. The tragic night when he accidentally shot his sister while under the influence of alcohol became a dark shadow in his mind, leading him to suppress the memory entirely. This repression triggered terrifying hallucination episodes, making it impossible for him to escape the guilt and trauma.

As he delved deeper into his sessions, he began to unravel the layers of pain, slowly piecing together his fragmented memories and acknowledging the truth of that fateful night. Each session felt like a battle, as he confronted his fears and insecurities, seeking to reclaim the peace that had eluded him for so long. With each step, he sought not only forgiveness from himself but also a chance to reclaim his life from the clutches of despair.

The process was intensive, requiring both courage and vulnerability, but with each step forward, he began to feel a sense of liberation. Through resilience and the support of his therapists, he began to see a glimmer of hope amid his turbulent past. He gradually uncovered the roots of his anxieties, learning to confront and dismantle the beliefs that had held him captive. Through this transformative experience, he discovered that healing was not just about a single moment of release, but rather an ongoing journey of self-discovery and growth. With newfound strength, Jabari emerged more resilient, ready to face the world with a clearer mind and an open heart. Malik continued to excel in his clothing business and all was well among the Frays and the Simpsons.

Whilst the Frays and the Simpsons distanced themselves from the seer, Njeri found herself forging new connections. As the early morning sun rose, Kwame strolled through the familiar streets, savoring the tranquility of the morning. His eyes brightened when he spotted Njeri, tenderly kneeling down to embrace a young child. They stood outside the creche, a place filled with laughter and the promise of new beginnings. Njeri's gentle smile radiated warmth as she reminded him to be brave and have fun, her nurturing touch evident in every gesture.

A surge of emotions rushed through Kwame and his heart jolted at the sight. Memories of their shared moments flooded back, leaving him with an aching sense of loss. Kwame stood in disbelief as the thought sank in - Njeri was married with a child. Memories of their encounters flooded his mind, and he suddenly realized he had never noticed a ring on her finger. Was it possible that not all women felt the need to show off their marital status? But why had he never seen any man accompanying her? Maybe her husband was simply out of the country. These questions spiraled in his mind, igniting an internal conflict. The uncertainty gnawed at him, making him feel as if he was losing a part of himself. He was overwhelmed by the fear of never truly knowing Njeri, the woman who had captured his thoughts in ways he could no longer ignore. Each revelation felt like a jolt, leaving him trembling in a mixture of confusion and longing.

Kwame was restless all through the day, anxiously waiting to see Njeri and put an end to his growing impatience. With zealousness, he drove directly to her plantation, hoping for a chance to talk. Upon arriving, he parked his car and inquired about Njeri's office. The workers were helpful but delivered disappointing news; Njeri had left to pick up her son from school and had closed for the day. Frustration swelled within him as he contemplated the missed opportunity, wondering when he would finally get to share his feelings. The long drive home loomed over him; Kwame's worries grew as he made his way back home, the weight of his thoughts pressing heavily on his mind.

In an unexpected turn of events, he encountered Njeri's mother. He stepped out of his vehicle and greeted her warmly, trying to shake off the unease that had been haunting him. Without hesitation, Kwame offered to drive her home, an offer she graciously accepted. The atmosphere lightened somewhat as they traveled, and upon arriving, Njeri was delighted to see him. Her bright smile brought a momentary relief to his anxious heart.

As Kwame was sharing the events of his day, Njeri's son suddenly dashed over and threw his arms around him, exclaiming, "Daddy, daddy!" Despite the commotion, the adults in the room decided to act as if they hadn't heard the enthusiastic outburst. With a warm smile, Kwame lifted the little boy into his arms, his heart swelling with joy. Remembering he had a toy and some sweets stashed away in his car, he swiftly took the child on an exciting trip to the vehicle. Junior was filled with joy as he clutched his new toy, feeling a sense of happiness that made him want to share it with the world. With a heartfelt thank you to Kwame and Njeri, he dashed back inside, excited to play. He made a promise to be good and not bother anyone again.

Kwame and Njeri remained outside, engaged in a delightful conversation, reminiscing about their adventures together. As the sun began to set, Kwame bid farewell to Maa-me with a friendly wave and a warm smile, cherishing her kindness that had added sweetness to his day. He made his way home, carrying with him the warmth of friendship and the joy that comes from small, meaningful moments shared. As darkness fell, Njeri and Junior drove home. By the time they arrived at their house, Junior had succumbed to a deep sleep, his little body worn out from a day filled with excitement and exploration. She smiled at the sight of him tiptoeing around the house, completing each routine task with care. Njeri equally nestled into her bed, the soothing rhythm of her routine lulled her into a state of relaxation, allowing the peaceful night to carry her into sweet dreams. Just moments after she snuggled under the covers, her phone buzzed with an incoming call - it was Kwame, checking in to ensure they had made it home safely. Their conversation flowed easily, filled with laughter and the warmth of their bond, providing a delightful end to Njeri's day. The night stretched on as they exchanged stories and dreams, the world outside fading away, leaving just the two of them wrapped in their shared moments of joy and connection.

As their conversation unfolded, Njeri decided to crack the lid on the jar a little bit. She opened up a little by sharing that she was a single mother. Kwame let out a sigh of relief, exclaiming, "Thank God!" He quickly realized how his earlier comments might have sounded and hurried to apologize, "oh my goodness, that was insensitive of me." Njeri couldn't help but laugh at his reaction; she understood his concerns all too well. It was clear that he had hoped she was unattached. He continued, "Once again, I'm sorry for how I said it, but on the bright side, it's a great opportunity for me to get to know you better." Njeri replied playfully, "We'll see about that."

With their new found understanding, they dove back into their earlier discussions, the clock ticking away unnoticed until midnight.

Next day, Njeri divulged in Maa-me about Kwame's date invitation. "I can see a spark all over your face and in your eyes: he looks responsible enough, handsome, charming, hardworking and most importantly, a native of our town. It wouldn't hurt to get to know him better. Just be cautious." Maa-me cautioned. "I know Maa-me and I will." Junior had a sitter who came around from time to time when Maa-me got engaged with community activities. The doorbell rang, Junior's sitter, hurried to answer it. Junior filled with excitement and curiosity, dashed downstairs clutching his homework in his small hands. He knew it was Kwame coming to visit. Proudly, he showcased his painting, a colorful depiction of himself with his mom. "This is amazing!" Kwame exclaimed, running his fingers through his hair and giving him a celebratory high five. The atmosphere was vibrant and filled with excitement as Kwame turned to Junior saying, "listen, big guy, Mom and I are heading out for some fun, is that okay with you?" Just then, Njeri gracefully descended the staircase, her radiant presence instantly captivating Kwame. He found himself completely mesmerized by her beauty, showering her with compliments and stealing glances. Every moment together felt special, as they enjoyed each other's company, creating memories that would last long after the night ended. It was a perfect evening, filled with genuine smiles and the thrill of blossoming affection.

As the clock struck ten-forty, Kwame gently escorted Njeri to her door. With a soft kiss on her forehead, he whispered a tender goodnight, leaving a warm glow in his heart. It was a night filled with warmth, connection, and the promising spark of something more, leaving both of them with smiles as they parted ways. Later, at eleven, he picked up the phone, eager to hear her voice once more. The sound of her laughter felt like a sweet echo of the delightful evening they had just shared. In that moment of reassurance, gratitude washed over him, reminding him of the beauty in their simple yet profound interactions. Their conversation stretched through the stillness of the night until the clock struck two in the morning. Realizing that Njeri had fallen asleep, her ears closed to both joy and sadness, Kwame took the hint that it was time for him to rest as well. He climbed into his bed, allowing the warmth of their connection to linger in his mind as he drifted off, content and ready for whatever tomorrow would bring.

Saturdays were a cherished time for Njeri and her son, Junior, a moment filled with the warmth of mother-son bonding. At around ten in the morning, Junior burst into her bedroom with excitement, his eyes wide and a smile stretching from ear to ear. Instead of asking for tickles, he inquired about Uncle Kwame. Njeri explained that he was at home but might visit soon, playfully calling Junior "little man." Junior, amused, countered with what Uncle Kwame called him - "big guy." Their laughter echoed in the room, creating a cozy atmosphere until the phone rang, jolting them from their moment. Junior's eyes sparkled with anticipation as he hoped it was Uncle Kwame. Njeri passed the phone to him, and the room filled with cheerful banter as they connected over the call, celebrating the joy of Saturdays together.

"Good morning, big guy!" Kwame greeted, to which Junior joyfully replied, "Good morning, Uncle Kwame!" Their lively chatter was playfully interrupted by a soft knock at the door. Seizing the moment, Kwame turned to Njeri and boldly asked her out on a second date. To his delight, she agreed but insisted he shares the intriguing tale of how a handsome young man like him found himself in the countryside. With that captivating condition, a date was set, infusing the day with a thrilling sense of anticipation for Njeri, who couldn't help but wonder about the stories and adventures that awaited them.

April heralded the arrival of planting season, a critical time for farmers eager to cultivate their crops. The term "April fools" had taken on a new meaning in the agricultural community, referring to those who neglected to plant during this crucial month. Farmers understood that skipping the April rains could significantly jeopardize their harvests, leading to a bumper crop for some and disappointing yields for others. As the days lengthened and the rain began to fall, many felt a sense of urgency, determined to avoid the stigma that accompanied missing this vital planting window. The pressure was on, as each farmer aimed to secure a prosperous future, ensuring they were not among those left to bear the unfortunate label of "April fools."

Njeri was fully engaged with her workers, ensuring that every necessary seed and planter was on site and in good condition.

She made her way to the newly acquired acres intended for corn cultivation, carefully inspecting the land to confirm it was adequately cleared and primed for planting. As she settled into her new office on the farm, she took the initiative to invite the field supervisor for a meeting. This gathering was crucial to discuss their level of preparedness and to ensure that all plans were on track for a successful planting season. With determination and diligence, she was committed to optimizing every aspect of the operation, laying a strong foundation for the upcoming agricultural venture. She had made a significant investment in her new project, channeling a considerable amount of money into state-of-the-art equipment designed to streamline the more arduous tasks. She employed a skilled team of operators, both men and women, to ensure the machines were used effectively.

Mr Amah, the field supervisor, knocked on Njeri's door, and she welcomed him into her new office, which was far cozier than her previous one. Njeri prioritized the comfort of her workers, providing a well-structured and ventilated space for them to rest when needed. The air-conditioned environment was pleasant, but everyone agreed that the natural coolness and freshness of the outdoor air were truly refreshing, creating a perfect atmosphere for productivity at the farm. As Mr Amah entered, Njeri noticed an unusual persona, his facial expression hinted something was amidst. She calmed her nerves down and offered him freshly squeezed mixed tropical fruits which he obliged. "Now tell me, is everything ready for this season for both farms?" asked Njeri. Mr Armah gave a big sigh, "the palm nut plantation is ready; both sites have been cleared and ready. The palm nut seedlings are also ready and on the ground waiting for planting." "I hope they are the local type (organic)" interrupted Njeri. "Yes Ma, they are" "However, the corn seedlings are not looking healthy and we might not be able to use them for planting." "Why is that?" "Ma, I think we got duped." "How so Mr Amah?" "Ma, I think the seedlings are not local (organic) like the seller promised. I think they are GMO." "Were the sacks of seedlings not inspected?" "We did Ma." "So how come, how could this have happened?" "I think they must have mixed them up somehow."

"This is not good, not good at all and has to be fixed ASAP. "Ma, I will handle this myself " Mr Amah assured Njeri. "But Mr Amah, this should have been detected long before now." "Yes Ma, I saw this sometime back but I thought the seedlings only needed more sunlight to dry properly so we dried them but today, the color and nature of the corn promoted my further investigation. It was through my investigation I realized it was fake. Truth be told Ma, the GMO's are very difficult to detect especially if the seller has every intention of duping you." "How do you know this will not repeat itself?" Ma, I have been directed to a specific village where their objectives is to preserve the natural seedlings passed on to us just like you are doing. Their prices are on the high side but I will do my best and negotiate with them. "Then be on your way already. But first, see the accountant. I must go with you to see this village and possibly have an alliance with them." Njeri instructed. "I think that will be great Ma."

Njeri and Mr Amah scheduled to leave early the next morning. She took a moment to call Kwame, sharing the news of their scheduled journey. As she spoke, Kwame felt regretful of not being able to join her on this important venture. He had always wanted to be by her side during crucial moments, offering support and companionship. He had already scheduled an on-site tour with the Technical School nearby. Every year, Technical and Vocational students from nearby schools visit Kwame's workshop to get on-site training and that Monday was the appointed day. But now, all he could do was offer his best wishes from afar, hoping that their mission would unfold smoothly and that Njeri would return with stories of success and excitement.

"You don't have to beat yourself up for this Kwame, I'm well aware of this appointment. I know you had this plan long time ago and what you do for these children and the schools is highly commendable and terrific. Besides, my issue just cropped up and there is nothing anyone can do about it. I will see you when I get back." "Safe trip Njeri." "Thank you and good luck with your training." The road leading to the village was very rough and terrible, despite her locally manufactured vehicle that had raised tires that was perfect for the countryside mud and bull terrain, she still felt her bones shaking. Nonetheless, the trip was a success. The town folks were elated to see someone with a vision to the local (organic) seedlings and as such were helpful with the transaction. Within days, the cleared land was planted with local corn kernels, (organic).

For days, Kwame felt the absence of Njeri, despite their nightly conversations that kept their bond alive. As the fourth night arrived, he picked up the phone, knowing this call was different; it was a reminder of their long-anticipated date the following day. Excitement surged through him as he rummaged through his wardrobe, determined to make a lasting impression. After several trials, he finally opted for an elegant outfit in olive green adorned with festive Adinkra symbols, a nod to his admiration for their rich meanings. Kwame believed these symbols conveyed deep messages, yet felt that many people lacked the understanding to truly appreciate their significance. He believed deeply that his people would soon awaken from their slumber, embracing the rich meanings of the adinkra symbols that defined their heritage. With night drawing closer, he was filled with both hope and anxiety, eager to connect with Njeri beyond their nightly calls. Njeri, captivated by both his appearance and the alluring scent of his perfume, couldn't help but express her admiration.

"You smell amazing," her eyes sparkling with appreciation. Njeri radiated an elegance reminiscent of royalty, draped in a stunning Sikaprint dress that beautifully complemented her figure. Her chic pompadour hairstyle framed her striking features, making her bright eyes twinkle with an enchanting brilliance. As she gracefully descended the stairs, Kwame found himself utterly entranced, momentarily speechless by her breathtaking presence. He gently held her hand and kissed it tenderly, his admiration pouring with compliments about her exquisite beauty. Each word he uttered only deepened his infatuation with her. As the night unfolded, Njeri couldn't help but be captivated by Kwame's outfit adorned with the striking adinkra symbol. It was a design she had never encountered before, and its uniqueness left a lasting impression on her. Intrigued, she expressed her admiration, revealing that she, too, was a big fan of adinkra symbols. However, she made it clear that the one he wore was something special, different from the others she had seen. This sparked a delightful conversation between them, where they exchanged insights about the meanings behind various symbols, ultimately deepening their connection and appreciation for their rich cultural heritage.

Kwame spoke passionately about the lesser-known adinkra symbols, which are often overshadowed by the more popular ones. He shared how his father, an adinkra enthusiast, had instilled in him a deep appreciation for these cultural icons. As he delved into their significance, Njeri shifted the conversation, curious about Kwame's life choices. "It's intriguing, how a young and handsome man like you could live comfortably in the USA but choose to settle in the countryside instead." Her interjection brought a smile to Kwame's face, as he appreciated her desire to understand his journey. The evening took a warm turn, blending the rich heritage of adinkra with the personal stories of their lives, as they both savored the connection between past traditions and present experiences.

Kwame tilted his head playfully, a mischievous smile dancing across his lips as he asked, "So you think I'm handsome?" Her eyes sparkled with a teasing glint, and Kwame couldn't help but chuckle at her boldness. The warmth of the moment enveloped them, and the carefree laughter that followed echoed their shared delight. It was one of those lighthearted exchanges that made the world seem a little brighter. They both knew it was just a playful banter, but there was an undeniable chemistry in the air; each wink filled with unspoken words and a promise of more laughter to come.

Now the ball was in Kwame's court. Njeri had already set it rolling by asking to know him more. Kwame held Njeri's hands, rubbed them gently as he looked into her eyes and started. "Well, I have always hoped to tell this story to someone and Im glad I found the right and perfect person to tell it to. One day, while paddling our canoe to school, I found myself among five children from different families, with me being the oldest. As the designated paddler, I took on the responsibility of steering us safely. However, just a few minutes into our destination, the canoe struck a rock, causing it to capsize. In an instant, all of us tumbled into the river. We managed to swim to the bank, but when we counted ourselves, we realized one friend; Kwesi, who couldn't swim was missing. Panic set in as we called out for him, but there was no response. Without hesitation, we sprinted toward the town where our school was located, desperate to alert the adults and seek help for our missing friend. Our hearts raced, knowing the urgency of the situation as we hoped for Kwesi's safe return. A lot of young and older adults run back to the spot where the incident occurred to rescue him. They dived into the river to search for him but there was no sight of Kwesi. The tragic incident that claimed the life of young Kwesi left a lasting mark on our community.

As news spread in our community, both young and older adults rushed back to the location where he had vanished, diving into the river in a desperate search for him. Despite their efforts, Kwesi remained elusive until the town's chief priest, after performing sacred rituals, finally located his body. This heartbreaking loss haunts me to this day.

Throughout my years of education, both at home and abroad, I reflected on the glaring inequities that stemmed from colonial rule. Despite the stated generosity of the colonizers, their efforts hardly translated into meaningful educational opportunities for the broader population. In the cities, only a handful of schools were established, while those living outside the urban centers were left completely devoid of access to education. This stark contrast reminded me of the systemic injustices that pervaded our society. As I navigated my academic journey, the thought of countless individuals denied the same opportunities weighed heavily on my conscience, fueling my desire to advocate for equitable access to education in all corners of society. Why should a child, with dreams of education to uplift not just himself but also his family and community, have to pay the ultimate price? Kwesi's story opened my eyes to the struggles some children endure in pursuit of education, often navigating dangerous paths just to attend school. Inspired by Kwesi's memory and the challenges I have witnessed, I made a solemn vow to build a school in my community once I had the means to do so. It became clear to me that every child deserves safe access to education, a place where they can learn and grow without fear. Creating a nurturing environment for learning is my way of honoring Kwesi's legacy and uplifting my community. I returned to my hometown not just to fulfill my promise, but to actively contribute to the educational welfare of my community. By establishing a school, I hope to ensure that every child has access to quality education without fear or danger. Together, we can create a brighter future where learning is a right, not a privilege. My mission is not just about buildings and classrooms; it's about transforming lives and empowering the next generation.

The second reason; during a walk with my father, he posed a thought-provoking question:" "Son, do you know why famine struck our country years ago?" "My ignorance prompted him to share a touching lesson from our past. He explained that the indigenous people once had a practical education system based on apprenticeship, which fostered skills and creativity rather than rote memorization. This old educational approach cultivated a deep respect for various trades, including farming. However, as the new system emerged, it focused on preparing individuals for lucrative positions, diverting attention from essential agricultural work. The allure of quick wealth led many to abandon farming, and before long, the nation found itself in crisis. This neglect resulted in widespread famine, claiming countless lives.

My father illustrated the profound impact of education on society's values and the importance of nurturing our roots. I envisioned a bright future where I could establish a technical school on our land. This school would serve as a hub of knowledge, teaching children about technology during the week - so our land will evolve and shape our world. On weekends, they would immerse themselves in the wisdom of our elders, learning the intricate art of farming. This dual education would cultivate a passion for both technology and agriculture, empowering the next generation to thrive in an ever-changing landscape. By bridging the gap between modern innovation and traditional practices, I hope to nurture well-rounded individuals who are equipped to face the challenges of tomorrow while honoring the roots of our community."

Kwame looked across the dinner table, his

storytelling abruptly interrupted by a drop of tears from Njeri. Engrossed in his tales, he hadn't noticed her quiet sorrow until now. Confused and concerned, he reached out, holding her hands gently and asking what was wrong. To his astonishment, Njeri revealed that she had been one of the children in the canoe that tragically hit the rock that fateful day. Kwesi, her only brother, had been two years older than her. Kwame felt a lump rise in his throat as he choked out, "oh dear, I had no idea. I'm deeply sorry for your loss." Regret washed over him as he realized his storytelling had unknowingly reopened old wounds. Njeri, however, reassured him, saying softly, "It's fine, Kwame. You didn't know." Their connection deepened, both understanding the weight of memories carried in silence. Kwame had an incredible ability to transform sorrow into joy, a talent he showcased during the dinner date. As the evening unfolded, laughter and stories filled the air again, allowing both him and Njeri to momentarily forget the heaviness of

Kwesi's death. They shared tales of their past appointments, reminiscing about victories and challenges, while dreams of upcoming aspirations painted a hopeful picture for the future.

The Festival of the Moon was just around the corner, and its vibrant energy was visible with preparations bustling all around them. Amidst the festivities, Kwame and Njeri found cheer in each other, embracing the beauty of the moment and the promise of brighter days ahead. The yearly festival of the moon was a treasured tradition passed down through generations. As old friends, neighbors, and families gathered, the atmosphere became filled with an undeniable sense of joy and connection. Each year, during the celebration, the moon shone brighter, illuminating the faces of those reunited under its radiant glow. The addition of a lonely star, twinkling in the night sky, added an air of magic and hope to the evening. It was during those enchanting moments that first kisses blossomed, friendships deepened, and new connections forged, all wrapped in the warmth of laughter and shared stories. The festival was not just an event; it was a celebration of love, unity, and the timeless bonds that wove the fabric of the community together. The gathering took place in a field adorned with mystical trees, fondly nicknamed by the townsfolk . As stories were shared and memories created, the essence of the festival evoked a profound sense of fellowship and love that lasted long after the moon and the star had faded from the sky.

On the brightest night of the moon, a cherished belief echoed among the festival-goers: those who stood beneath the ancient trees would see their wishes granted. The celebration, which kicked off on a bustling Thursday, welcomed families and friends arriving in groups from the cities, each filled with excitement and hope. The air was alive with unforgettable sounds, drumming, dancing, and the harmonious melodies of various musical groups, creating a vibrant atmosphere. Food overflowed from open kitchens, generously provided by the affluent members of the community, ensuring no one went hungry. As Saturday approached, anticipation reached its peak, when in a breathtaking spectacle, the moon radiated its fullest light. With joyful shouts ringing out, many stood beneath the luminous glow, whispering their dreams to the night sky, believing wholeheartedly in the magic of the moment. The people of the land adhered strictly to every aspect of this festival as it brought blessings upon their lives especially couples.

It was believed in ancient times that the moon goddess extended her conjugal bliss to couples on the night that the moon shone brightest. The night was also dedicated to honoring the beloved souls who had departed from the community. While mourning was strictly forbidden, joy and cheerfulness reigned supreme throughout the festivities. Families gathered under the starlit sky, sharing laughter and stories, ensuring that the spirit of their loved ones remained alive in their hearts. Fresh flowers adorned the tombstones, a beautiful tribute symbolizing love and remembrance. Each bloom represented cherished memories, and as the light flickered from lanterns, it illuminated both the graves and the joyful faces of those who gathered. This festival was a unique blend of celebration and remembrance creating a night where spirits were revered and joyous laughter echoed in the air.

Kwame and Njeri knew the importance of the festival of the moon very well. They made sure all work activities were either done on time or postponed in order to fully enjoy with families and friends. They each contributed to the success of the festival. The king had called both to intimate them of the budget for the festival. They not only contributed financially but they also gave new ideas for the success of the celebration.

After their lively dance filled with laughter and rhythm, Kwame gently took Njeri by the hand, guiding her away from the bustling crowd. The energetic sounds of the festivities faded as they walked towards the enchanting magic tree, its branches adorned with glimmering lights that flickered like stars in the night sky. The air was filled with the sweet scent of blossoms, and a soft breeze rustled the leaves, creating a serene atmosphere just for them. Underneath the tree's protective canopy, Kwame and Njeri shared whispers and dreams, their bond deepening in this secluded, magical space. It felt as if time had stopped, allowing them to savor the moment, surrounded by the beauty of nature and each other's presence. It was a memory they would cherish forever, a perfect pause from the world.

Under the glistering glow of the moon, Kwame and Njeri's love story began to unfold beneath the enchanting branches of the magic tree. Their first kiss was filled with youthful exuberance, reminiscent of first graders capturing the thrill of innocence. As they embraced, the air around them sparkled with the promise of romance, marking the dawn of their journey as the newly dubbed 'power couple.' Together, they breathed life into Tsetsebo, transforming it from a quaint country-side into a well-planned town, where the old beautifully intertwined with the new. With the support of the diaspora, they ensured that the essence of their beloved town remained intact, preserving its lush greenery and clean environment.

Their blossoming love became a beacon of hope and progress. Njeri and Kwame found love and decided to marry, uniting their families and solidifying their bond. Their marriage marked the beginning of a new era, as the two families ascended to become the Odogwu's - respected figures known for their wealth and wisdom throughout the land. Their legacy became a testament to the harmonious blend of tradition and progress, leading the path for future generations to thrive both economically and culturally.

CHAPTER FIFTEEN

*"Said the Hen: If You Will Not Have
The Rain, You must Also Miss the Worms"*

Despite the distance and circumstances that kept Njeri from saying goodbye to Abeba, she and Abeba managed to rekindle their friendship. Their bond remained strong, as they frequently reached out to each other, sharing updates and reminiscing about old times. Njeri missed being part of the family farewell, but she knew that their connection was unwavering. They found solace in their conversations as they navigated their separate lives. The clarity and warmth of their rekindled relationship brought comfort and joy, reaffirming the significance of their lasting friendship.

Abeba found the transition from her first degree to medical school to be a challenging experience, especially as she studied abroad without the comfort of family nearby. While her undergraduate years were filled with excitement and social connections, medical school demanded intense focus and dedication, often leaving little room for leisure or connections. The rigorous curriculum and high expectations created a sense of isolation, making her long for the close-knit support system she had back home. Despite the pursuit of her dream to become a medical doctor, she sometimes struggled with loneliness and the weight of academic pressure. Yet, she remained determined, hoping that the sacrifices she made would eventually lead to a fulfilling career in medicine.

Deeply passionate about her studies in human anatomy, a field that captivated her with its complexities and intricacies. Each lecture and practical session presented a new challenge, requiring her to apply intense concentration and unwavering dedication. She approached her studies as a thoughtful and careful endeavor, knowing that understanding the human body was not just an academic pursuit but a responsibility that could impact lives. The more she learned, the more her enthusiasm blossomed, fueled by the profound connection between her studies and the art of healing. Despite the demands of her course-work, she found joy in deciphering the mysteries of anatomy, eagerly absorbing every detail and appreciating the journey of knowledge that lay ahead. For her, it was more than just education; it was a calling that she embraced wholeheartedly.

All said and done, Abeba graumated with honors, a testament to her remarkable intelligence and dedication. From a young age, it was evident that she was always a bright student, excelling in her studies and displaying an insatiable curiosity about the world around her. Her teachers and classmates recognized her talent, often citing her ability to grasp complex concepts with ease. This achievement was not just a reflection of her academic capabilities but also of her hard work and perseverance. Balancing her studies with extracurricular activities, she continuously demonstrated a strong commitment to her personal and academic growth. As she moved forward, her honors graduation served as a solid foundation for her future endeavors, further motivating her to chase her dreams and make a meaningful impact in her chosen field.

During her time in medical school, Abeba found herself drawn to Kevin, a charming native of the United States. Their connection blossomed amidst the rigorous demands of their studies, providing a much-needed breathing space from the challenges of medical education. Late-night study sessions often turned into laughter-filled conversations, where they shared their hopes and dreams for the future. Abeba appreciated

Kevin's unwavering support as she navigated the complexities of her course-work, while he admired her dedication and passion for medicine. Together, they explored the city, forging a bond that intertwined their academic aspirations with personal growth. As they balanced exams and romantic dinners, Abeba and Kevin discovered that love could thrive even in the busiest of times, enriching their lives as they prepared for their future careers in healthcare. With cultural disparities, their relationship became complex. At times, their connection grew as they discovered the beauty in each other's traditions, celebrating holidays and sharing culinary delights that spanned their diverse backgrounds. However, these cultural disparities also became a source of tension, leading to misunderstandings and disagreements that tested their bond.

It was during one such moment, fueled by love and commitment, that Kevin found the courage to propose to Abeba. Her acceptance not only solidified their bond but also symbolized their willingness to embrace their differences and join their lives together. However, their union remained shrouded in secrecy, as no family member from Abeba's side was informed about the marriage. This choice to keep their vows private added a layer of complexity to their already problematic relationship, leaving Abeba caught between her love for Kevin and his expectations of acknowledgment from her family regarding their marriage. As they embarked on this new chapter together, both were aware that their journey would require more than just love; it would demand understanding, openness, and a willingness to confront the repercussions of their choice.

On the day of their honeymoon, Abeba's excitement was overshadowed by an unexpected revelation. She encountered a document that left her heart racing: Kevin had purchased the dream home they had both envisioned, but he had done so solely in his name. Their dream house, meant to symbolize their shared hopes and aspirations, was now tainted by secrets. Unbeknownst to Abeba, Kevin had crafted an illusion, presenting it as a rental property while she had been unknowingly paying rent to him. What she thought was a step towards their future together now felt like a betrayal, casting a shadow over what should have been a blissful beginning to their married life.

The revelation left her questioning not only their plans but also the very foundation of trust that their relationship was built upon. Did Kevin truly envision their future together, or was this a sign of something deeper creeping beneath the surface? What seemed like a blissful beginning quickly turned into a moment of reckoning. As the reality of the situation sank in, her dreams of a perfect honeymoon began to unfold; what should have been a celebration of their love quickly turned into a moment of doubt.

The joyous atmosphere of their trip

evaporated, leaving behind an agonizing sense of uncertainty about their future together. This painful revelation reshaped her reality; not only had Kevin deceived her about the purchase of their home, but he had also hidden the truth regarding her wedding ring and the lavish wedding, which had all been financed through the house's equity. Each detail she uncovered felt like a dagger, piercing the trust she had once held dear. In her mind, she had envisioned a partnership built on love and shared dreams, yet instead, she was left grappling with feelings of being used and dishonored, struggling to reconcile the image of their life together with the harsh reality she now faced.

With clenched fists and a resolute heart, she decided it was time to stand up for herself. This wasn't just about a ring or a wedding; it was about her dignity and the respect she deserved. No longer would she be a pawn in Kevin's antics; she was ready to reclaim her life. Abeba glanced at Kevin one last time, feeling a dart of guilt as she explained that something urgent had come up, prompting her to return to the house. She assured him she would be back soon, but deep down, she knew that wasn't the plan. In a hurry, she packed her belongings, her heart racing as she bought a ticket back to her family. The weight of her decision settled heavily on her chest, but the thought of leaving behind her current situation felt liberating. Once at the airport, she switched off her phone, knowing Kevin's calls would go unanswered as she crossed borders, heading towards a sense of safety and familiarity. She was determined to carve out a new path, one that wouldn't include the unanswered questions Kevin would inevitably have, once he realized she was gone.

Kevin found himself drowning under the weight of responsibilities he never anticipated. With the burdens of a high mortgage and the cost of an expensive engagement ring that Abeba refused to return, he felt trapped. The wedding plans that had once filled him with excitement now seemed like cruel reminders of what could have been. Ultimately, he was forced to abandon the home that held so many hopes and dreams, retreating back to a modest apartment. The down payment he had worked hard for dissipated, leaving him with a ruined credit score as a bitter souvenir of the relationship's end. In the back of his mind, he couldn't shake the feeling that Abeba's actions were a twisted form of revenge, leaving him with a heavy heart and an uncertain future.

Abeba stepped off the aircraft, her heart pounding with conflicting emotions. The relief of returning home mingled awkwardly with the guilt that weighed heavily on her conscience. What was meant to be a joyous honeymoon had spiraled into chaos when she made the heart-wrenching decision to leave Kevin behind. Memories of their plans together danced in her mind, each one laced with the bittersweet taste of regret. As she stood there, the bustling airport around her faded into a blur, and she felt an overwhelming sense of loneliness despite the crowd. The adventure she had envisioned had unraveled into a confusing mess, leaving her to grapple with the consequences of her choice. The sights and sounds of their romantic getaway felt hauntingly vivid in her mind, reminding her of the moment she decided to break free: excited for independence, downhearted for what could have been. Abeba realized that returning home was just the beginning of a transformative journey, one that she needed to navigate with courage.

The airport filled with the sounds of travelers and announcements seemed to fade away. Abeba's eyes searched the crowd, and then she spotted him - Joe, standing there with his usual warm smile. It was a smile she had come to rely on, a beacon of comfort amidst the chaos of her life. The world around her felt overwhelming, yet Joe's presence brought a wave of stability that grounded her. His relaxed demeanor suggested that everything would be alright, and for Abeba, that moment was a reminder of the bond they shared. As she approached him, the stress of her journey melted away, replaced by his warmth and the anticipation of the adventures that lay ahead. Their connection rekindled effortlessly, as if no time had passed since their last encounter. They slipped back into their routine, sharing laughter and intimate conversations that reminded Abeba of the bond they had nurtured before her trip. It was as if fate had intervened, bringing Joe back into her life when she needed him most. With him by her side, she felt hopeful and excited about what the future might hold, eager to explore the depths of their relationship once more.

Abeba felt a mix of excitement and apprehension as she stepped into her father's private practice for the first time. Although her heart yearned for the bustling environment of the public sector like her father had once experienced, she couldn't ignore the comfort of having Dr Fray by her side. He had promised to guide her through every challenge, teaching her the essential skills needed to thrive in this new role. With his reassurance, Abeba slowly began to embrace her position as the second in command at the private hospital. She realized that while the path might not align with her original preferences, it was an invaluable opportunity to learn and grow under her father's mentorship. As days turned into weeks, she found herself increasingly appreciative of the knowledge and experience she was gaining, a foundation for her future career in medicine.

Njeri and Kwame's family continued to grow as they welcomed three more children into their lives, complementing their joyful experience with their little-big-man, Junior. Each new arrival brought a unique personality and charm, enriching the family's dynamic and creating a lively atmosphere in their home. With laughter and playtime filling the air, Njeri and Kwame embraced the challenges and joys of parenting their expanding family. They worked together to ensure that each child received love and attention, fostering a sense of belonging and togetherness. As they navigated the ups and downs of family life, their bond grew stronger, and their hearts swelled with pride and affection for their beautiful family. Junior, now a big sibling, delighted in the opportunity to guide and play with the younger ones, filling the household with even more warmth and love.

One day at Junior's school, something unusual happened that sparked curiosity among the students. A stranger, dressed in a dark coat and sunglasses, stepped out of a shiny black car and made his way towards the playground. The children, playing games and laughing, paused for a moment to catch a glimpse of this unfamiliar figure. Whispers spread among them as they wondered who he was and why he was visiting their school.

Some felt a thrill of excitement while others felt a sense of apprehension. The air was thick with anticipation as the stranger approached, his intentions unknown. Junior and his friends exchanged glances, contemplating whether they should continue their games or keep a watchful eye on the mysterious visitor. The day suddenly felt different, filled with the promise of adventure or perhaps a hint of danger waiting just around the corner. The stranger made his way towards the playground, he spotted Junior. "Hi, young man," he greeted with a friendly smile. "Hi, sir," replied Junior, his eyes wide with curiosity. "My name is Mr Orji. What's yours?" "My name is Junior," With a glimmer of excitement, Mr Orji reached into his pocket and handed Junior a card. "Can you please give this card to Njeri, your mother?" he asked kindly. Junior nodded enthusiastically, eager to take on the small responsibility. What began as a simple exchange of pleasantries quickly evolved into a profound bridge of connection between the two, creating a warm atmosphere filled with the innocence of youth and the kindness of strangers.

Njeri's fury boiled over as she replayed the encounter Orji had with Junior in her mind. "What the nerve!" she exclaimed aloud, her thoughts racing. It wasn't just the audacity that infuriated her; it was the timing. "Why now?" she wondered, feeling a mix of betrayal and disbelief. Njeri had always believed that certain boundaries should never be crossed, especially within their close-knit circle. The way Orji had approached the situation felt like a blatant disregard for her feelings. As she paced back and forth, frustration swelled within her, pushing her to confront Orji and demand an explanation. The anger coursing through her was not just about what happened, it was also about the principle of loyalty and respect. Njeri knew she had to take a stand; confrontation loomed in her mind despite Kwame's efforts to soothe her, she couldn't shake the feeling of betrayal. Determined to seek answers, they set off the next day to confront Orji at his lodging place.

The atmosphere was tense as they approached, each step heightening Njeri's resolve. She needed to understand why Orji had engaged with her son, a situation that had left her feeling uneasy. Kwame stayed close, offering silent support, but Njeri knew it was time to face Orji and demand answers. As they approached his lodging place, Njeri steeled herself for the confrontation that would reveal the mysteries surrounding their lives. As she and Kwame approached, the atmosphere was charged with unspoken tension, each step drawing them closer to a crucial moment. Orji noticing their arrival, hurriedly stood up to greet Kwame with an air of appreciation before turning to Njeri, his demeanor shifting to one of regret. With a sincere tone, he offered an apology for his earlier encounter with Junior, expressing that his fear had kept him from addressing Njeri directly. There was a brief moment of silence in the air, creating a fragile bridge between their fractured pasts and the uncertain future that lay ahead.

Njeri's heart raced as she processed Orji's revelations, the weight of their shared history looming over her like an impending storm, ready to release its long-held secrets. Orji intimated Njeri and Kwame, revealing the fruitless efforts of private detectives he had hired to locate Njeri over the years. Despite their persistence, it seemed as though she had disappeared without a trace, leaving no clues behind. The detectives combed through various leads, but each attempt only deepened the mystery surrounding her whereabouts. Orji's frustration grew as he realized that a crucial piece of the puzzle - the name of Njeri's village - had slipped from his memory. It was as if the place where she once belonged had faded along with her, leaving him with a sense of loss and unanswered questions. Desperate to reconnect, he felt a heavy weight on his heart, knowing that the bond they once shared was shrouded in uncertainty.

Throughout their time together, Njeri rarely spoke of her past, mentioning only her aunt, with whom she lived during her college years, and her best friend Abeba, who had mysteriously disappeared. The absence of concrete information left him feeling lost, as he realized that those two individuals were the only people who held the key to finding Njeri. With nothing but a fading memory and vague connections to guide him, he felt the weight of uncertainty pressing down, intensifying his desperation to uncover the truth and bring Njeri back into his life. Time slipped away like sand through his fingers, until one day, while sifting through a supplier's list for his company, he stumbled upon a name that piqued his interest - a woman listed as the leading supplier. Curiosity ignited, he delved into her profile, and to his astonishment, every detail aligned perfectly with what he remembered about Njeri.

Fueled by a renewed sense of hope, he turned once more to a private investigator, seeking to unravel the threads of a mystery that had long haunted him. As he stood before the investigator, a whirlwind of emotions engulfed him - anticipation, anxiety, and a flicker of excitement danced within him, a moment he had yearned for, the countless sleepless nights and unanswered questions. Each piece of the puzzle he had been hoping to find was now drawing closer to completion, lighting a fire within him. Yet, he couldn't shake the remnants of doubt, wondering if the answers would bring clarity or simply open the door to more confusion.

His heart ached with the weight of his longing; he recognized that he needed his son more than ever. Life had dealt him a harsh blow, leaving him to grapple with the reality of his wife's inability to bear children - a truth that he conceded as his own failing. The dreams of fatherhood, once vivid, now faded into a distant hope, but the yearning in his soul remained unabated. He understood that the bond between a father and son was irreplaceable, and he could no longer ignore the emptiness that echoed through their home. As he stood there, uncertain yet determined, he resolved to confront the complexities of his feelings and fight for the family he wished to build, one that defied the shadows of their past. Orji confided in Njeri, revealing the heavy burden his mother felt over his failure to secure an heir for the empire they had worked tirelessly to establish. The weight of this expectation pressed down on him, as he sought to reconcile years lost and fulfill his duty by bringing his estranged son back into the fold.

Frustration bubbled within Njeri, leading her to hurl the spoon across the breakfast table in response to Orji's revelations. It was Kwame, her husband, who gently reminded her of their current situation and the delicate balance they needed to maintain within their standing in society. The tension in the air became real, as each of them grappled with the looming responsibilities that entwined their lives and futures. Kwame, sensing the unease, stepped in to ease the situation by asking Orji to excuse them for a moment. He handed him his card, urging him to ensure that his family joined him on his next visit. Orji was appreciative of Kwame's patience and understanding amidst the turmoil. It was a small gesture, yet he was grateful. As the two men exchanged words, a brief moment of clarity emerged, offering a glimpse of hope for what lay ahead for both of them.

Njeri and Kwame arrived home, their minds heavy with the thoughts of their challenging circumstances. They settled down with Maa-me, who had always been a pillar of support. As they spoke, Maa-me shared her wisdom, offering her perspective on the situation at hand. Njeri listened intently, absorbing every word, yet deep inside, she held onto her belief that Junior would only truly be able to leave her care when he was an adult, capable of standing on his own two feet. This conviction pressed heavily on her heart, as she recognized the intricacies of their lives and the responsibilities that lay before them. The conversation deepened their understanding, intertwining their hopes and fears for Junior's future. The discussion was emotional yet necessary. Njeri felt a sense of responsibility toward her son and was determined to protect him until he was ready to face the world on his own.

A week later, Orji's entire family gathered at Njeri and Kwame's home, where they were guided to Njeri's family house to address their issues per tradition. Orji's mother, feeling the weight of the situation, offered heartfelt apologies to Njeri and her kinsmen acknowledging the inhuman way she treated her. In accordance with local customs, a customary fine was imposed on Orji's family as part of the resolution process. Following this, important rites were conducted to solidify their claim to kinship with Junior fostering a sense of unity and healing between the two families. The gathering not only served to mend relationships but also reinforced the cultural values that bind the two families together, ensuring that such matters were respectfully resolved in the spirit of community and family.

After the important rites carried out by Orji's family to validate their biological connection to Junior, Njeri firmly communicated to Orji and his kinsmen that, although Junior was now officially recognized as part of their family, he would not be relocating to the city with them. Njeri's stance underscored her desire to keep Junior rooted in his current environment, emphasizing the importance of stability and continuity in his life. The decision stemmed from a deep understanding that Junior would thrive better in the familiar surroundings he had always known, where his relationships and community ties were firmly established. She elaborated on the situation, clarifying that she and her husband were unwilling to allow Junior to venture out of their sight until he reached maturity. This revelation caught Orji and his family off guard, but they quickly understood the gravity of the concern.

With a newfound respect for their wishes, they decided to postpone their plans. As the time to depart approached, Orji and his kinsmen gathered to discuss their options. Rather than clinging to the hope of Junior joining them, they faced the reality of the situation with grace. They came to a mutual understanding; the decision, though difficult, leaving without him was a decision born not from disappointment, but from love. They acknowledged the bittersweet nature of the moment, aware that prioritizing Junior's well-being was paramount. Plans were made to ensure he would be supported in their absence, reinforcing their commitment to his happiness. With heavy hearts, yet clear minds, they set their sights on the city, trusting that this sacrifice would ultimately lead to brighter days for Junior.

CHAPTER SIXTEEN

"A Rich Man Cannot Keep a Poor Man's Chickens from Brooding"

◆ ◆ ◆

The passing of the revered king of Tsetsebo marked the end of an era, leaving behind a legacy that echoed through the ages. With the weight of tradition upon their shoulders, the townsfolk awaited the moment when their deity would unveil the next ruler. The air was thick with anticipation, as elders whispered tales of the past, recounting the qualities that a true king must possess. Communities gathered to pray and seek guidance from the divine, hopeful that the new leader would bring prosperity and unity. Each day as the sun began to set, everyone felt a deep connection to their history, poised on the brink of a new chapter, ready to embrace the figure that would rise to lead them into the future. The spirit of the town hung heavy with hope, awaiting the deity's decree to mark the dawn of a new reign.

Njeri felt a 'willy-willy' of emotions as she repeatedly saw her name emerge as the chosen leader for the people of Tsetsebo. The weight of this unexpected fate pressed on her, leaving her perplexed and unsure of what to do next. "How could she be the one chosen for such a significant role"? She questioned her abilities and the responsibilities that lay ahead. The people of Tsetsebo had their hopes pinned on her, but she struggled to believe in herself. As whispers of hope and expectation surrounded her, she knew she had to confront her doubts and summon the strength within herself to rise to the occasion. With determination slowly replacing confusion, she resolved to embrace this challenge and lead her people toward a brighter future, even if the path ahead was uncertain.

At first, she dismissed the idea of being

chosen as the new king, attributing it to her benevolent nature. It seemed absurd to her; her husband, Kwame, with his wisdom and charisma, was far more deserving of the title. She pondered the irony of the situation, feeling both honored and uneasy. While her instincts told her that the crown should rightfully rest upon Kwame's head, she could not ignore the weight of the responsibility now resting on her shoulders. In her heart, she yearned for Kwame to step forward, to claim the position that felt so ill-fitted for her. Yet, as she took a deep breath, she recognized that this unexpected turn of events might be an opportunity for growth, not just for herself but for the kingdom as well. In stepping into this role, perhaps she could prove that benevolence in leadership could forge a new path for all.

Tsetsebo, an ancient village on its ancient grounds, nestled amidst the serene embrace of mountains and gentle hills. It offered a picturesque landscape that captivated both residents and visitors alike. The village's unique location granted it a breathtaking view of rolling landscapes, where lush greenery met the rugged heights of the surrounding peaks. Through the relentless efforts of Njeri and her husband Kwame, Tsetsebo, the once small-size ancient village, steeped in history and the echoes of ancient wars, underwent a remarkable transformation. What was once a quiet reminder of past conflicts blossomed into a thriving town, beaming with life and opportunities. The couple's dedication to revitalizing the area brought new businesses, cultural initiatives, and a renewed sense of community spirit. As the town prospered, it attracted visitors curious about its rich heritage and vibrant present. Njeri and Kwame's vision not only preserved the village's history but also paved the way for future generations to enjoy a bustling, dynamic environment. The children were uniquely positioned at the crossroads of technology and agriculture, gaining invaluable skills that would shape their futures. They learned not just about innovative practices but also the significance of their cultural roots and the festivities that celebrated them.

Njeri and Kwame's journey stood as a testament to the power of determination and love for one's roots, illustrating how history can be honored while also embracing the promise of a bright and prosperous future. In the town of Tsetsebo, the beauty of its damsels was renowned, and the fabric of the community was woven tightly with the threads of family names. There, everyone knew each other, and the significance of a good name reverberated through every interaction. The phrase "a good name is better than riches" was not just a saying but a guiding principle that shaped the town's values. Residents took great pride in their family heritage, understanding that reputation and integrity outweighed material wealth. Relationships blossomed, and the bonds of kinship created an atmosphere of respect and admiration, where legacy of each families served as a foundation for collective pride.

The townspeople celebrated their connections, ensuring that the essence of their identities thrived in harmony whiles flourishing under an unconventional yet nurturing system of upbringing. Every adult took on the role of a guardian, embracing a collective responsibility for the well-being of the children. It was not uncommon for a child to be corrected, rebuked, or even disciplined by any adult they encountered, irrespective of their actual family ties. This practice fostered a strong sense of unity and accountability among the townspeople, reinforcing the belief that raising a child is a communal endeavor. Such an arrangement ensured that children were guided with care and respect, learning from various perspectives and experiences. As a result, Tsetsebo became a place where discipline was shared, and moral values were collectively upheld, contributing to the town's rich tapestry of social bonds and mutual respect.

With Maa-me's voice trembling yet resolute, she summoned Njeri to discuss troubling rumors that had begun to circulate throughout the town. She revealed the whispers of the townsfolk - speculations about why the gods had chosen her as the new king. It was an unprecedented occurrence, as the town had never seen a queen in such a significant role. The air was full with anticipation and apprehension, and her mother implored her to understand the weight of her destiny. Each word carried the gravity of tradition, as well as the hope of change, as they pondered what the gods intended for her reign, Njeri listened intently, feeling the ambition and responsibility stirred up within her, unsure of whether to embrace her fate or resist the path laid before her by unseen forces.

In a quiet village like Tsetsebo, where secrets lingered like shadows, Njeri lived her life unaware of the truth that bound her to the recently deceased king. The man she called 'Papa' had raised her, cloaking her in a veil of affection while withholding the most profound truth of her lineage. Unknown to her, the kind heart that beat within her chest was not just the legacy of Papa but also of the departed king, her biological father. The whispers of this hidden story were confined to a select few, who understood the dangers of revealing such truths. The villagers, though curious, kept their lips sealed, preserving the facade that had become woven into the fabric of their lives. Njeri roamed through life, blissfully ignorant of the royal blood that flow through her veins, a truth later unveiled. Maa-me recounted the early days of her marriage to the departed king, a union that lasted for three years before everything changed. When Njeri was just a year old, her father ascended to the throne following the death of his own father. He inherited not only the crown but also the responsibility of a betrothed, which meant sacrificing his love for Maa-me. In this, Maa-me became a silent observer of royal politics, as her husband was compelled to take a new wife who would be crowned queen.

Njeri, unaware of the complexities of her family's history, grew up surrounded by hardships and burdens. Her young life forever shaped by the decisions made in the palace long before she could understand their implications. In a cruel twist of fate, her father, the newly crowned king, was forcibly relocated from Tsetsebo to the sprawling capital as the ruler of over twenty villages, leaving behind the family he cherished. His sudden departure added salt to an already festering wound. Manipulated by his betrothed queen, whose ambitions overshadowed the king's family bonds, the king found himself ensnared in a complex web of political intrigue, where every whispered secret carried the weight of betrayal. His once-loyal advisors transformed into shadowy figures, each with their own hidden agendas. In the opulent halls of the palace, alliances shifted like the sands of time, and the king struggled to discern friend from foe. The townspeople looked to him for leadership and guidance, unaware of the turmoil brewing within his heart as separation from his loved ones haunted him daily. Njeri's father was left to grapple with the absence of his family, feeling the weight of his sacrifice while clinging to the hope that one day, he might return to their humble village.

Njeri felt an overwhelming surge of anger as she contemplated the stark contrast between her father's lavish lifestyle and the struggles she and Maa-me endured daily. Each day, while they toiled to make ends meet, her father reveled in his wealth, oblivious to their hardships. The richness that surrounded him felt like a betrayal to Njeri, who longed for a sense of fairness in their fractured family. Thoughts of missed opportunities and unfulfilled promises consumed her, feeding her frustration and deepening the divide between them. She could not understand how he could enjoy such luxury while they grappled with the harsh realities of life, leaving her to question not just his choices but also his love for them.

Her heart ached for justice, but her mother gently took her hands and spoke in soothing tones, urging her to let go of the anger that tightened her chest. "You need to forgive your father," she said, her eyes filled with love and understanding. "He made mistakes, but he was still your father, and he loved you. Now the kingdom needs a strong leader, and that leader is you, Njeri, embrace your destiny and accept the throne. Your people are depending on you to guide them towards a brighter future." Njeri listened, feeling the weight of her mother's words settle in her heart. Although uncertainty lingered, she realized that forgiveness was the first step toward healing, both for her family and her kingdom. With a deep breath, she began to consider the path that lay ahead, one where she could honor her father's legacy while forging her own.

Kwame and Njeri were thriving as their business flourished, bringing them both joy and prosperity. The Bounty Festival, a vibrant celebration that coincided with the enthronement of a new king, was just around the corner, and the excitement was evident in the air. Njeri, with her infectious spirit, was particularly enthusiastic about the festivities, eagerly preparing for the celebrations that would showcase their culture and heritage. As the festival approached, the couple felt an overwhelming sense of gratitude for their bond, filled with love, success, and the promise of new beginnings amidst the joyous chaos of the upcoming events. The days ahead promised to be unforgettable, brimming with laughter, music, and shared moments that would strengthen their bond even further.

The Bounty Festival celebration that year, promised to be an extraordinary affair, with an impressive array of sophisticated machines at the disposal of the townspeople. Participants eagerly gathered to explore innovative methods of transforming the abundant bananas and other harvested produce into long-lasting delicacies. From banana chips to dried fruit snacks, creativity multiplied as locals shared their ideas and techniques, fostering a spirit of collaboration and excitement. The atmosphere buzzed with energy, as families and friends came together to celebrate not only the harvest but also the ingenuity of their community. With each new invention, the festival became a testament to the resilience and resourcefulness of the townspeople, ensuring that their cherished harvest would be enjoyed for months to come. For the first time in its storied history, the Bounty Festival celebration was set to dazzle audiences far beyond its local roots with live television coverage. This groundbreaking event promised to showcase the colorful parades, spirited dances, and the joyous atmosphere that defined the festival. As preparations unfolded, excitement buzzed through the community, with vendors gearing up to serve traditional delicacies and performers rehearsing their captivating routines.

Families gathered in anticipation, eager to witness not only the festivities in person but also to share the celebration with loved ones who could tune in from afar. The event was a testament to the rich cultural heritage and community spirit, now amplified by modern technology, creating memories that would be cherished for generations to come. The Bounty Festival not only celebrated the bounty of the season but also served as a reminder of the richness of relationships that thrive over time and distance. Njeri enthusiastically shared her idea of incorporating a reunion with her friends into the upcoming festival celebration. She believed that such a gathering would not only enhance the festive spirit but also strengthen the bonds among long-time friends. Kwame listened intently, nodding in agreement.

"That sounds interesting and laudable," he responded, clearly impressed with the concept. They began brainstorming ways to organize the reunion, considering various activities that would make it memorable for everyone involved.

The prospect of reconnecting with friends amidst the joyous festival atmosphere filled Njeri with excitement, and she couldn't help but imagine the laughter and stories that would unfold. Together, they felt inspired to create a meaningful event that would celebrate both the festival and the friendships that had stood the test of time. Kwame thoughtfully contemplated the integration of a special scholarship initiative into the festive activities designed for technical and vocational students. Recognizing the importance of education and support for the students, he envisioned a program that would not only celebrate their achievements but also provide them with financial assistance to further their training. By adding this scholarship component, Kwame aimed to inspire and motivate students, encouraging them to pursue their passions and enhance their skills in their respective fields. The festive activities would serve as a platform to raise awareness about the scholarship, fostering a sense of community and support among students, educators, and local businesses. In doing so, Kwame hoped to create a positive impact that would empower the next generation of skilled professionals.

They organized an unforgettable reunion, inviting everyone in their circle to come together for this special occasion. They made sure to extend invitations to Abeba and her family, Orji and his family, as well as Ayanda and her family, ensuring that all their loved ones could share in the joyous event. Excitement filled the air as families reunited, laughter echoed in the air, and the aroma of delicious food wafted through the gathering. Stories were shared, memories were created, and bonds were strengthened, making it the biggest reunion ever. Njeri and Kwame's thoughtful planning brought everyone closer, reminding them of the importance of family and friendship.

The invitation to the Bounty Festival celebration from Njeri and Kwame was a significant moment for the Frays, particularly for Dr Fray. It represented his first return to Tsetsebo since their departure, stirring a mix of apprehension and eagerness within him. As the festival approached, memories of their life in Tsetsebo flooded back, igniting his excitement to reunite with old friends and revive the deep connections formed during their stay. The anticipation of exchanging stories and reminiscing about shared experiences from the years spent apart created an infectious buzz, promising a reunion filled with joy and cherished moments. Dr Fray looked forward to celebrating not just the festival but also the bonds that had endured over time, making the occasion an unforgettable chapter in his life.

Maa-me, though aged, held onto vivid memories of the Frays, particularly the challenges faced by Abeba. She recalled how Abeba would often seek comfort and reassurance from Njeri whenever the other kids picked on her. It was a bond forged in the face of adversity, a silent understanding that anchored their friendship. Njeri, though young herself, instinctively stepped in to protect Abeba, showcasing a strength that contrasted her years. These memories lingered in Maa-me's mind, even as life moved on, the echoes of those carefree days and the struggles they faced together remained a cherished part of her life.

Abeba and Joe found themselves in the cozy home of Njeri and Kwame, a space that felt very welcoming. It was a rare opportunity for the two friends to reconnect and catch up on the lost years that had slipped away in the busyness of their lives. While the others opted for the comfort of a nearby hotel. The evening was alive with laughter as Abeba and Njeri reminisced about their shared past, recounting stories that had once shaped their lives. Each tale brought them closer, filling the air with warmth and rekindling a bond that had faded over time. In those moments, they cherished the significance of their friendship, recognizing how some connections can endure the challenges of distance and time. They felt a deep sense of gratitude for this reunion, understanding that the best relationships often lie in wait, ready to blossom anew when the moment is right. This precious time spent together reminded them of the joy found in reconnecting, making new memories that would last a lifetime.

That year, Tsetsebo town erupted in celebration as they welcomed Dr Fray, their beloved physician, who had dedicated himself to improving the health and well-being of the community. His selfless contributions during his time practicing medicine in their land had not gone unnoticed, and the townsfolk expressed their deep gratitude with heartfelt cheers and joyous festivities. Banners adorned with messages of appreciation adorned the streets, while children sang songs of admiration.

The warmth of the community surrounded Dr Fray as he walked through the town, each smile reflecting the profound impact he had made on their lives. It was a moment of unity and thanks, showcasing the bond forged between the healer and the people he served. Dr Fray was not just a doctor; he was a true hero, celebrated for his unwavering commitment to the health of the town.

Subsequently, as the day gradually faded, in the warmth of the setting sun, Dr Fray found himself standing solemnly before Madam Feli's tombstone. In his hands, he cradled a bouquet of special flowers, each bloom symbolizing the deep affection and profound wisdom she had imparted to him since their paths first crossed. Memories of their conversations echoed in his mind, reminding him of the lessons she taught and the kindness she shared. He felt an overwhelming sense of gratitude for the enormous gift she had given him, the courage and inspiration to pursue his dreams. With every petal, he remembered the countless stories she had told, the lessons she had imparted, and the unwavering support she had offered. In that solemn moment, he reflected on how her belief in him had helped transform his aspirations into reality. As he laid the flowers down gently, he whispered promises to continue living a life that would make her proud, knowing that her legacy would forever be a part of him.

As he knelt beside Madam Feli's tombstone, a heavy weight settled in his heart. The vibrant flowers he had chosen, a mix of her favorite blooms, felt inadequate against the starkness of the granite. He bowed his head, letting the cool breeze carry his whispered apologies into the quiet cemetery. "I'm so sorry, Madam Feli. Life had pulled me in countless directions, each task more demanding than the last, but nothing could erase the guilt of not being here to honor your memory sooner." He spent a few moments in silence, reflecting on the lessons she had taught him, the love she had shared unconditionally.

With a deep breath, he placed the flowers gently at her grave, hoping they conveyed the depth of his feelings that words could not capture. He promised himself he would visit more often, cherishing the bond they still shared. Dr Fray made a heartfelt promise to visit Madam Feli more often, understanding the importance of maintaining a connection with her memory. To honor her legacy, he took an additional step by contracting a caretaker dedicated to keeping her tomb site clean and presentable. This commitment not only ensured that her resting place was respected and cared for, but it also reflected his deep affection and remembrance of the love she had shared throughout her life.

At the evening gathering following Njeri's

coronation, Ayanda, a vibrant presence in their circle of friends, with a warm smile and infectious enthusiasm, took the opportunity to introduce her family, painting a lively picture of their personalities and unique identities As she spoke, laughter and cheers filled the air, creating an inclusive atmosphere that sparked curiosity about each family member. Ayanda's love for her family was evident, and her passion made the introductions felt like a joyful celebration rather than a simple introduction. The warmth of their connections brightened the gathering making the celebration of Njeri's accomplishment even more special. The rest of them leaned in, eager to learn more, as Ayanda effortlessly wove stories that highlighted the deep bonds and cherished memories they all shared. It was a moment that not only showcased Ayanda's vibrant presence but also strengthened the ties among friends and family, united in joy and celebration.

With a warm smile and infectious energy, she stood confidently beside her husband, Judge Ayola, the esteemed Supreme Court judge whose remarkable legal prowess was recognized nationwide. As she spoke about her husband's achievements, her admiration was obvious, highlighting the profound impact he had made in the legal field. Judge Ayola's reputation as a fair and dedicated judge had earned him respect from colleagues and citizens alike. He embodied the spirit of integrity and service, inspiring those around them to value the rule of law and the importance of upholding justice in society. The room buzzed with excitement as she introduced her three children, each radiating their mother's enthusiasm. The children, with their bright eyes and playful demeanor, instantly captured the hearts of everyone present, making the gathering even more memorable. Laughter and joyful conversations filled the air, showcasing the strong bonds of friendship and family that

Ayanda cherished.

Ayanda, through the passage of time, remained a great force against her husband's undeniably strange behavior. She stood resolute amidst the shifting sands of her marriage, an unwavering beacon in the face of her husband's increasingly peculiar actions. As months turned into years, she grappled with a profound dilemma that tested her values and identity. The allure of affluence shimmered tantalizingly before her, promising a life of luxury and comfort. Yet, deep down, she felt an inward struggle, as her self-respect tugged at her conscience, urging her to consider the cost of such wealth.

Ultimately, the temptation was too great, and she made her choice. She prioritized material gain over her dignity, convinced that the security and status that accompanied affluence would overshadow the quiet unrest within her soul. This decision, however, left an indelible mark on her, challenging her to reconcile her outward success with the inner turmoil that accompanied it. In choosing wealth, Ayanda embarked on a path that promised external validations but threatened to erode the very essence of who she was meant to be. She had long understood that being wed to the elite carried a heavy burden, one that weighed upon her spirit like a stone. The societal expectations, the endless scrutiny, and the constant striving for perfection in a world of privilege drained her.

With each passing day, the facade of a perfect marriage chipped away at her freedom, suffocating her individuality. She yearned for the simplicity of authentic existence, far removed from the judgmental eyes of high society. Ayanda realized that her dream of love and companionship was being stifled by the very ideals that were supposed to elevate her. Thus, she found herself at a crossroads, grappling with the decision of whether to remain trapped in gilded confines or to break free and reclaim her identity - even if it meant facing the unknown. Soon after, the cost became clear; it was her soul's peace that she was unwilling to forfeit.

Equally, she found herself at a crossroads as she navigated the complexities of impending motherhood. With her first child on the way, the thought of returning to her previous life felt increasingly daunting. Each day, the weight of her pregnancy brought forth a mix of excitement and anxiety, reinforcing her resolve to move forward rather than retreat to what once was. The idea of going back seemed not only impractical but also incompatible with the new identity she was beginning to embrace. Embracing the changes ahead, she recognized that the journey into parenthood would shape her life in ways she could only begin to imagine.

Determined and hopeful, she focused on preparing for the challenges and joys that lay ahead, knowing that the future held both uncertainty and promise. Her decision to remain married to her husband extended beyond the simple fact of her pregnancy.

She had grown accustomed to the luxurious lifestyle that accompanied her role as a judge's wife, gloating over the high social standing it afforded her. The elegant parties, refined society meetings, and the admiration of her peers created a world she found difficult to relinquish. This sophisticated life, filled with connections and status, shaped her identity and offered her a sense of security. While love may have initially bound her to her husband, it was this opulent life and the promises of prestige that ultimately reinforced her commitment, making the thought of leaving felt like a step into an uncertain and less glamorous future. She understood that her marriage provided more than companionship; it offered her a ticket to a life of comfort and influence that she was not ready to give up.

Ayanda felt the weight of disdainful glances directed her way from her husband's ex's, and it left her feeling uneasy. She couldn't quite pin down the source of their animosity;

was it jealousy over her current relationship, or was it a reflection of their own complex histories with him? The tension in the air was obvious, and Ayanda tried to brush it off, but the judgment seemed almost personal. Each interaction was steeped in unspoken stories that lingered, creating an invisible barrier. She wondered if their past experiences with her husband, perhaps tied to difficult moments in their shared past, colored their perception of her.

Despite the unease, Ayanda resolved to rise above the negativity, focusing on her own dilemma determined not to allow the shadows of the past to overshadow her present. Her heart raced as she grappled with the grim reality of her husband's troubling behavior. The weight of his abominable acts hung heavily over her, pressing down with an urgency she could no longer ignore. With each passing moment, the implications of his actions became more apparent, and deep down, she knew that inaction was not an option. She felt a fierce determination boiling over inside her; it was time to confront the darkness that had taken root in her life. The shadows of doubt and fear twisted around her, but she braced herself, resolved to take swift and deliberate measures. She would not allow his misdeeds to define her future. Whatever it took, she would make her stand, not just for her sake, but for the sake of her young family. The clock was ticking, and she understood that change had to come, and it had to come quickly.

In her quest for clarity and guidance, Ayanda turned to the spiritual realm, seeking the wisdom of a renowned fetish priest. She approached him with an open heart, ready to embrace the ancient rituals and practices that had long been revered in her culture. The priest, adorned in traditional attire and surrounded by sacred artifacts, welcomed her with a gentle smile. As he began to perform the rituals, she felt a profound connection to the spiritual energies around her. Through divination, the priest revealed insights that resonated deeply with her innermost struggles and aspirations. This experience not only offered Ayanda solace but also ignited a newfound sense of purpose within her, empowering her to navigate the challenges of her life with renewed strength and determination.

The revelation made by the fetish priest regarding her husband sent a wave of fear coursing through her veins. As the priest laid bare secrets that intertwined the fates of the judge and his fortification, her heart raced with anxiety. Doubt clouded her mind, casting shadows on her once unwavering trust in her husband's integrity. As whispers echoed in her ears and unsettling visions haunted her thoughts, she grappled with the realization that the foundation of her marriage might be more precarious than she ever anticipated. Her trust wavered, and a sense of impending doom loomed over her, transforming the safe haven of her home into a place of uncertainty and fear. The revelation from the fetish priest left her in a whirlwind of confusion and distrust.

As she reflected on her husband's actions during their intimate moments, doubts gnawed at her mind like an insatiable beast. Were these acts mere expressions of love, or were they sinister gestures woven into a tapestry of dark rituals? Each touch felt tainted, each whisper shadowed by the eerie implications of what she had learned. The once warm embrace became a source of chilling speculation, making her question the very foundation of his humanity. Were the sacred bonds of marriage a front for something more abominable? She felt entrapped in a web of uncertainty, yearning for clarity in the chaos. As she struggled to reconcile her feelings with the unsettling truths being unveiled, the essence of their union seemed to hang in a delicate balance, staggering on the edge of revelation and betrayal.

As Ayanda pondered over her multitude troubles, the weight of her spiritual quest became increasingly burdensome. The thoughts danced in her mind, each one more tangled than the last, leading her to a critical decision: perhaps it was time to back out. Deep down, she recognized that her problem was not just like any other; it was unique problem, demanding a unique level of attention and resolution that felt beyond her current capabilities. "A unique problem requires fixing," she murmured to herself, grappling with the notion that perhaps solutions were not one-size-fits-all. The journey inward had been enlightening yet exhausting, and Ayanda felt it necessary to step back, reassess, and approach her troubles with a fresh perspective.

Ayanda came to an important realization: life is not just about applying spiritual or logical solutions to every challenge. Sometimes, the best approach is to confront problems head-on, embracing them with courage and creativity. It's about taking the bull by the horns and dressing each issue in an appropriate outfit, tailored to the specific circumstances at hand. She took the bull by the horn and gradually her husband's abilities began to fade, she knew it was time to take control of the situation. As they prepared for the arrival of their third child, intimacy dwindled, leaving her husband increasingly disconnected from reality. Ayanda was aware of what was going on but in a way he was not, his decline was a slow process, and she had intentionally contributed to it. The time had come for her to reclaim her own freedom.

Ayanda had been trapped in the dark confines of Judge Ayola's twisted fantasy factory, a place where her spirit was slowly siphoned away, leaving her weak and despondent. Each day felt like an eternity, as she fought against the insidious hold that sought to consume her entirely. But now, unknown to him, Ayanda was slowly weakening his abilities to her freedom, his fantasy factory was shut down and Ayanda free, free at last from a horrifying experience of losing oneself to such an abominable act all because one could. The factory's shutters were finally closed, marking the end of her torment. With every step away from that harrowing realm, Ayanda could feel her strength returning, like a Bennu rising from the ashes of despair. She was free at last, liberated from the horrifying experience that had threatened to strip her of her very identity. It was a new beginning, a chance to reclaim herself and rise above the shadows of what once was. She embraced her freedom with newfound resolve, determined to rebuild her life and never allow another abominable act to define her existence again. She was ready to navigate the uncharted territory of her life, one where she could finally define her own identity beyond the roles of wife and mother.

Ayanda reveled in the glow of victory, her mind racing with the possibilities of what it meant to have it all. As she raised her glass to cheer with her friends, a big smile spread across her face, reflecting the joy of the moment. It wasn't just the triumph that made her heart race; it was the sweet taste of revenge that lingered in the air, more satisfying than any success. In that instant, surrounded by laughter and cheers, with a clink of each glass, she felt invincible as if the universe was finally aligning with her dreams.

As the night drew to a close and the final moments of their gathering approached, Joe, stirred by the gestures that captured the essence of the evening, raised his own glass high, a signal for everyone to join him in celebration. The soft clinking of glasses filled the air, friends leaned in, eyes sparkling with joy and appreciation, ready to embrace the toast that would mark the end of a wonderful night.

Joe looked around at the familiar faces, each one a testament to the bonds they had forged over time. With a heartfelt smile, he raised his glass, his voice steady yet filled with emotion. "To the countless memories we've created together, Abeba," he began, his words flowing effortlessly like a beautiful tribute to their journey. He spoke of late-night conversations, laughter echoing through the years, and the quiet moments that spoke volumes. Each sentence was infused with a promise of future adventures and shared dreams. As he poured out his heart, the atmosphere around him shifted, anticipation hanging thick in the air. "I want to spend my life with you," he declared, his gaze locking onto Abeba's, the sincerity of his intention conspicuous. The moment was more than a toast; it was a proposal filled with hope, love, and the commitment to embrace whatever life would bring their way together.

After Joe declared his heartfelt proposal to Abeba, she was overwhelmed with joy, and without hesitation, she accepted his proposal. Their sparkling eyes met with warmth and unspoken promises of dreams and a shared future. Friends and family, who had been waiting with anticipatory breath, erupted in cheers. Abeba's cheeks flushed with happiness, she couldn't contain her excitement as she envisioned the life they would build together. Joe, equally overjoyed, felt a surge of relief and love, knowing that their journey was just beginning. Amidst the jubilant atmosphere, they both recognized that they had taken the first step towards a beautiful adventure filled with love, laughter, and endless possibilities.

In the wake of accepting Joe's proposal, Abeba felt a rush of excitement mingle with anxiety as memories of Kevin, her jilted secret husband, surged to the forefront of her mind. She recalled the moments they had shared, the promises whispered in the quiet of the night, and the reasons they had been forced to part ways. The thought of Kevin searching for her sent a shiver down her spine. What if Joe discovered her old life, her marriage to Kevin? Could he forgive her for choosing a different path? Abeba's mind raced with questions, weighing the possibilities and consequences that lay ahead. She couldn't shake the feeling that the past has a way of catching up with the present, and the looming uncertainty made her heart race. Would she be able to fully embrace this new chapter, or would Kevin's shadow forever haunt her choices?

Abeba glanced around the room, the weight of unspoken secrets hanging heavily in the air. For now, her own secret remained securely tucked away, hidden behind a facade of lively conversation; after all, every person had their own layers of hidden truths and untold stories. Each laugh and smile masked the complexities underneath, and she couldn't help but wonder how many secrets lay dormant, waiting for the right moment to be revealed. For the time being, she would keep her own close to her chest.

"While the world still stands, tantalizing thrill of mystery will fill it." As she stood there, a delicate smile played on her lips, her own thrill of mystery wrapped around her like a soft blanket. Joe's proposal hung between them, ripe with possibilities and unspoken dreams, nonetheless, she allowed herself to savor and rejoice every second of the warmth of his gaze. What lay ahead was uncertain, but the promise of the journey ignited a spark of excitement within her: for now, she would embrace the moment, letting it unfold like the pages of a captivating story, ready to explore the path that their hearts might carve out together. The seduction of the unknown beckoned, and she was more than willing to follow wherever it would lead.

The coronation of Njeri's enthronement was truly a spectacular event, marking a significant milestone in the history of the kingdom. The grand hall was adorned with vibrant flowers and radiant banners. The atmosphere buzzed with excitement as nobles, dignitaries, and citizens gathered, eager to witness the moment where tradition and ceremony intertwined. Dressed in a dazzling gown crafted from the finest Kente, Njeri radiated elegance and tranquil as she made her way to the throne. The air was filled with the harmonious sounds of music and cheer as she accepted her crown, a symbol of her commitment to shoulder the responsibilities, the hopes and the dreams of the kingdom. Everyone present knew they were stepping into a new chapter in their shared story, where hope and unity would reign supreme, Njeri stood at the forefront, radiating strength and inspiration, her voice echoed through the anticipated crowd, with the promise of change, encouraging each person to become a beacon of hope. Njeri's reign was destined to be one of inspiration and unity, promising a brighter future for all. Together, they embraced the dawn of her reign.

The ceremony was a historic occasion, rich with tradition and significance. Kwame, her devoted husband, was by her side, offering unwavering support as they embarked on this new journey of responsibilities together. Maame, a pillar of strength and wisdom, stood beside them, beaming with pride. As they looked toward the future, hope grew in their hearts for a prosperous kingdom. The three of them formed a united front, ready to face the challenges ahead as they worked collectively to uplift their community, assuring the people of Tsetsebo that their new era would be marked by love, strength, and determination.

At Njeri's coronation, Orji's mother stood in a mix of regret and admiration, her thoughts revolving around the choices that had led her to this moment. She couldn't help but reflect on the idiocy that clouded her previous judgment about her, a woman she once dismissed, now adorned as paramount queen over a vast kingdom. As memories of their past encounter flooded her mind, Orji suddenly appeared beside her, a teasing glint in his eye. "How do you like her now?" he asked, a playful smirk tugging at his lips. His mother rolled her eyes and clicked her tongue in mock disapproval, replying, "The sun doesn't shine in one place; some days are cloudy, but tomorrow, it will be sunny somewhere."

Few hours later, Queen Njeri was summoned into the grand throne room, a place steeped in history and tradition. As she entered, she felt the expectations upon her shoulders worrisome, knowing she was to meet the king she had succeeded. The room was adorned with portraits and statues of the past kings, each one a testament to the legacy they had built. Their names, etched into the walls, echoing the triumphs and tribulations of the kingdom, reminding Njeri of the challenges ahead. Every figurehead seemed to gaze down at her, as if assessing her worthiness to continue their lineage. With a mixture of hope and unease, she stepped forward, ready to embrace her destiny and honor the legacy of those who reigned before her. She felt frightened by the history of their reigns, understanding that she was not merely stepping into a role; she was stepping into a complex narrative woven with threads of power and history. With each breath, she steeled herself for the challenges to come, determined to forge her own path while honoring the ghosts of those who had come before her.

As she gracefully entered the throne room, her gaze was immediately drawn to a striking figure of a king that stood proudly in the corner. The craftsmanship was exquisite, each detail reflecting a rich history and a sense of nobility that shuddered her deeply. Intrigued, she approached the statue, her curiosity piqued by its regal presence. Just then, the throne room guide, a knowledgeable figure with a passion for the kingdom's lore, hurried to her side to share the story behind the statue. Together, they delved into the past, exploring the legacy of the king it depicted. The guide indicated that the impressive statue that situated before her was a striking likeness of the king she had just succeeded, a figure whose reign had been marked by strength and wisdom. Intricately designed, each detail of the statue seemed to embody his values, vision, and the legacy he cultivated throughout his life. The gold adornment captured the essence of his leadership, with every detail reflecting the legacy he left behind.

Queen Njeri's heart felt heavy as she gazed upon the statue, knowing that it represented not just the past, but also the weight of responsibility she now bore. From then on, she realized that the path ahead would require her to honor his memory while forging her own legacy, inspiring her subjects to embrace the future with hope and courage. The throne room echoed with the stories of generations, and she was determined to add her own chapter to this rich history. As she stood before the statue, the striking resemblance of the statue's face captured her attention. Memories danced at the edges of her mind, urging her to recall the moment she had encountered that face in real life. The intricate details of the statue seemed to come alive, intertwining with her past experiences. Each curve and expression penetrated her, deepening her sense of connection. How could she possibly fill those shoes, she wondered, when the legacy of this face called to her with such familiarity?

After battling with her memory for what felt like an eternity, she finally recognized the striking resemblance between the statue in the throne room and the mysterious man she and Abeba had met beneath the ancient tree during their adventurous teenage escapades deep in the forest. The vivid image of that encounter flooded back to her, igniting a sense of remembrance intertwined with perplexity. What had once seemed like a whimsical moment now held deeper significance, hinting at connections woven through time and fate. The old man had recounted tales of the revered deity, a mysterious figure whom she and Abeba dubbed as the "Mo Swine."

This enigmatic figure, hidden beneath a cloak of a wealthy man, had a singular purpose: to guide them away from the perilous paths that threatened to tarnish their bright futures, steering them toward choices that would preserve their destinies. Their precarious moment in the forest served as both a warning and a blessing, reminding them of the potential dangers lurking in their youthful adventures.

Her heart raced as she pondered the implications of this revelation, her mind abound with questions about the man's identity and the secrets he might hold. The forest, a backdrop to their youthful adventures now felt shrouded in an air of mystery, beckoning her to uncover the truths hidden within its depths and linking her past to her present in unexpected ways.

During Queen Njeri's reign, the kingdom boomed with prosperity. Tsetsebo town remained a splendid locale of peace and natural beauty. The land became remarkably fertile, infused with essential minerals and nutrients that created an ideal environment for agriculture. Rich soil supported a diverse range of crops, enabling farmers to cultivate everything from grains to fruits and vegetables. The abundance of mineral resources further enhanced the agricultural capacity, ensuring that the land remained productive year after year. The unique combination of natural assets not only contributed to local food security but also positioned the area as a potential hub for sustainable farming practices. The flourishing landscape, teeming with life, showcased the harmony between nature's gifts and human endeavor, ultimately fostering economic growth and community well-being.

Queen Njeri understood the wealth her kingdom possessed: gold, lots of it; she had gazed upon its gleaming in the forest, yet, as much as her heart yearned for the prosperity that the precious metal could bring, she knew that true strength lay in the toil and dedication of her people. For the moment, the focus would be on nurturing the land, cultivating crops, and ensuring that her subjects embraced the fundamental practices of agriculture. By turning the soil and investing their labor into the earth, Queen Njeri envisioned a thriving community that would, in time, be enriched not just by gold, but by resilience and growth. Together, they would forge a better life, one rooted in the virtues of hard work and collective effort, laying a foundation for the future where both the land and her people could flourish.

As the residents harnessed their resources responsibly, they created a thriving agricultural sector that benefitted both current and future generations. In times of adversity, the townsfolk stood united, facing challenges head-on with a courage that inspired not only each other but also those who wandered into their midst. This steadfast resolve and deep-rooted sense of honor forged a close-knit community where empathy reigned supreme and respect was a guiding principle. The children greeted strangers with warm smiles, offered assistance to anyone in need, showcasing their inherently good nature.

Market days became vibrant events where the streets were filled with the sights and aromas of fresh produce, reflecting the abundance that characterized the golden era. The people took pride in their harvest. Money flowed easily, as both locals and merchants gathered to trade their goods, fostering a sense of community and celebration. The joy of sharing bountiful meals brought families and friends together, making every mealtime a feast of gratitude and the spirit of generosity thrived.

Queen Njeri and her husband, Kwame, alongside the Frays and the Tsetsebo diaspora, united their efforts to establish the most advanced and well-equipped modern hospitals. The facilities were not only a gain for the twenty towns under Her Majesty's rule but also extended their care to distant kingdoms that desperately needed healthcare services. Their collaboration demonstrated a profound commitment to the well-being of all, bridging gaps between communities and ensuring that essential medical care was accessible to everyone, regardless of their location. The hospitals became a symbol of hope and vitality, fostering a sense of unity and health across a wide expanse of lands. Through their visionary leadership, Queen Njeri and her partners transformed the landscape of healthcare, leaving an indelible mark on the lives of countless individuals seeking assistance.

In the heart of Tsetsebo, a small ancient town, the spirit of the people shone brightly through the unwavering kindness and bravery of three families. Each family carried a sense of dignity that was woven into the very fabric of their daily lives that shaped the town's identity. The brave souls who once walked the soil - defenders of the helpless, guardians of hope - left behind echoes of their compassionate deeds. A beautifully crafted plaque stands proudly at the square, bearing the names of those whose stories continue to echo. The laughter of children, mingled with the soft notes of a musician's song, is heard each day, reminding all passersby that these stories are not merely relics of the past, but vibrant threads in the tapestry of life. Each corner hold a memory, each shadow a testament to the enduring legacy of those who dared to act with courage. Such moments invite reflection, ensuring that the legacy of these remarkable individuals continues to inspire future generations.

ACKNOWLEDGEMENT

I am deeply grateful to all my family and well-wishers who have supported and encouraged me throughout my writing journey. Your kind words and unwavering belief in my abilities have been a constant source of motivation. Each message of encouragement has fueled my passion and inspired me to strive for excellence in my craft. Whether through thoughtful feedback, sharing my work, or simply cheering me on, your support has made an immense difference in my growth as a writer. I cherish each individual who has taken the time to uplift me, and I look forward to continuing this journey with your encouragement by my side. Your faith in me serves as a reminder that the path of creativity is a collaborative one, enriched by the kindness of others. As I move forward, I carry your support in my heart, propelling me to reach new heights in my writing endeavors.

I would like to take a moment to express my heartfelt gratitude to my fans, who have graciously welcomed me into their reading lives. Your support and enthusiasm inspire me every day to create and share stories that resonate deeply. It is a profound honor to share my thoughts and imagination with you, knowing that you take the time to explore the worlds I craft. Each book, each page, and each word comes to life with your engagement, and for that, I am truly thankful. Your trust and openness allow me to connect in ways I could never have imagined, and for every moment you spend with my work, I am deeply appreciative. Together, we embark on journeys that transcend the pages, and your presence makes all the difference. Thank you for believing in me and for letting me be a part of your literary adventures.

ABOUT THE AUTHOR

Ama Nkrumah

Ama Nkrumah is a novice Author whose enchanting narratives blur the lines between fiction and true stories. With a background in philosophy and experience as a Publicist, she brings a unique depth to her writing, skillfully weaving human emotions into her characters' journeys. Her fascinating worlds are crafted with a fine balance of suspense and rich character development, drawing readers into the heart of her stories and fostering a deep connection with her characters. Each book reflects her innermost thoughts and life experiences, capturing her evolution towards becoming a celebrated author. Filled with hope and determination, Ama Nkrumah is excited to share more tales that resonate with audiences and leave a lasting impression, ensuring her voice and stories continue to inspire and uplift.

BOOKS BY THIS AUTHOR

Nyankonton Be Yourself

"If a man be not enlightened within, what lamp shall he light?" Nyankonton, despite her immense power and abundance, embarked on a perilous journey driven by a profound lack of self-awareness. She quickly learned that her quest was akin to jumping from the frying pan into the fire, facing challenges that tested her resolve. Through her trials, she discovered that time progress relentlessly, much like an arrow shooting through the air. This realization was coupled with the understanding that, just as no ten fingers share the same length, every being has its unique purpose to fulfill. Nyankonton's journey became one of a self-discovery, as she began to appreciate the distinct roles that each individual, including herself, plays in the grand tapestry of existence.

In a moment of reckless abandon, she tossed a stone into the well, the very source of her sustenance, unaware of the chaos it might unleash through the influence of her malicious guardian. Time was of the essence, and the fate of the universe teetered on the brink of disaster. Yet, amid the uncertainty, a flicker of hope remained. As she grappled with the gravity of her choices, she began to realize that the true power lay not just in her actions, but in her recognition of self-worth and resilience. With every moment counting, she was determined to harness the inner potential she had yet to fully embrace, for it was the key to saving not only herself but the entire universe

www.ingramcontent.com/pod-product-compliance
Lightning Source LLC
Chambersburg PA
CBHW071957150426
43194CB00008B/904